The CHIANG Family History

A Tale of Three Cultures and Chia Keng Village

Related Titles

My Maternal Roots: A Story of Family, Faith and Freedom
by Cyprian Lim
ISBN: 978-981-140-182-4
ISBN: 978-981-140-183-1 (pbk)

The CHIANG Family History

A Tale of Three Cultures and Chia Keng Village

BERNARD CHIANG

Genealogy Society Singapore, Singapore

Genealogy Society Singapore
新加坡族譜學會

Celebrating SG Families

World Scientific

Published by

Genealogy Society Singapore
3 Jalan Arif
Singapore 548790

and

World Scientific Publishing Co. Pte. Ltd.
5 Toh Tuck Link, Singapore 596224
USA office: 27 Warren Street, Suite 401-402, Hackensack, NJ 07601
UK office: 57 Shelton Street, Covent Garden, London WC2H 9HE

National Library Board, Singapore Cataloguing in Publication Data
Name(s): Chiang, Bernard. | Genealogy Society Singapore, publisher.
Title: The Chiang family history : a tale of three cultures and Chia Keng Village / Bernard Chiang.
Description: Singapore : Genealogy Society Singapore : World Scientific Publishing Co. Pte. Ltd., [2022]
Identifier(s): ISBN 978-981-12-5243-3 (hardback) | 978-981-12-5333-1 (paperback)
Subject(s): LCSH: Chiang, Bernard--Family. | Families--Singapore. | Singapore--Biography. | Singapore--History.
Classification: DDC 929.2--dc23

British Library Cataloguing-in-Publication Data
A catalogue record for this book is available from the British Library.

Supported by

National Heritage Board

DISCLAIMER: *The views expressed here are solely those of the author in his private capacity and do not in any way represent the views of the National Heritage Board and/or any government agencies.*

Celebrating SG Families

Strong families support the development of resilient individuals, and this forms the bedrock of our society.

All of us have a part to play in building strong, resilient families.

In support of Celebrating SG Families 2022

For any available supplementary material, please visit
https://www.worldscientific.com/worldscibooks/10.1142/12728#t=suppl

Desk Editor: Nicole Ong

Printed in Singapore

Celebrating SG Families

Strong families support the development of resilient individuals, and this forms the bedrock of our society.

All of us have a part to play in building strong, resilient families.

In support of Celebrating SG Families 2022

Acknowledgements

I would like to thank the following:

Mr Baey Yam Keng Senior Parliamentary Secretary, Ministry for Transport and MP for Tampines GRC for his message.

Mr Seah Kian Peng MP for Marine Parade GRC for his message.

My late father Chiang Boon Lim and mother Lim Poh Neo for archiving all the old photos and documents related to the publications.

Fourth Paternal Aunty Chiang Guet Seng and cousin Teo Chee Hong and family members for sharing the family photos and history.

My cousin Chiang Choon Tiang from China and nephew Nack Prayadrat from Thailand for sharing the family history and photos.

My maternal relatives, granduncle, grandaunt, uncles, aunties and cousins of Singapore for their kind assistance in sharing their photos and knowledge regarding our family history.

My brothers, sisters, brothers-in-law, sisters-in-law, nephews and nieces for their support. Especially my brother Melvin Chiang, nephews Ray Chiang, Nack Prayadrat and my niece Dr Bernita Chiang for their write-ups.

All the former patrons, sponsors, committee members, villagers and supporters of the Yio Chu Kang Villagers' Mutual Help Association for their contributions and strong support in promoting the true kampong spirit at Chia Keng village.

Dr Wee Sip Leong, Sister Leonora Pau, Sister Maria Kiang and the team from Franciscan Missionaries of Mary for their invaluable voluntary medical services rendered to the villagers.

National Heritage Board
Genealogy Society Singapore
Mr Ng Yew Kang, President of Genealogy Society, for his message and invaluable advice and kind assistance.

Mr Cyprian Lim, Secretary of Genealogy Society, for his encouragement, input and assistance.
Mr Tay Bak Tee, former Braddell Heights CCC Secretary, for his input on the relocation of the various temples and markets.

Mr Lee An Ko, for helping me in the Chinese translations.

All former Advisers, current Adviser, past and current grassroots leaders and friends of Braddell Heights for their support and encouragement.

All those who had, in one way or another, helped me in my research and contributed to the publication.

About the Author

Bernard Chiang Kheng Joo (Singapore Fourth Generation; China 22nd Generation) was raised in Kampong Chia Keng and studied at St Gabriel's School. At the young age of 12, he was already active in community services, serving as a volunteer firefighter, helping in the village free clinic, becoming a musical percussionist and performing in the village's amateur Teochew opera troupe. He worked as a florist for almost half a century, beginning at a pre-war house along Upper Serangoon Road. After his National Service, he joined the renowned Nanyang Academy of Fine Arts (NAFA) in 1972 and graduated in 1975. He was so influenced and impressed by his father's artist friend Mr Yang Ping that he decided to enrol in the art course at NAFA. Mr Yang helped to paint the backdrop scenes for the Teochew opera performances and Bernard was his assistant. After his graduation, his father roped him in to join the family florist business. He worked there for two years; unfortunately, the shop, which was founded in 1972, had to be relocated to Lorong Lew Lian HDB Estate due to urban redevelopment and road extension.

It was a turning point in his life as he settled down in a new environment and became inspired to follow his father's footsteps to revive the legendary kampong spirit. His father was a very passionate and devoted leader of the former kampong at Chia Keng village. He was encouraged by his father to be a volunteer in the grassroots organisations and became a member of the Braddell Heights Zone A Residents' Committee in 1980. He became the second person to chair the Residents' Committee in 1986. Ultimately, he was recruited to help in the Citizens' Consultative Committee, Civil Defence Co-ordinating Committee, Community Centre Management Committee and Town Council. In 2005, he was appointed as the chairman of Inter-Racial and Religious Confidence Circle. Apart from that, he was also an Executive Committee Member in the St Gabriel's School Old Boys' Association since 1990. In 2011, he was invited to join the management committee of the Serangoon Moral Family Service Centre.

With his forty years of involvement and experience in grassroots organisations, together with his father's lifelong collection of valuable old kampong photos and documents, he decided to publish this memoir. The family's rich cultural and historical background had also inspired him to trace his ancestral roots from China, Thailand and Singapore. He wishes to ensure and encourage the current and future generations to learn from the past and gain a better understanding of their family roots. He also urges future generations to reflect on this analogy — 'A family tree will perish if its roots are unattended.'

Preface

This book is dedicated to my parents, family members, relatives, friends, leaders, benefactors and villagers of the former Kampong Chia Keng. Many of the villagers and our family members had benefitted from the perseverance and hard work of the kampong elders. They were instrumental in uniting the people and motivated the villagers to embrace the iconic Kampong Chia Keng spirit. The strong sense of bonding within the cohesive community helped build a united and peaceful kampong where the villagers enjoyed living for more than half a century.

Without the community's selfless contributions and vision, the kampong wouldn't have lasted for so many years as we were very vulnerable to fire and disease outbreaks. One little spark of fire could wipe out the whole kampong, as was the case in Bukit Ho Swee. The prevalence of contagious diseases during those days, such as Asian Flu, Hong Kong Flu, tuberculosis and leprosy, could have caused unimaginable fatalities in the overcrowded environment of the kampong.

During the kampong days, juvenile delinquency was a serious issue, and many children would have ended up joining secret societies, if not for the intervention of the kampong elders and the village community. We are indebted to the unsung heroes for their dedication, sacrifice and leadership to lead and protect the villagers. We appreciate their selfless contribution in providing healthcare, recreation, education, safety and security to the villagers.

Coincidentally, when I was drafting this book, Singapore was going through a difficult period, fighting the COVID-19 pandemic since January 2020. My family business was suspended, and we were placed under the circuit breaker from 7 April to 4 May 2020. Subsequently the circuit breaker period was extended till 1 June for the reopening of the first phase targeting at essential services only. Our florist business and other such businesses, classified as unessential retail shops, were rescheduled to reopen on 19 June under the second phase, and I took this opportunity to spend over three months staying at home to concentrate on my research for this book.

It was a challenging task as I struggled to trace my family roots and search for the missing links, while at the same time improving my computer knowledge and Chinese translation. I had to persevere at the time when my health and eyesight were troubling me. It was a tough decision to trace our long-lost family history and follow the family values passed down from my ancestors. These were the factors that motivated me to push on to gather these records for future generations. The remarkable die-hard spirit and legacy of the village volunteers of Kampong Chia Keng must not be forgotten. The pioneers of our nation had laboriously planted the trees for the future generations to enjoy the fruits of their labour. We must treasure and salute them for making this place we called home. There were many lessons we learned from our role models, and we were also fortunate to tap into their life experience. These records will give our future generations a better insight to honour the past, celebrate the present and embrace the future.

My interest to pen this book was sparked by the availability of many old photographs and documents of historical interest archived by my parents since the 50's. I started to collate and archive them in digital format since the year 2005. Initially my focus was to capture the history and experience of our kampong days as our maternal family members and relatives spent their formative years there. We were very sentimental and had strong emotional attachment to this kampong as most of us were born and grew up together there. As a big family, and guided by the values of the village elders, we had the passion to contribute our services to the kampong folks. We were motivated to join the Yio Chu Kang Villagers' Mutual Help Association to be trained as volunteer firefighters as well as participate in other community services. We also helped and supported the operation of the free clinic jointly operated by the Association and the Franciscan Missionaries of Mary. Our family members were also involved in the setting up of the amateur Teochew opera troupe as a form of recreation for the villagers, which was vital in building social cohesion and harmony.

As I was chronicling the past events and happenings of the good old days in the kampong, I was also inspired to trace our maternal family roots as six generations of our family have been living here. It was a challenging task to dig further into the roots of our earlier ancestral generations as there were missing links and resource limitations.

The other interesting area was the different cultural aspect of our maternal roots. Our great grandmother and grandmother were traditional Peranakans, as they dressed up and communicated with a mixture of Malay and Teochew lingo. When it cascaded down to our mum, the traditions were diluted as she was married to a traditional Chinese Teochew migrant. Unfortunately, when it passed down to our generation, the Peranakan traditions and practices tapered off, although we still craved for the traditional signature cuisines.

Another area of bicultural interest was from the second family of our paternal grandfather. Paternal grandpa migrated to Thailand as his business in Shantou, China, was disrupted during the tumultuous years. The future in the village where he lived was bleak, and he had to support his family as the sole breadwinner. Like many other immigrants, he took a big risk to travel in a big junk to reach Thailand. There, he started as a humble street hawker before venturing to rent a shop to start his rice business. Years later, he married a second wife in Bangkok, who was also a Thai Chinese. Gradually he sowed another seed to grow a new family tree in Thailand. This tree had grown and branched out to five generations. Under the rich Thai traditions and education system, the third generation of descendants were naturally exposed to the Thai culture and language. The Teochew mother tongue was not relevant to their society as the young generations communicated mainly in Thai language, embraced their cultural practices and enjoyed Thai cuisines.

Our communication with the Thailand relatives of the same generation was challenging as we could only depend on our youngest aunty to be the translator. Fortunately, most of the fourth-generation nephews and nieces were better educated and able to communicate in English and Mandarin. With the advancement in technology, we were luckier to be able to break the communication barrier through social media and the Internet. They might be disconnected with their Teochew roots, but over time we hope some of them would develop an interest in learning the Teochew language and culture with the aim of keeping a line of communication open with our China relatives. This could be achieved by strengthening the bonding and immersing them in the Teochew-speaking environment, with greater frequency of educational visits to the ancestral village.

The future is bright with the modernisation of China. An increasing number of Chinese nationals are travelling abroad. The younger generations have better opportunities to study overseas in English-medium schools and universities. A common language could be adopted for the convenience of communication through the social media platform. The world is getting smaller with virtual connectivity, and it is more easier to keep in touch with those family members who married foreigners or have settled down in a foreign country. In the time to come, new branches of the family tree would sprout in other countries outside South East Asia, and these records of the family genealogy would be useful for the future generations.

Contents

Contents

Foreword

The Genealogy Society Singapore is proud to publish The Chiang's Family History — A Story of Three Cultures and the Chia Keng Village by Mr Bernard Chiang. This is the second in a series on Singaporeans' family history, and the fourth publication of the Genealogy Society Singapore.

Bernard's father hailed from the historic Zhanglin Ancient Port 樟林古港in Cheng Hai District 澄海区 of Shantou City 汕头市 in Guangdong Province 广东省, China. Before the establishment of the Shantou Port 汕头港, all migrants from the Chaoshan area 潮汕地区 travelling to South East Asia departed from Zhanglin Port in junks painted with a red bow with two black eyes. This feature distinguished it from the junks sailing from Fujian Province, which had green bows with two black eyes. The Zhanglin Port was succeeded by the Shantou Port when the river feeding the Zhanglin Port was silted up.

The migration of Bernard's grandfather and father to South East Asia took on an unusual pattern. His grandfather used to have a thriving rice business in Zhang Lin. However, as he imported rice from Japan to boost business, he was met with great displeasure and resistance from local rice growers and other rice businessmen. This was aggravated by the civil war raging between two forces for the control of China. The situation became so untenable that both the father and son, the two main breadwinners of the family, had to seek their fortunes overseas. To spread the risks, the father decided to migrate to Siam (Thailand) and son to Singapore

Both men left behind their respective wives and children in Zhanglin. As they established themselves in Thailand and Singapore, they set up families in each place, but continued to remit money to their families in their ancestral homeland. The three families in Zhanglin, Bangkok and Singapore did not visit one another until very much later. They have now happily reunited and enjoy the three cultures.

Bernard's father settled in the then Kampong Chia Keng in Yio Chu Kang Road and raised a large brood there since the 30's until the village was demolished to give way to development. Life in the kampong was austere but eventful, with family members actively involved in the formation and operation of the village's voluntary firefighting squad, the village clinic, grassroots organisations, and even the establishment and operation of a Teochew opera troupe, with family members participating in the orchestra and performing as actors and actresses. The close kampong spirit was much treasured by villagers long after the demolition of the village.

Bernard has long cherished the idea of compiling his family history and the rich life in Kampong Chia Keng. He spent several years researching the materials, which has finally come to fruition.

In promoting an awareness and knowledge of family history among Singaporeans, the Genealogy Society actively encourages Singaporean families to rediscover at least the Singapore chapter of their family histories and to record them for the benefit of family members and their descendants. It would of course be better if they could trace their roots to their country of origin. Each family has rich stories to share among themselves that give each member a sense of who they are and where they come from. These stories should not be lost with time but cherished and recorded by each generation

In the wake of rapid development and modernisation, Singaporeans have embraced modern lifestyles and enjoyed the exclusivity of nuclear family units. In the process, many Singaporeans have lost a significant part of their heritage: the knowledge of who their ancestors were, where they originated from, why and how they came to Singapore, how they led their lives, who their current extended family members are and how they are faring in life.

The Society believes in the value of preserving every family's history. It regularly organises public talks, forums and workshops to share with Singaporeans on why it is worth our time and effort to compile our family history and how to go about doing it.

To further promote interest in compiling family histories in Singapore, the Society has been spearheading a sustained project to publish well-researched and written family histories of ordinary Singaporeans of all ethnic groups. While the Society helms and sources for funds for this project, we hope clan associations, trade unions, trade guilds and other civic and sociocultural associations as well as religious bodies can also encourage their members to compile their family histories and to help publish them if the authors so wish.

Apart from benefitting family members and their descendants, the published family histories of Singaporeans will collectively form a valuable part of Singapore's social history. A collection of these family histories in the National Library will ensure their preservation for posterity. They will also be made available for public consultations.

By recording one's family history, one's descendants will not suffer the predicament of not knowing the stories of their ancestors and extended family members. In the process of compiling one's family history, one gets to know all members of the extended family better, and family relationships can be bolstered. A closely knit family is the bedrock of a cohesive society, and an appreciation of our shared past can only help to strengthen our familial and social bonds.

Ng Yew Kang
President
Genealogy Society Singapore
26 February 2021

Foreword

It is always important to know our roots. Without our forefathers, we will not be around. We also get to appreciate that the many good things we enjoy today were started during much difficult times.

Mr Bernard Chiang's family tree started its roots in Singapore when his father Mr Chiang Boon Lim (章文林) sailed from Zhanglin (樟林) village in China in 1936 to seek a better life. Surviving a near-death accident in his hometown rice mill, the senior Chiang worked as a janitor when he arrived in Singapore, with just a loaned foldable canvas bed for his room. With his entrepreneurship, writing and interpersonal skills, he progressed in life and survived the Japanese occupation. Even though he lost money when his businesses failed, he found his interest in serving the community.

Among the various initiatives he was involved in, Mr Chiang Boon Lim started Chung-Lim Community Oversea Association (樟林旅外同乡会) in 1960 as a founding member. My late grandfather was a member of the association, having migrated from Zhanglin village as well. Throughout my education in the 70's and 80's, I was fortunate to receive academic awards from the association every year. The annual dinner and ceremony became a motivation for me to do well in my studies. Today, my father and brother are members of the association and our children receive the academic awards when they achieve good results.

After more than twenty years serving on the Management Committee as Secretary, Vice President and then Adviser, Mr Chiang Boon Lim retired from the association in 1994. His son Benson (章庆平) became the President from 1994 to 1999. In addition, Mr Chiang's other son Melvin (章庆隆) is also a long-serving member of the Management Committee since 2004.

Subsequently, Ray Chiang (章瑞书) from the following generation, who has been a recipient of the academic awards, was invited to be the association's Legal Adviser in 2002. The long-running and sustainable contributions of the Chiang family to the Chung-Lim Community Oversea Association are evident and I thank them for it.

I would like to congratulate Bernard for penning this book. It offers me and many others the chance to learn so much from this illustrious family with a heart for service. It is a reminder for us to contribute what we can, however little, to our community.

I wish all a happy reading.

Baey Yam Keng (马炎庆)
MP for Tampines GRC
Senior Parliamentary Secretary, Ministry of Transport
Senior Parliamentary Secretary for Sustainability and Environment
Honorary Advisor, Chung-Lim Community Oversea Association

Foreword

This is a remarkable book that traces the Chiang family over six generations. It was painstakingly and beautifully put together by Mr Bernard Chiang and his extended family.

I first met Bernard when I became the MP for Marine Parade GRC in 2006. You could say Bernard is a kampong chief in the Lorong Lew Lian area in particular. Those who have lived there for some time are almost likely to know him. Bernard has been an active grassroots leader in Braddell Heights since 1981, and in his 40 years of community work, he has held various key positions in different committees.

In my mind, there are many highlights to be gleaned from his distinguished services to the community. I would highlight the following for special mention:

- His tenure as Chairman of our Zone B Residents Committee;
- Being the first Chairman of our Inter-Racial & Religious Confidence Circle (IRCC) appointed by MCCY; and
- Being in the pioneer batch of Singapore Civil Defence Force (SCDF) Volunteer group, which was involved in the rescue efforts during the catastrophic collapse of Hotel New World — Bernard was actually the company commander of the Braddell Heights Civil Defence volunteer company. For his many contributions to the community, Bernard was accorded National Day Award honours in the form of the Pingat Bakti Masyarakat (The Public Service Medal) in 1998.

Bernard is a natural leader with a big heart for anyone who needs help. He is particularly passionate about promoting and strengthening the bonds in our community — building bonds between the young and old and across all social strata and building bonds across races and building bonds across faiths. Little wonder that, as the current co-chair of our IRCC, a position he has held since 2005, he has been a key and inspirational pillar of the committee. His tireless efforts and sterling leadership has developed strong bonds and trust amongst members in the committee which comprise leaders of religious organisations, schools, voluntary welfare organisations and grassroot organisations. This is the same energy, commitment and leadership which Bernard has brought over from his earlier tenure as Chairman of the Zone B Residents Committee.

In publishing this book, I can see the dedication, commitment and passion that he has to get the Chiang's family history documented and completed. It is a wonderful achievement and a fascinating book — one which the Chiang family and clan can look back with pride over how each member of the family has grown and chosen their own paths whilst remembering their family history.
Congratulations, Bernard and the Chiang family.

Seah Kian Peng
MP for Marine Parade GRC

Foreword

Growing up as a young boy in 80's Singapore, the world of my grandparents seemed alien and distant. A chief reason for this was my inability to communicate well with them. My grandparents spoke exclusively in the Teochew dialect, while I spoke mostly in English. This was a common struggle for many people of my generation, arising from governmental policies to eradicate the use of Chinese dialects and establish English as the main functional language of Singapore.

As someone with a keen interest in history and the migration of our forefathers to Singapore, the history of my own family's origins and establishment in Singapore remained a mystery to me. How did my forefathers first arrive in Singapore? What drove them to migrate from Southern China? What were their experiences and emotions in their early years of resettling in Singapore? I never got to ask my grandparents these questions due to the language barrier. With the years passing, memories fading and generations departing, there was a genuine risk of never knowing some of these answers.

I am thus deeply grateful to my uncle Bernard Chiang for writing such a comprehensive book tracing not only the history of my forefathers and their migration to Singapore and South East Asia, but also many other aspects of our family's history, including life in Singapore in the yesteryears. As a compendium of precious family history, I am sure each member of our tight family will hold each copy sacredly and with a deep sense of pride. But this is not merely a book about a random family in Singapore. This is the Singapore story: of migration to a foreign land for better opportunities, of communal living and the community spirit, of tradition and identity and of the central role of family in our social fabric. It is a nostalgic walk down the memory lane, with evocative photos of old Singapore and descriptions of life in past generations.

One can only imagine the emotions of my grandfather as he left China in the 30's under crippling economic conditions and with the backdrop of civil strife. Travelling in an overcrowded and unsanitary junk, the uncertainties must have been foremost on his mind. This must have reflected the emotions of early migrants to Singapore, to whom we are all eternally grateful to for taking the chance and eventually building the foundations of our nation and allowing us this chance of a prosperous life. I hope that anyone who picks up this book feels a sense of connection with it. While the characters and context may be different, it is ultimately a mirror of many families' journeys in the last century.

Ray Chiang Rui Shu
Singapore - 5th Generation, (China - 23rd Generation)

Origin of the Surname Zhang
章氏起源

Part 1:
The Zhangs are said to be descendants of the legendary Emperor Yan 炎帝神农, who lived in the pre-dynastic times. He was said to be the first person who discovered the art of farming in ancient China, hence he was dubbed the God of Agriculture 神农.

His name was Shaodian 少典, and he married Madam Jiao 娇 and had a son Shi Nian 石年 and lived in Jiang Sui 姜水 (present-day Shaanxi Province, Qishan County West 陕西省岐山县西). He thus adopted the surname Jiang 姜. He also discovered the use of fire to cook food and was known as Yan 炎 Emperor, or the Flaming Emperor.

His initial capital was in Chen 陈 (Henan Province, Kaifeng County, Chenzhou 河南省开封府陈州) . He later shifted the capital to Qufu (曲阜) in Shantung Province (Confucius' birth place). His reign lasted one hundred and twenty years. He was succeeded by six emperors, Quai 魁, Cheng 承, Ming 明, Xuan 宣, Lai 来 and Guo 裹, lasting three hundred and twenty-five years.

The last Emperor Guo 裹 had two great-grandsons: Yugan 褕罔 who reigned for fifty-five years. The second great-grandson Qi 器 had a son Zhurong 祝融. He was a disciple of Emperor Huang 黄帝. He assisted Xiayu 夏禹 in taming floodwaters and was conferred the state of Lv 吕 and given the surname Jiang 姜.

Part 2:
The Viscount of Lv had four sons living in the State of Lv until the tenth-generation Lvshang 吕尚, popularly known as Jiang Tai Gong 姜太公. In 1140 BC, he met Xibai 西伯 at the north bank of Wei Shui 渭水and was conferred the title of Wu Wang Shi 武王师, the Adviser to Wu Wang. In 1122 BC, he contributed to the defeat of Shang 商 and was given the state of Qi 齐 as his reward, with Yingqiu 营丘 (Shandong Province Qingzhou County 山东省青州府) as capital. His grandson Mu Gong Hu 穆公虎 was also conferred the state of Zhang 鄣 (Shandong Province Dongping Zhou 山东省东平州). The Zhang State was a subordinate state of Qi.

Part 3:
Wei 伟, the eighth-generation grandson of Mu Gong, during the period of Zhou Yiwang 周夷王, declared himself Zhang Cheng Wang 章成王. Notice that he had dispensed with the right side of the word 鄣. His seventh-generation grandson was Hu Gong Xiang 胡公祥, whose state was exterminated by the state of Qi 齐 in 664 BC. Hu Gong's son Xian 显 decided to use Zhang 章 as the surname for his family, and moved to settle at Hejian 河间 (in present-day Hebei Province 河北省). He was the progenitor of the Zhang surname 章姓始祖.

Why was the Root of the Zhangs in China in Pu Cheng in North Fujian 闽北浦城?

The descendants of Xian 显 lived in Hejian until the Jin Period 晋代, and the Minister for Defence, Zhang 章岩, settled in Fujian Province, Nan An county 福建省南安县。In late Tang Dynasty 唐末, Zhang Ji 章及, the tenth-generation grandson of Zhang Yan, moved from Nan An to Pu Cheng. His son, Zhang Xiu 章修 was the Military Judge in Fuzhou 福州. Zhang Xiu had two sons, the elder was Zhang Zi Jun 章仔钧 and the younger Zhang Zi Chuan 章仔釧. Zhang Zi Jun can be said to be the first ancestor of the Zhangs in China.

According to Ouyang Xiu 欧阳修, the historian who created the system of recording genealogy in China, it was difficult to trace the genealogy of the Zhangs before Zhang Zi Jun because of the long time lapse. The records of Zhang Zi Jun and his wife Mrs Lian 练夫人 were traceable as there were only about thousand years.

Zhang Zi Jun had fifteen sons and sixty-eight grandsons, all of whom had attained high levels of scholastic and officialdom achievement. Over a thousand years, the family spread all over China. Its achievements culminated in the Song Dynasty. The entire family produced over four hundred Jinshi 进士 (equivalent to present-day Bachelor's degree). The branch in Pu Cheng alone produced twenty-five Jinshis, two zhuanyuans 状元 (top imperial scholars), three 宰相 (prime ministers) and nine shangshus 尚书 (cabinet ministers) .

There are still numerous relics, books and genealogy materials of the Zhangs in Pu Cheng today. In recent years, Zhangs' relics such as An Lang Bridge 安廊桥, Zhang Zi Jun Tomb in Bai Yang Cemetery 白羊坟章仔钧墓, Nan Feng Temple Merit Hall 南峰寺功德院, Xian Yang Lian Village 仙阳练村 (Mrs. Lian's ancestral village?) and Kuang Shan Zhang Yi Monastery 匡山章溢苦斋 have been progressively approved as Provincial Cultural Heritage places to be preserved for posterity.

Source: **Chaozhou Zhang Shi Genealogy 潮州章氏族谱**
Compiled by: **Zhang Shi Genealogy Editorial Committee 潮州章氏族谱编委会**
November 2013

章氏家训

怀疑别人的心不可有，不要听不利团结的话，不能干引起公愤的事，不要有贪图公众利益的行为，不良行为在萌生意念时就应当及早遏制，切不可发养成恶习惯，最要紧是事实就是，万事以诚为本。

子孙虽多而庸碌无才，是最大的不幸；家产虽富而喜于铺张，是贫穷的根源；门庭虽闹而调理无度，是最大的败落；交际虽广而结恶从邪，是最大的罪行。

不肖子孙眼底无几句诗书，胸无一段道理，精神萎靡不振，为人的礼仪如痴人一般漫然不知，却纵欲如狂，气度如乞丐一样卑鄙，败祖宗家业，辱母名声，乡邻为之羞耻，妻妾为之哭泣，像这种人怎配列入我宗祠谱中，死后怎配葬我列祖坟地呢？
以上安家处世格言，应日夜诵读，切记在心

The Zhang Family Mottos

Do not be suspicious of others, do not listen to words that are unfavourable to unity, do not do things that arouse public outrage, do not behave in ways against public interest, nip bad behaviours in the bud, never allow them to develop into undesirable habits, honesty is the best policy.

It is the greatest misfortune to have many mediocre and incompetent descendants; excessive extravagance is the root cause of poverty; unregulated entertainment will surely lead to downfall; having a wide social network particularly with evil elements is the greatest crime.

Unscrupulous and lowly educated children and grandchildren could not distinguish right from wrong, they are sluggish in spirit, ignorant of manner like idiots, have excessive indulgence in desires, exhibit beggarly demeaner, ruin ancestral fortunes, humiliate their parents' reputation, put neighbours and fellow villagers to shame and make wives and concubines cry in misery. Such persons do not deserve to be included in family genealogy book lodge in ancestral hall, and are unworthy to bury in the ancestors' burial ground upon death.

The above mottos should be read day and night, and be constantly remembered.

Our Family Tree

我们的家谱

CHAPTER 1

Paternal Roots

Our paternal grandfather, Chiang Sia Hua (章聲和) was brought up in the village of Zhanglin (樟林), which was part of Cheng Hai (澄海) County, Guangdong (广东省) Province. He inherited his rice processing business from his father Chiang Huan Chew (章芳州), based in Shantou (汕头) City, and his business was doing very well. He had remarkable acumen in business matters and later ventured into importing Japanese rice. As the business expanded, he faced rivalry from the local rice growers, who boycotted his services in rice processing. All the debts owed to him were never recovered, and he was stopped from importing Japanese rice, while the investigations of the allegation of price undercutting by the farmers took a long time to resolve. Grandpa had to look after his wife and seven children, while his future in the village was bleak and uncertain. He had to think out of the box and brace himself for new challenges in order to survive.

As such, his business was heavily disrupted and inevitably had to be folded up. The future in Shantou was bleak, therefore he decided to move out to Thailand to seek greener pastures. It was a difficult decision to make as his seven children were still young and they had to fend for themselves. There was no guarantee that he could make it in a foreign land without the support of his friends and family. The next question was how long would he be away; in the worst scenario, he might not even return to China to be with his family. This was indeed a big risk and a difficult decision he had to take.

With his departure as the head of the family, the responsibility of looking after his wife and children fell on grandma Cheo Ah Sian (蒋亜婵). It was heart-breaking for grandma too as she had to play dual roles as a breadwinner and head of the family. Another disappointment was that her eldest son, Chiang Boon Lim (章文林), also wanted to leave the family and head for Singapore to explore other job opportunities. Father and son decided in desperation to migrate to different destinations of South East Asia for better prospects and chances of survival in order to bring home the bacon for the family. Around the mid-1950s, after the communists took over China, our fourth aunt Chiang Guet Seng (章月笙) decided to migrate to Singapore to unite with her husband Teo Kwee Seng (张贵成). It was also a difficult decision as she had to bring along her young son and endure the long journey on board an overcrowded passenger liner to reach Singapore.

During those tumultuous years, my father Chiang Boon Lim migrated from Zhanglin village, a district in Cheng Hai County, to Singapore in 1936. He was just over 20 years old when he sailed for more than a week to Singapore with just some cash and small pieces of gold ornaments. The journey to Singapore cost about one hundred yuan, with no proper sleeping space. He was squeezed in an overcrowded steam passenger liner with about one thousand refugees and sailed toward a new destiny, hoping to build a better future to support his mother, younger brother and sisters.

At that time, he was already married to Teo Siew Lan (張秀兰) and had a son called Kheng Soy (章庆先). He too had to sacrifice and leave them behind in Zhanglin village to look for greener pastures elsewhere. It was a big risk he had to take as his aspirations might not have turned out as expected. When he first landed on the shores of Singapore, all the refugees were required to be quarantined. All passengers, male and female, were stripped naked and covered only with a small towel for thorough medical examinations near the wharf area. After the check up and clearance, he was allowed to proceed to his destination, but to his great disappointment, a relative who promised to pick him up did not show up. It was a bad start to his journey to seek a better future in a foreign land. With utmost desperation, he braced himself to take a rickshaw to Boat Quay to meet up with the relative who worked at the Yong Ann Kai Kee Rice supplier company.

All newly arrived immigrants had to start from scratch and work very hard. My father started his first job at the Boat Quay area as a janitor, a far cry from his position as the son of a rice processing merchant who employed more than thirty workers. There was no proper room for him to rest after work, and he was paid only six dollars monthly. He was loaned a foldable canvas bed to sleep at the corridor of the shop. He worked for half a year before he moved on to become a shop assistant at 5th mile Upper Serangoon area. The job has been recommended by a former classmate, and he had to walk from Boat Quay to Upper Serangoon for an interview with the boss. As a newly arrived migrant, he had to be frugal and save for his survival. It was in the late evening when he arrived at the shop, barefooted, as the pair of clogs he was wearing had given way. He was offered dinner by the shopkeeper, but he turned down their offer politely even though he was hungry and tired after the long journey. He discreetly went to a tap with drinkable water to fill his empty stomach and to quench his thirst. After the interview, he was supposed to return to Boat Quay, but was asked to stay by the boss who agreed to employ him and offered him a place to sleep for the night.

"During those tumultuous years, my father Chiang Boon Lim was just over 20 years old when he sailed for more than a week to Singapore with just some cash and small pieces of gold ornaments. The journey to Singapore cost about one hundred yuan, with no proper sleeping space."

It was not a bed of roses here as his new boss took advantage of him. He was not paid for the first two months but continued to be his slave. To his disappointment, after the third month, he was reimbursed with just eighteen dollars and given another four dollars as a Red-Packet for Lunar New Year. He had to continue working in such exploitative conditions until he came up with the idea to improve the business by providing free letter-writing services and assisting in free remittance matters in order to draw more customers. With his writing and interpersonal relationship skills, the business flourished, and his salary was increased to sixteen dollars per month. Under demanding circumstances, he also forced himself to learn to speak in the Malay language to communicate with customers who could not speak the Teochew dialect or Mandarin. Another challenge he had to overcome was to learn the names of the products, vegetables and fruits in Malay in order to communicate with the customers and increase sales for the shop.

Unfortunately, after a few years, the island was invaded by the Japanese and his career was disrupted. Fortunately, he did not run into trouble with the Japanese soldiers or else he would have been rounded up with the rest of the innocent civilians to be executed at the Sook Ching Massacre site at Punggol Point beach. With his past experience in dealing with the Japanese rice suppliers in Shantou, he was used to their culture of paying obeisance and impressed the Japanese soldiers. After the Japanese surrendered in 1945, he ventured out on his own and started a small shop dealing with animal feeds and household products. He was doing well with his business, and when it was stable, he was in a better position to start a second family and be rooted in Singapore.

However, it was not smooth sailing all the way. He had to face another setback because, when the British took over Singapore from the surrendered Japanese army, all Japanese currencies were deemed invalid. He lost a fortune and his business had to be folded up. From then on, his dream to be a businessman never materialized, and he began to develop an interest in community and social services.

He devoted his time to helping Mr. Tan Kah Kee (陈嘉庚), a well-known philanthropist and community leader, to raise funds to rebuild China, which was extensively destroyed by the Japanese occupation. Finally, he joined the Chia Keng village temple management committee and devoted his time to serve the villagers. With his past experience, he was in a better position to help the villagers to write letters and arrange remittance. With his contacts and influence, he soon gained the confidence of the elders, who made him hold more responsible roles in the community.

With more added responsibilities and heavy commitments in managing the association, he had to sacrifice his business and do part-time trading jobs. Our older family members had to chip in to help whenever and wherever they could. We too had to fend for ourselves and take care of our schoolwork and examinations. It was very tough and challenging for him as he had to take care of thirteen children and his two wives. We considered ourselves very blessed and lucky that he was able to raise us and provided us with a good education. More importantly, the most important lesson we learned from him was to give back to the society. He always instilled in us to respect and help the poor and underprivileged. He was heavily committed to his community services rendered to the kampong folks, and looking after the family was left to my mother. As such, his plan of returning to China for a reunion with our grandma, uncle and aunties was difficult to materialize due to his heavy commitments, travel restrictions and financial constraints.

Our beloved mother had also left a strong impact on us with her patient and caring nature as she had to struggle and take care of her own ten children. To supplement the family income, she did part-time sewing and manufactured joss papers for the cottage industry from home. Our maternal aunties, uncles and relatives were also very cooperative and helped to take care of us while we gathered to have fun and had meals with our cousins in their houses.

Fortunately, by the early 60's, my dad was able to secure a canteen stall at the Sing Ming High School, and our eldest brother Kheng Soy was in charge of the operations. The income from the canteen food stall helped to lessen the financial burden and supplement the household expenses. By the 70's, our other older brothers and eldest sister had started working and helped to defray the education expenses for my younger brothers and sisters.

It was around this period that dad wanted to try and venture into the florist business at 621 Upper Serangoon Road. He started the business as a partnership operation with my fifth brother Gary and some friends at the rented premises of a pre-war-period stilt-house. The business kicked off with a good start with strong support from the community leaders and his circle of friends from various associations and business associates. Running a small retail business with many partners was not easy, and after a few years, the partners left to start their own shop as the number of clientele had grown and the business was making good progress.

With the growing numbers of English-educated clients, more help was needed to handle the operations of the shop. As such, my younger sister Audrey and I were roped in to help with the operations and handle orders from English-speaking customers. At that time, the business was already in a steady stage and I had just completed my studies at Nanyang Academy of Fine Arts. The Fine Arts education had in a way helped me finetune and improve the flower arrangements and presentations. As sales picked up, I had to help in the delivery services and as such forced myself to learn driving after my art classes. Audrey was in charge of taking orders from walk-in customers, managing telephone orders and issuing invoices.

Nothing was permanent and unfortunately we had to face another stage of uncertainty, as by the mid 70's the house owner wanted to take back his rented premises to prepare for redevelopment. Our family was left with no other choice but to find an alternative site to carry on with the business. It was a blessing in disguise as, at that time, HDB was already building eight blocks of flats with shops opposite our flower shop. We managed to secure a shop unit and move our operation to Lorong Lew Lian Estate in 1977. The shop was built with a dwelling unit, and our parents and younger family members prepared to move over. Mum had to prepare lunch and dinner for all of us, and it made sense to have a central kitchen. With most of the family members living under one roof, we had the advantage of having more helping hands in the flower shop. My youngest brother and sister, Melvyn and Ivy, along with my sister-in-law Florence, were recruited to help in the shop.

A new chapter opened as we began operations at the new shop at Lorong Lew Lian. We met more friends and immersed ourselves in a new environment. Our family members continued to be involved in community services and served in grassroots organizations to revive our kampong spirit.

The Early Zhangs (Chiangs) Ancestors

Emperor Yan, said to be the progenitor of the Zhangs (章)

Jiang Ziya (姜子牙), popularly known as Jiang Tai Gong (姜太公), said to be one of earliest ancestors of the Zhangs.

Zhang Zi Jun (章子钧), the first traceable ancestor of the Zhangs. He was the first Zhang to settle in Pu Cheng (莆城) in North Fujian.

Mrs Lian (练夫人), wife of Zhang Zi Jun.

Source: Chaozhou Zhang Shi Genealogy 潮州章氏族谱

Chiang Family Tree　章氏世系谱 (中国,泰国和新加坡)

17th 代 Generation

章作本 x 陈明金
Great Great Great Grandfather / Grandmother Chiang Chak Poon x Tan Meng Kim

18th 代 Generation

章孝长 x 许敬发
Great Great Grandfather /Grandmother Chiang How Chian x Koh Ken Huat

19th 代 Generation

章芳州 x 刘庄肃
Great Grandfather / Grandmother Chiang Huan Chew x Low Chng Sock

20th 代 Generation

章聲和 x 蒋亜婵/陈娥芝
Grandfather /Grandmothers Chiang Sia Hua x Cheo Ah Sian /Tang Ngoa Jue

21st 代 Generation

1	2	3	4	5	6	7	8
章文林 X	章月枝 X	章月吟 X	章月娥 X	章月笙 X	章月全 X	章文定 X	章赛柔 X
張秀兰/林宝娘	林天敏	陈进樑	郑传芳	张贵成	陈亿秋	郑佩粧	夏森发
Boon Lim X	Guet Kee X	Guet Ngim X	Guet Ngoh X	Guet Seng X	Guet Chuan X	Boon Thia X	Sai Jieu X
Teo Siew Lan/ Lim Poh Neo	Lim Thiam Meng	Tan Chin Lian	Tay Tuan Huan	Teo Kwee Seng	Tan Aik Chew	Tay Puay Chuan	Hay Siam Huat

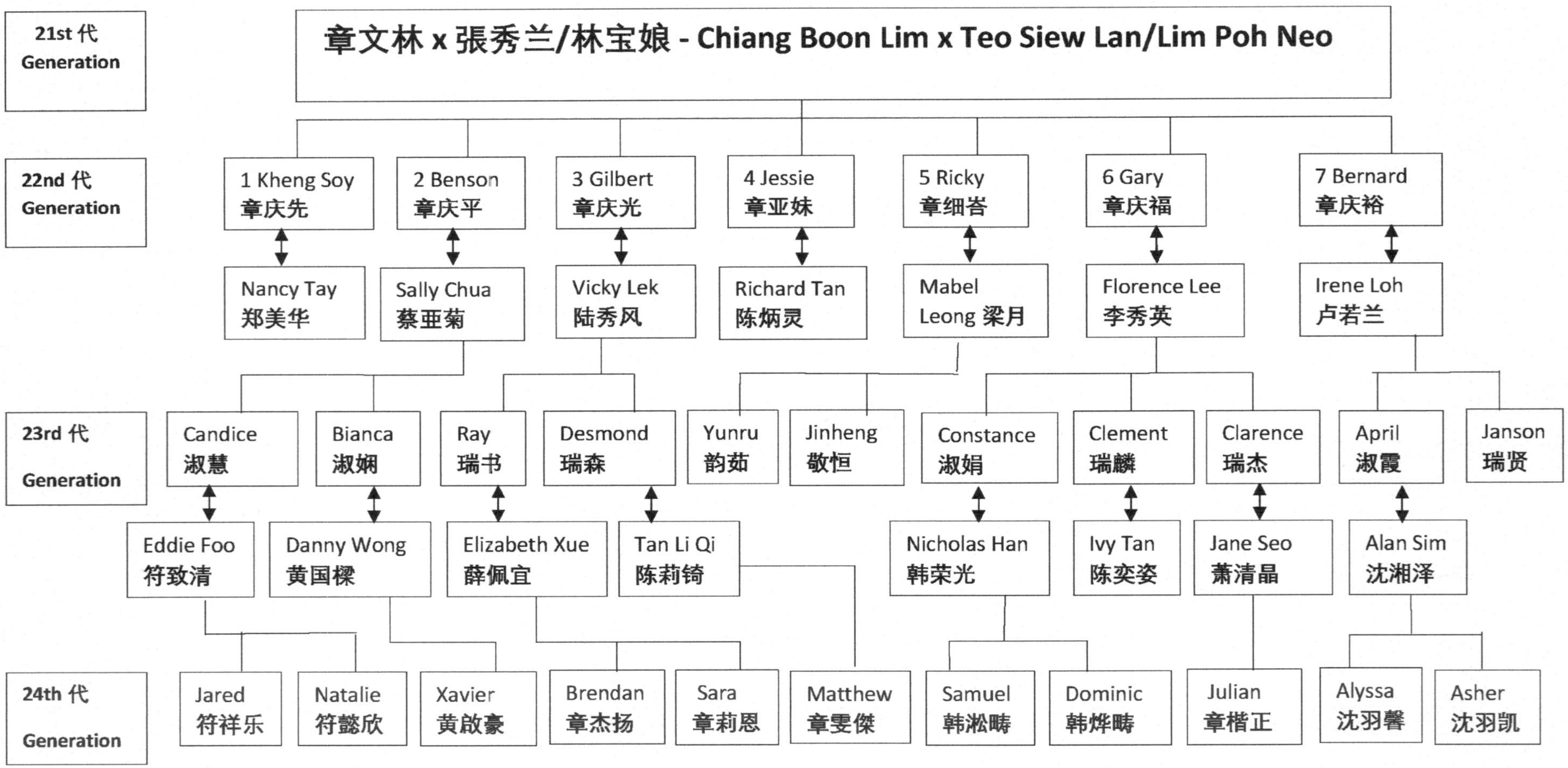

21st 代 Generation
22nd 代 Generation
23rd 代 Generation
24th 代 Generation
章文林 x 張秀兰/林宝娘 - Chiang Boon Lim x Teo Siew Lan/Lim Poh Neo
1 Kheng Soy 章庆先
Nancy Tay 郑美华
2 Benson 章庆平
Sally Chua 蔡亚菊
3 Gilbert 章庆光
Vicky Lek 陆秀风
4 Jessie 章亚妹
Richard Tan 陈炳灵
5 Ricky 章细岺
Mabel Leong 梁月
6 Gary 章庆福
Florence Lee 李秀英
7 Bernard 章庆裕
Irene Loh 卢若兰
Candice 淑慧
Eddie Foo 符致清
Bianca 淑娴
Danny Wong 黄国樑
Ray 瑞书
Elizabeth Xue 薛佩宜
Desmond 瑞森
Tan Li Qi 陈莉锜
Yunru 韵茹
Jinheng 敬恒
Constance 淑娟
Nicholas Han 韩荣光
Clement 瑞麟
Ivy Tan 陈奕姿
Clarence 瑞杰
Jane Seo 萧清晶
April 淑霞
Alan Sim 沈湘泽
Janson 瑞贤
Jared 符祥乐
Natalie 符懿欣
Xavier 黄啟豪
Brendan 章杰扬
Sara 章莉恩
Matthew 章雯傑
Samuel 韩淞畴
Dominic 韩烨畴
Julian 章楷正
Alyssa 沈羽馨
Asher 沈羽凯

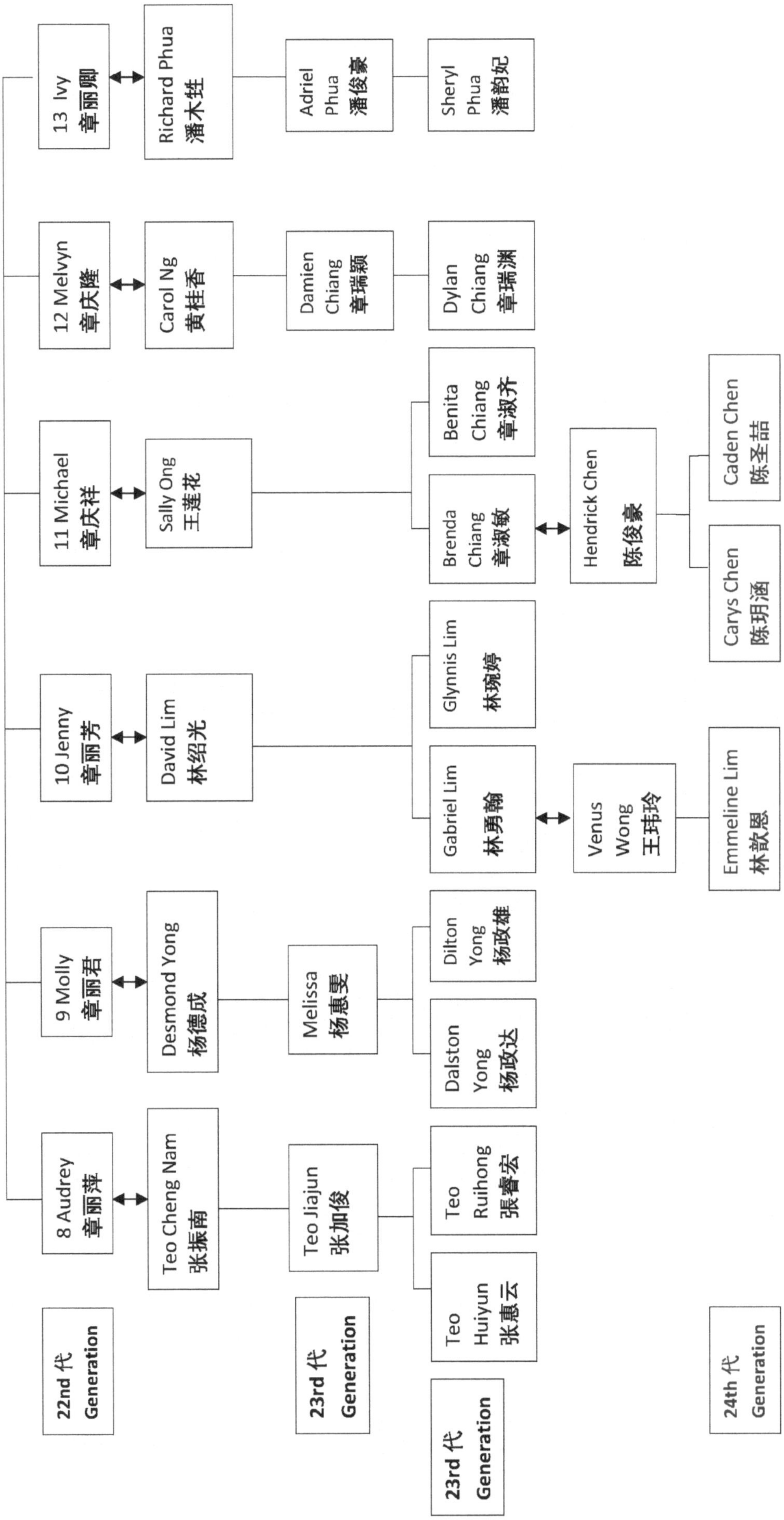
22nd 代
Generation
23rd 代
Generation
23rd 代
Generation
24th 代
Generation
8 Audrey
章丽萍
Teo Cheng Nam
张振南
Teo Jiajun
张加俊
Teo
Huiyun
张惠云
Teo
Ruihong
張睿宏
9 Molly
章丽君
Desmond Yong
杨德成
Melissa
杨惠雯
Dalston
Yong
杨政达
Dilton
Yong
杨政雄
10 Jenny
章丽芳
David Lim
林绍光
Gabriel Lim
林勇翰
Venus
Wong
王玮玲
Emmeline Lim
林歆恩
Glynnis Lim
林琬婷
11 Michael
章庆祥
Sally Ong
王莲花
Brenda
Chiang
章淑敏
Hendrick Chen
陈俊豪
Carys Chen
陈玥涵
Caden Chen
陈圣喆
Benita
Chiang
章淑齐
12 Melvyn
章庆隆
Carol Ng
黄桂香
Damien
Chiang
章瑞颖
Dylan
Chiang
章瑞渊
13 Ivy
章丽卿
Richard Phua
潘木牲
Adriel
Phua
潘俊豪
Sheryl
Phua
潘韵妃

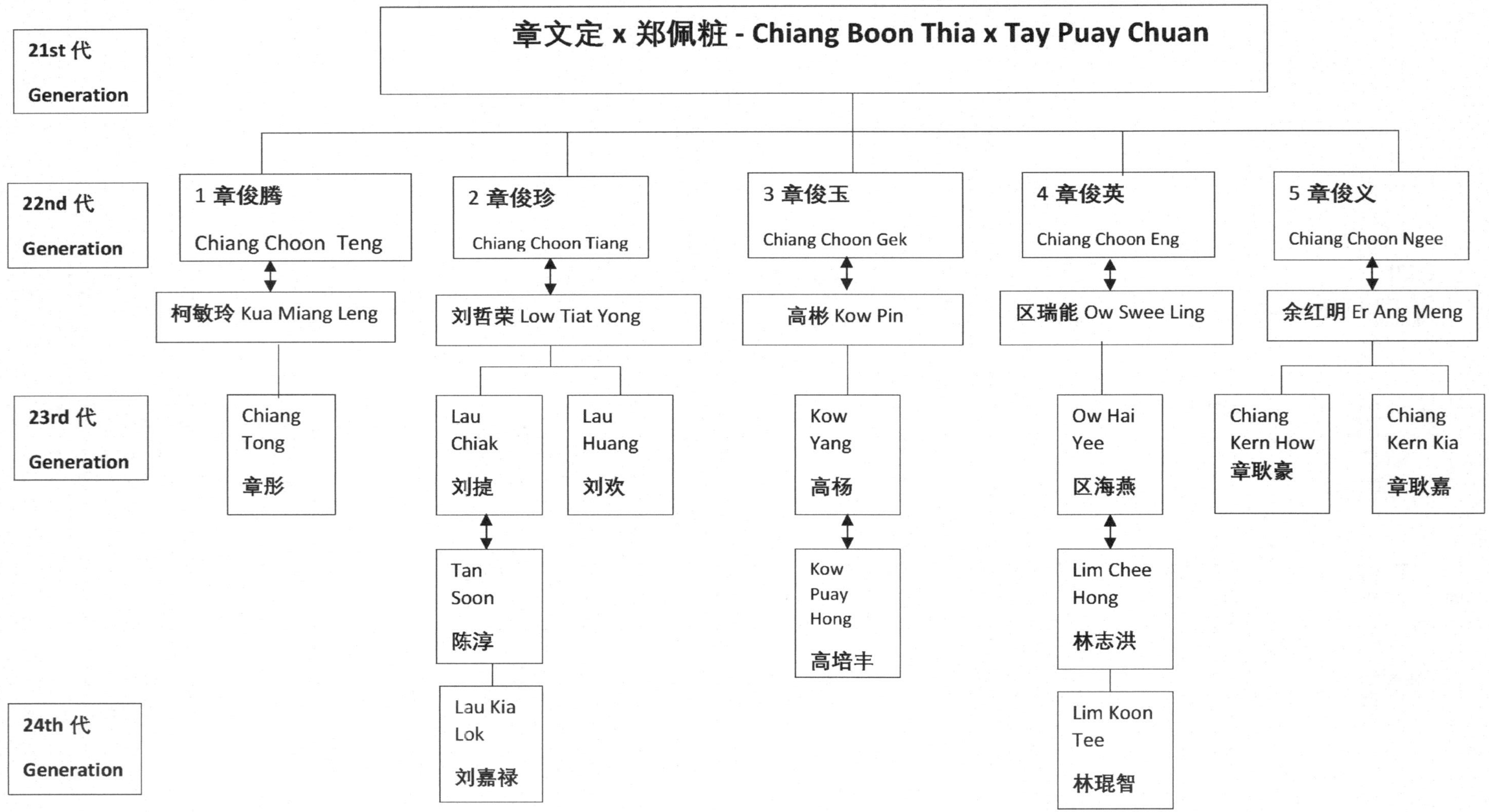
21st 代 Generation
22nd 代 Generation
23rd 代 Generation
24th 代 Generation
章文定 x 郑佩粧 - Chiang Boon Thia x Tay Puay Chuan
1 章俊腾 Chiang Choon Teng
柯敏玲 Kua Miang Leng
Chiang Tong 章彤
2 章俊珍 Chiang Choon Tiang
刘哲荣 Low Tiat Yong
Lau Chiak 刘捷
Tan Soon 陈淳
Lau Kia Lok 刘嘉禄
Lau Huang 刘欢
3 章俊玉 Chiang Choon Gek
高彬 Kow Pin
Kow Yang 高杨
Kow Puay Hong 高培丰
4 章俊英 Chiang Choon Eng
区瑞能 Ow Swee Ling
Ow Hai Yee 区海燕
Lim Chee Hong 林志洪
Lim Koon Tee 林琨智
5 章俊义 Chiang Choon Ngee
余红明 Er Ang Meng
Chiang Kern How 章耿豪
Chiang Kern Kia 章耿嘉

17th 代
Generation

Great Great Great Grandfather & Grandmother
Chiang Chak Poon
&
Tan Meng Kim
章作本
陈明金

18th 代
Generation

Great Great Grandfather & Grandmother
Chiang How Chian
&
Koh Ken Huat
章孝长
许敬发

19th 代
Generation

Great Grandfather
Chiang Huan Chew 章芳州

Great Grandmother
Low Chng Sock 刘庄肃

20th 代
Generation

Grandmother
Cheo Ah Sian 蒋亜婵
(China)

Grandfather
Chiang Sia Hua 章聲和

Grandmother
Tang Ngoa Jue 陈娥芝
(Thailand)

Paternal Family Tree 父系家谱

Family picture taken in the 50's with Paternal grandmother, grandaunties and relatives from our ancestral village at Chung Lim.

1950年代与祖母在樟林村的家人合影。

Descendants Of The Chiang Family 章氏家族的后裔

21st代
Generation

1st wife
Teo Siew Lan (China)
張秀兰

Eldest son
Chiang Boon Lim
章文林

2nd wife
Lim Poh Neo (Singapore)
林宝娘

Children by first wife :
L to R: Kheng Soy, Jessie & Ricky
庆先, 亚妹, 细明

22nd代
Generation

Children by second wife :
L to R: Melvin, Michael, Gary, Benson, Bernard, Gilbert, Molly, Jenny, Audrey & Ivy
庆隆, 庆祥, 庆福, 庆平, 庆裕, 庆光, 丽君, 丽芳, 丽萍, 丽卿

Eldest daughter Chiang Guet Kee and husband Mr Lim Thiam Miang and family members Tai Poh, Suan Chin, Kee Suan, Kee Hwee, Koon Kwang and Keng Kwang.

大姑章月枝, 姑丈林天敏和家庭成员: 岱波, 旋琛, 琦旋, 琦辉, 群光, 庆光。

2nd daughter Chiang Guet Ngim and Children Chiap Chin, Chiap Kern and Chiap Chay with grandchildren.

二姑章月吟和家庭成员: 泽深, 泽勤, 泽静。

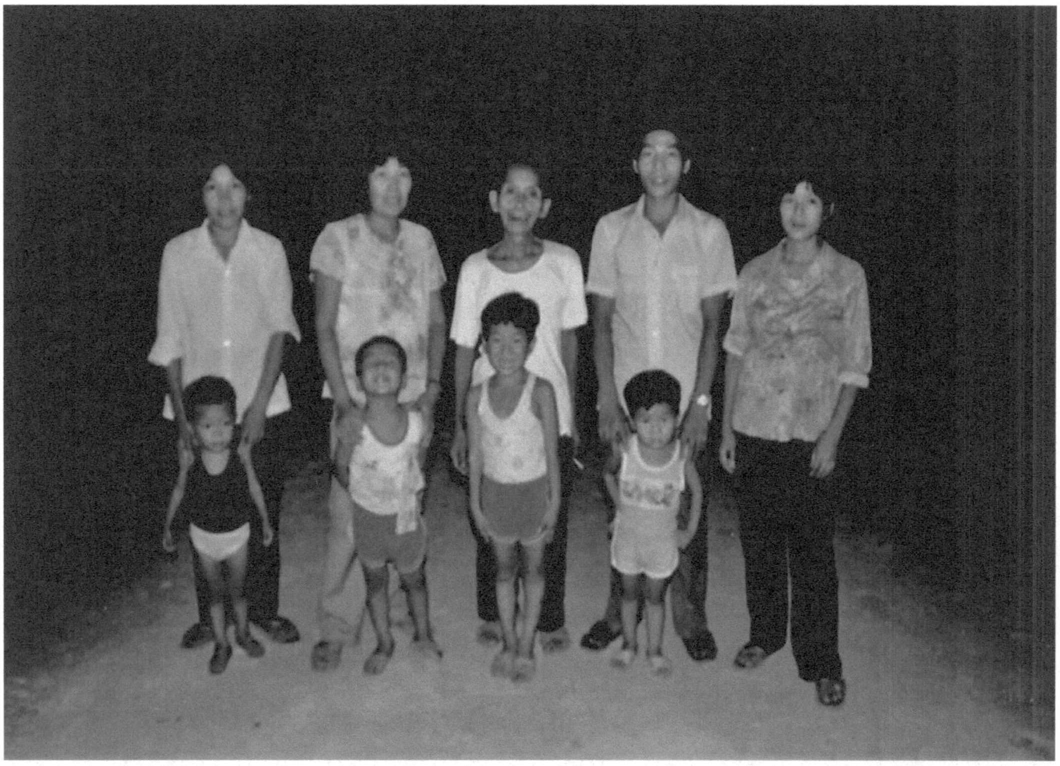

Third daughter Chiang Guet Ngo, husband Mr Tay Tuan Huan with family members Sock Koon, Sock Hoon, Kay Chiap and grandchildren.

三姑章月娥, 姑丈郑传芳和家庭成员: 淑君, 淑芬, 家哲, 媳妇, 和孙子。

4th daughter Chiang Guet Seng and husband Mr Teo Kwee Seng with children Chee Kwang, Chee How and Chee Hong. Daughters-in-law Chia Fui Keng and Seah Geok Suan.

Grandchildren Lee Tong, Lee Hee, Lee Yong, Hutt Wang, Shun Xie and Hutt Soon.

四姑章月笙, 姑丈张贵成和家庭成员: 张志光, 张志浩, 张志宏, 媳妇: 谢慧娟, 谢玉宋和孙子。

5th daughter Chiang Guet Chuan and husband Tan Aik Chew with family members Koon Hiong, Swee Hong, Koon Wee, Swee Nah, Swee Ling and grandchildren.

五姑章月全, 姑丈陈亿秋和家庭成员: 群雄, 瑞宏, 群伟, 瑞娜, 瑞玲, 媳妇, 和孙子。

Youngest son Chiang Boon Thia and wife Tay Puay Chuan with their children, son-in-laws, daughter-in-laws and grandchildren. Eldest son Choon Teng, Kua Miang Leng and Chiang Tong. Eldest daughter Choon Tiang, Lau Tiat Yong, Lau Chiak, Lau Huang. Second daughter Choon Gek, Kow Ping and Kow Yeo. Youngest daughter Choon Eng, Koo Swee Ling, Koo Hai Yan Youngest son Choon Ngee, Er Ang Meng, Chiang Kern How and Chiang Kern Kia

叔叔章文定,亜婶郑佩妆和家人(章俊腾,柯敏玲,章彤)(章俊义,余红明,章耿豪,章耿嘉)(刘哲荣,章俊珍,刘捷,刘欢)(高彬,章俊玉,高杨)(区瑞能,章俊英,区海燕)。

Youngest daughter Saijai and husband Somchai with family members Wanna, Rewat, Nipa, Pacharee, Thanyatorn and grandchildren.

泰国六姑章赛柔, 夏森发姑丈和她的家庭成员。

CHAPTER 2

My First Visit to OurAncestral Village at Zhanglin (Chung Lim)

My first visit to China was in 1988 when I followed Dad, maternal granduncle, fourth paternal aunty and her two friends to our ancestral village. We landed at Shantou Waisha Airport and dad chartered a van to transport the entourage to our ancestral village in Zhanglin (樟林), which was part of Cheng Hai district (澄海) in Shantou (汕头) Prefecture. Cheng Hai was invaded and occupied by the Japanese from 1939 till 1945. It was recaptured by the People's Liberation Army a few years later. From 1994 onward, Cheng Hai was upgraded to a county-level city and was later administrated by the Shantou Provincial Government as a Special Economic Zone in 2011. The streets were overcrowded with many makeshift stalls, shoppers and pedestrians, making it very difficult for the hapless driver, who had to blast the vehicle horn intermittently to get the pedestrians to make way. The noise levels multiplied, with other drivers on the road also honking incessantly. We stayed in the guest house built specially for overseas relatives and guests in the village. Dad, granduncle and I shared one room and they slept on beds while I slept on the floor covered with straw mat. The fourth aunt and her friends stayed nearby with some other relatives. The noise from the crickets outside the courtyard was very irritating and disrupted our conversations with the relatives.

I was very happy to meet up with so many relatives for the first time but was emotional to see many of them undernourished and frail. I could understand why, in the 60's, dad had to send many sacks of used clothing and foodstuff back to the ancestral village to support them. All the village residents were very poor and almost everyone was expecting the overseas relatives to lift them out of poverty as there was not much opportunities in the village. The main objective of this visit was for dad to pay his tribute to

"Most of the relatives had missed a decent meal for a long time. They had been starving for a long time and were too poor to enjoy this luxury as they had to live within their means."

grandma at her final resting place. They had not met for decades, and due to many restrictions and financial constraints, there were slim chances of reunion when she was still around.

I remembered we were there in the month of July, which coincided with my birthday, and most of the relatives who visited us would bring a bunch of homegrown lychees and other fruits. Many of them had to walk for many hours from distant suburbs to meet us as they could not afford to buy a bicycle, not to mention there was no public transportation at all. Everyone was very happy and engrossed in catching up with one another to reminisce their childhood days. We spent the whole day in our room, engaging in chitchat and consuming lychees and peanuts with Chinese tea.

Due to excessive consumption of lychees, I ended up with a bowel problem. I was down with diarrhoea for a couple of days as my body system was not conditioned to the hygiene standards of the village. The whole room was filled with cigarette smoke from many chain smokers. Practically everyone was a smoker, whether young or old, and it was common to see their teeth were tarred by the nicotine in the tobacco.

While the relatives were busy catching up on lost time with Dad and fourth aunt, I took the opportunity to snap pictures and record their moment of happy reunion with the video recorder. I was fortunate to have borrowed the video recorder from my neighbour Heng Chee Meng, who was a full-time photographer. The earlier model of the Sony video recorder was heavy and bulky, and I needed help from my relative to carry the extra load of my photography equipment. Many of the relatives had never seen this gadget and were inquisitive about the operations and the final stage of production. At that time, we needed a cassette tape for the recording; however, storage was an issue — the tape turned moldy and destroyed all my precious recordings. My heart sank when I discovered fungus growing on the tapes, but I managed to retrieve certain parts of my historical recordings. As a novice to this new gadget, I was also afraid that the recordings might not turn up well. Luckily, I managed to capture some of the historical moments with the conventional camera, or else my trip to China would have been futile.

On the following day, Uncle Boon Thia managed to borrow two bicycles for us to tour the village and meet up with dad's childhood friends and relatives. Uncle Boon

Thia rode with dad in the back while I rode with my granduncle on the backseat of my bicycle. My fourth aunt and her friends had their own plans. We made our rounds in the village and stopped occasionally to take pictures. This experience reminded me of our kampong days in Singapore, where I learned to ride the bicycle and helped my maternal uncle to deliver groceries to his customers. We managed to visit our ancestral home where grandpa and grandma started their family. Unfortunately, I was told that the house had been sold after grandma passed away as the young uncle and all the aunties had their own matrimonial homes.

We had a peek at the small shed where our grandparents once lived, with a built-in well, and the bed that belonged to grandpa and grandma. The house was pitch dark and poorly ventilated, and their room had a very small window to let in natural sunlight. There was no electricity, running water, and proper sanitation. I could not imagine how my grandparents had managed to squeeze in their seven family members into the small shed. At that time, I was living in a three-room flat with my wife and two young children at Lorong Lew Lian, and I considered myself very lucky compared to their living conditions.

In the evening, Dad engaged the caretaker of the guest house to prepare a sumptuous meal for all the relatives and close friends. Probably during that period, most of the relatives had missed a decent meal for a long time. They had been starving for a long time and were too poor to enjoy this luxury as they had to live within their means. It was an eye opener as I witnessed this happy reunion of my dad and fourth aunt with their immediate family members. This historical moment was very touching and is always fresh in my mind. They certainly missed each other dearly for many decades. Unfortunately, our grandparents and first and third aunts did not survive the tumultuous years to witness the happy reunion with their loved ones.

The next day, our young uncle and his family helped to prepare offerings for us to pray and pay our tribute to our beloved grandma who passed away in 1978. Dad had missed her badly as he never saw her again after he left for Singapore. He took time to reflect on his childhood days with grandma and pray for forgiveness for the lost years. Uncle Boon Thia had prepared some of grandma's favorite dishes to be offered to her. At this momentous occasion, I could see that dad was emotional when he knelt down to pray in front of the tombstone. It was a blessing from grandma as I managed to capture this episode with my camera and some of these pictures turned up to be useful when I wanted to trace my family roots. The inscriptions on the tomb stone led me to discover the name of my great grandfather and my grandma's second name.

The following day, we visited a preserved fruits factory owned by a Singaporean friend, who was one of the earliest businessmen to venture into Zhanglin village. After a short tour of the factory and village, we visited our granduncle's relatives. Granduncle was happy to meet up with his cousins and their children, and they were surprised that I could converse in Teochew dialect and greeted them in accordance to decorum.

Their impression was that my mum was a Peranakan and therefore we would be conversant in the Malay and English languages only. Grandüncle had helped them build a house in the village and needed to iron out the transfer of ownership. It was another great reunion that I witnessed with maternal granduncle and his relatives. To them, I was an alien as I dressed differently in shorts and a colored polo T-shirt while most of the villagers donned different hues of sober grey-colored dresses.

After tying up the loose ends probably after the third day, granduncle left for Hong Kong by ship to take a flight back to Singapore. He was very busy with his business back home and could not join us for a short tour, whereas we stayed back for a couple of days before we travelled by bus to Guangzhou to take a flight to Guilin for a short holiday with the fourth aunt and her friends. At that time, China was just opening up, and the airports were not well administered as we were stuck at the Guangzhou airport for many hours and there were no fans, warm water, or food stalls available. With the unexpected disruption, we were lucky to have simple dinner catered for us as we waited for the plane to take off after our dinner.

My first trip was very fruitful and fulfilling as we managed to meet up with our close relatives and experienced their living conditions in the village first hand. We also had a better understanding of their plight and their limitations in finding jobs and business opportunities. We had heard bad things from friends who had visited their relatives in China. Some of them had had bad experiences and were disappointed with how demanding and possessive their relatives were.

Conversely, if we were in their position, we would also hope our better-off relatives could help lift us from poverty. History took a twist later when my granduncle's son told me that he was astonished when his relatives from Zhanglin visited them few years after our trip. They came to Singapore, hunting for expensive branded products!

Paternal ancestral home at Zhanglin village and the ancient bed of our grandparents.

参观我爷爷奶奶的故居，及他们古老的床。

Our ancestral village at Zhanglin.

爷爷奶奶故居的一口井及樟林村街景。

Our ancestral village at Zhanglin.

樟林村街景。

Fourth aunt and her youngest son Chee Hong visited the Chiang Ancestral Hall at Zhanglin after the reconstruction with contributions and support from overseas relatives and members.

新加坡四姑和她的小儿子张志宏参观了由海外亲友捐资重建的章氏祠堂。

Our Ancestral Hall was almost collapsed and rebuilt with contributions from relatives overseas.

我们的祠堂几近倒塌，侨胞捐资重修。

In the early 80's, relatives from Singapore were transported by manual and motorised three-wheelers to the village.

在80年代，人力及机动三轮车是前往乡村的常见交通工具。

Relatives from Singapore walking down the memory lane to reminisce their childhood days in Zhanglin village.

新加坡的亲戚回味儿时的村在樟林。

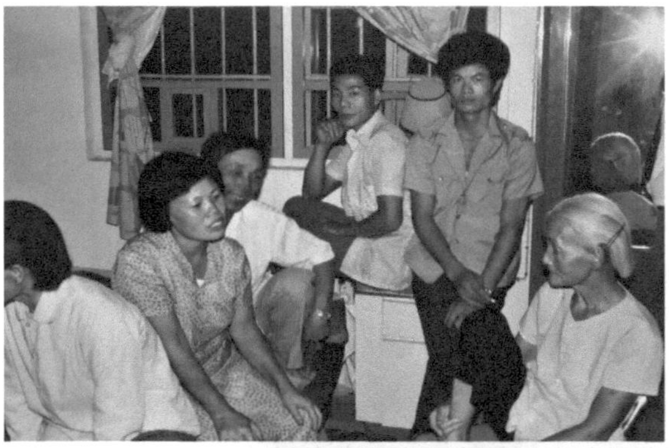

My first meeting with our China relatives in the village guest house in 1988.

1988年，我第一次在招待所与中国亲戚见面。

We visited the tomb along with his brother, sisters and brothers-in-law, niece and grand-nephew in 1988.

1988年爸爸和我与中国亲戚一起向在樟林的祖母墓地致敬。

Relatives visited the final resting place of paternal grandmother to mark the completion of the tombstone in the late 70's.

中国的亲戚在我们心爱的祖母重修墓地后合影。

CHAPTER 3

The Glorious Days of Zhanglin Ancient Port: The Birthplace of Our Ancestors

The Zhanglin Ancient Port (樟林古港) is located in Dongli (东里) town of Cheng Hai (澄海) district in Shantou (汕头) city. In the ancient days, it was a small and undeveloped port but later became a popular port under the Song Dynasty. The port was well known and became the busiest port in Guangdong (广东省) Province from 1723 to 1791. Zhanglin Port was chosen as the centre of rice trade with Siam, currently known as Thailand, because of its strategic location. Rice trading with Thailand intensified due to the shortage of the grain in China as the population multiplied tremendously after peace was restored by the Qing government. According to historical reports, no import duties were imposed on imported rice during the reigns of Emperor Kangxi and Emperor Qianlong from 1722 to 1796.

With regular and intensive trading activities between the two countries, soon Thailand became one of the most popular destinations for many Teochew migrants. Many of the Teochew traders, including my grandfather, preferred to migrate to Thailand, which offered better opportunities in agriculture and trade. According to historical records, more than one million Chaoshan ancestors disembarked from Zhanglin Port to migrate to Siam.

The shipping vessels were wooden sailing junks with the bow painted in red colour and with two big eyes on each side, which was called Hongtouchuan (红头船). The olden-day sailors believed that the pair of painted eyes could help them navigate speedily to the right destinations. As the birthplace of the Hongtouchuan, Zhanglin Port was an important gateway to foreign trade and became one of the larges ports in eastern Guangdong.

The first Hongtouchuan from Zhanglin Port sailed to Singapore in 1821.[1] Initially the vessels functioned as cargo ships transferring goods such as dried food stuff and ceramics to South East Asia, and in return the sailors would bring back opium and dried shark fins back to China. Later on, the ships were used to ferry passengers to South East Asia.

Most of the junks were made in Thailand because of the availability of lasting wood and cheaper labor costs. To differentiate the origin of the junks, the government mandated the colour codes for the bows to be painted in red for junks from Zhanglin Port, which was under Guangdong Province. Fujian province used green, Zhejiang used white, and Jiangsu used black.

With abundant opportunities in Thailand, the numbers of Teochew immigrants multiplied in great numbers, especially in the Bangkok area. Some of the immigrants and their descendants soon rose and became prominent politicians and businessmen in Siam. Historical records revealed the most notable and prominent Teochew immigrant was Tay Sin (鄭信), who became King Taksin of Siam. His father was known as Tay Yong (鄭鏞) from Teng Hai county in Guangdong province. He founded the

[1] Zhou, Y. (2018, October 10). Zhanglin port, once the largest port in eastern GD. Life of Guangzhou. Retrieved June 9, 2022, from https://www.lifeofguangzhou.com/wap/article/content.do?contextId=8342

The glorious days of Zhanglin may have faded, but the remnants of the historical sites remind us of its rich culture and incredible heritage.

Thonburi Dynasty and ousted the Burmese occupation of Ayutthaya and ruled from 1767 to 1782.[2] According to historians, there were other prominent and influential Teochews who became Prime Ministers and Deputy Prime Ministers.

Unfortunately, Zhanglin Port soon outlived its usefulness as the riverbed became silted and was replaced by Shantou Port to cater for the arrival of steamships in 1865. Shantou Port was officially opened in 1860. Many more migrants from Shantou took this opportunity to travel by steamships to head to South East Asia. The second wave of millions of Teochew immigrants departing from Shantou to South East Asia began in 1912 with the establishment of the Republic of China. Subsequently the volume of trade in Shantou Port ranked in the third

[2] Carl Parkes (2001). Moon Handbooks: Southeast Asia 4 Ed. Avalon Travel Publishing. ISBN 1-56691-337-3.; Bertil Lintner (2003). Blood Brothers: The Criminal Underworld of Asia. Macmillan Publishers. ISBN 1-4039-6154-9.; Woodside, A. B. (1988). Vietnam and the Chinese Model: A Comparative Study of Vietnamese and Chinese Government in the First Half of the Nineteenth Century. Council on East Asian Studies, Harvard University.

position after Shanghai and Guangzhou. Eventually the red-bow junks were replaced by steamships, and many Teochew migrants used Shantou Port to travel to South East Asia without limitations caused by the monsoon seasons. The steamships were more efficient as they could make many trips with higher volume of passengers.

In 2019, I revisited Zhanglin village with a group of childhood friends and was amazed by the transformation of the Ancient River and the restoration of surrounding streets and ancient buildings. I did not pay much attention to its historical background until early 2020, when I was reminded by the President of Genealogy Society Singapore, Mr Ng Yew Kang, that my ancestral village had formerly been a prosperous and popular place in the olden days. I researched about its history and was surprised to find out the interesting story of the birthplace of our ancestors. As such I would like to encourage the younger generations to find an opportunity to visit and trace their family roots, enrich themselves with their family history, and be connected with their relatives in China.

After visiting the historical birthplace and witnessing the living conditions of our ancestors, I considered myself to be very lucky and grateful. Apart from poverty, they had to struggle and survive tumultuous years of upheavals and uncertainties.

Drawing from their past experience, we can better understand and appreciate our ancestors' sacrifices to give us a good upbringing and provide us with the luxury of a good life and education. These lessons and values should be imparted to the younger and future generations.

The glorious days of Zhanglin may have faded, but the remnants of the historical sites remind us of its rich culture and incredible heritage. The arch of Xinxingjie Street (新兴街), Tianhou Temple (天后宫), Nanshengli Street (南盛里街), Shanhai Xiongzhen Temple (山海雄镇庙) and many other interesting architectural façades with both Chinese and Western designs were the testimonies of the days of glory of this ancient port.

These artifacts were the best evidence of economic and cultural exchanges between China and foreign countries in the olden days. According to historical reports, a stone tablet and the remnants of an ancient port site were discovered recently at Xinxingjie Street. I'm confident that, with greater publicity of these attractions, more overseas Teochews could consider this area as part of the itinerary when they visit Shantou city.

A replica of the red-bow ship on which many early migrants from Zhanglin village sailed from the Ancient River to Singapore.

许多移民从樟林古巷航行到新加坡的红头船复制品。

My friends and I revisited the conserved Ancient Port and River at Zhanglin in 2019.

2019年我和朋友参观了受保留的樟林古港。

永安楼

CHAPTER 4

The Values and Experience We Learned from Dad

Dad's purpose in traveling to Singapore was to look for an opportunity to have a new start in life and bring home the bacon to support his younger sisters and brother in China. As the eldest brother in the family, he was supposed to help grandpa to look after the younger ones in the family. After the family business in Zhanglin folded up, there was no future remaining in our ancestral village. There was no guarantee that his mission would be successful in Singapore, but he took the risk to seek greener pastures here, even after knowing from relatives that many people perished during travel due to hunger and sickness. We admired his guts and foresight to venture into a foreign land where he could not even speak the local working lingo.

His ability to make a living and be rooted in a foreign country with a second family was unimaginable. Having to take care of and feed so many children here was a great challenge and difficult to emulate. At the same time, he had to support his younger sisters and brother back in China. With his limitations, he was able to raise us and provide a sound education. He imparted good family values and instilled in us to give back to the society. He always reminded us to respect the elders and stressed the importance of mutual respect. According to him, filial piety and love and care for our parents and family always must be practiced. He often reminded us to remember the Chinese idiom — "When we drink water, think of its source" [饮水思源]. In other words, he reminded us not to forget or ignore our roots and know where we came from.

He was very lucky to once escape death while working in the family rice mill. He tried to fix the faulty rice-husking machine and was seriously injured when the machinery gave way and pinned him down. He was motionless while family members and workers tried to extricate him from the heavy machinery. He was blessed to survive the mishap and took many months to recover. It was an unforgettable lesson that he learned, and from then onward he swore not to meddle with any heavy machinery. Dad led a simple lifestyle and devoted his precious time to serving the community and advocating for the true kampong spirit among the villagers. He was a dedicated leader who cared and looked after the welfare of the villagers at Kampong Chia Keng since the 50's.

He was passionate about serving the community and, along with several other leaders from the village, established a firefighting unit to prevent and prepare for any eventual disaster. With the community preparedness and knowledge of fire prevention, the kampong folks were more assured and had peace of mind when they were away or working.

He and his team also initiated the opening of a free clinic to help poor villagers, since in those days the people were very vulnerable to contagious diseases as they had no knowledge of personal hygiene. Along with other village leaders, they managed to rope in members of Franciscan Missionaries of Mary to collaborate on this project.

In order to strengthen community bonding, the leaders organized an amateur Teochew Opera group to engage the villagers in performing arts. The successful setting up of the amateur opera troupe turned out to be a blessing as it was also used for fundraising activities. The troupe was engaged in many fundraising projects for the setting up of the free clinic, building of new schools and community centers and the establishment of the Arts Council and Defence Fund. When Kampong Chia Keng was affected by resettlement, we moved over to Lorong Lew Lian HDB Estate, and Dad continued to lead and serve the community resettled from various parts of Singapore. Initially, he and some other shop owners and coffee shop stall owners helped organize the first 7th Moon Celebrations Committee in order to create a sense of camaraderie among the people who were mostly relocated under HDB resettlement schemes. The intentions were to allow the newly resettled residents to build rapport and strengthen the old kampong spirit.

It was also a subtle move to scout for leadership prospects in the newly formed community to take on leading roles and be decision-makers. These small pools of leaders would be trained and nurtured to lead and help the community. When the Community Centre (CC) Management Committee and Residents Committee (RC) in Lorong Lew Lian were formed in 1979, dad was approached to recommend some of the 7th Moon Celebrations Committee members and shop merchants to help out in both committees. The idea came from Mr Lee Khoon Choy, who became a Member of Parliament and Adviser of Braddell Heights in 1980. He wanted to have a more balanced mix of representatives from both private and public sectors to sit in both committees.

At the onset, the members of the RC comprised mainly staff from the civil service and government agencies. The voices and the contributions from the ordinary citizens were absent, and it was easier to recruit members from the civil service to play leading roles and set the ball rolling. When Mr Lee Khoon Choy became the MP for Braddell Heights in 1980, he tasked the community leaders to recruit more members from the private sector to join the RC and CC Management Committee.

By 1983, my dad Chiang Boon Lim was approached by the RC and Lorong Lew Lian CC Management Committee to help organise and head the Senior Citizens Club. It was an uphill task as many of the elderlies were resettled from different areas and had different mindsets. Extensive efforts were needed to network and strengthen the team spirit before the committee could be formed. The task force had to choose the right person for the right job and ensure it was sustainable. Most of the senior citizens were from different dialect groups and majority couldn't speak Mandarin. That was another challenging task the pro tem committee had to handle. As the majority who were nominated to spearhead the committee were Teochews, the meetings were conducted in Teochew dialect and translated to Mandarin for those who couldn't understand. The Senior Citizens Club under his leadership grew from strength to strength, with more than a few hundred members, and he initiated the self-supporting system by appointing patrons to finance the annual anniversary celebrations and other activities.

To sustain the interest of the club members, he also initiated the formation of the Taiqi and Qigong Club with the help of a renowned martial arts instructor Mr Tan Geok Hoe. He also initiated wake visits and funeral send-offs for members and their parents and parents-in laws. To defray the expenses of the grieving family, a token of one hundred and fifty dollars was also contributed by the club. After more than thirty years, both the Senior Citizens and Taiqi clubs were still functioning well and in the good hands of his successor Heng Joon Chaik. I approached Mr Heng to lead the Senior Citizens Club as there was conflict of interest when I was appointed to succeed the RC Chairman Mr Loke Wah Heng, who passed away suddenly from a severe heart attack in 1986. By 1988, the Lorong Lew Lian Estate was demarcated and came under the purview of Aljunied GRC, with Mr Chin Harn Tong as the new MP. From then onwards, Mr Heng gradually recruited more new and younger members into the Senior Citizens Club and continued to nurture the legacy of my father.

Dad was a founding member of the Chung-Lim Community Oversea Association located at Hong Kong Street since the 1950s. The association was founded in 1960 to touch base and provide mutual help to the fellow Teochew immigrants from Zhanglin village in Cheng Hai County. With his experience and leadership, he was given leading roles to expand the club memberships and reach out to youth members. Like all organisations, leadership succession was crucial and youth played an important part to rejuvenate the ageing committee. As such, the association committee had to plan activities to attract and sustain the members' interest. The objective of the association was to provide a platform for fellow members to meet and engage in recreational activities in order to strengthen camaraderie. After about ten years, he was relegated to an advisory role and succeeded by younger leaders, with the Member of Parliament Dr Michael Lim Choon Leng, whose parents hailed from Zhanglin village, taking charge as the association's first Honorary Adviser in 1992. My second brother Benson Chiang

Kheng Peng, third brother Gilbert Chiang Kheng Kwang and youngest brother Melvyn Chiang Kheng Long were recruited to join the association in the 1980s. By 1994, my second brother Benson Chiang Kheng Peng was groomed to take over the chairmanship for the next six years. By year 2000, he handed over the chairmanship to a much younger member Mr Tan Kay Chuan, Project Director with the Institute of Technical Education (ITE). Mr Tan's late father, Mr Tan Boon Keng, was a founder member of the association.

With a team of younger leaders in the committee, they too have to infuse new blood into the association and prepare for the next innings. It was not easy to recruit and get younger members to join the traditionally ingrained club activities due to changing lifestyles. The younger family members were more interested in Country Club and Reservists Club facilities and activities. The committee members had to think out of the box to involve the members' children to generate a sense of belonging and affinity by providing educational bursary and commendation awards. The yearly awards were presented during the anniversary celebrations in order to provide an opportunity for members and their families to meet up and strengthen their bonding. This platform could provide opportunities for the younger members to strengthen their bonding. By 2007, another Member of Parliament, Mr Baey Yam Keng, whose ancestors were also from Zhanglin, was appointed as Honorary Adviser to the association. Mr Baey is currently appointed as Senior Parliamentary Secretary at the Ministry of Transport. Coincidentally I used to meet Mr Baey at some official events when he was with the Ministry of Culture, Community and Youth. By 2012, there was a ray of hope for rejuvenation when a member of our fifth generation Ray Chiang Rui Shu was recruited as the association's Legal Adviser. Ray is a practising lawyer and the eldest son of our third brother Gilbert Chiang. This was in line with our father`s expectation to have the new generation to continue his legacy and serve in the Chung-Lim Community Oversea Association.

Towards the end of the 90's, Dad's health deteriorated, with just one of his kidneys functioning, and he was admitted to the hospital occasionally for medical treatment. He had to be carried down two flights of stairs and wheeled to the driveway for transportation to seek medical consultations and treatments. He was in and out of the hospital frequently and passed away after a short admission at Changi Hospital on 19 October 1998. The wake was held for one week in front of our flower shop at Blk 2 Lorong Lew Lian. We were humbled by the visits of the former Speaker of Parliament Mr Tan Soo Koon and Mrs Tan. Members of Parliament Mr Goh Choon Kang, Dr Ker Sin Tze, Dr Michael Lim, Mrs Lim Hwee Hua, Mr and Mrs Chin Harn Tong, grassroots leaders, business associates, residents, friends and relatives.

Chiang Boon Lim 章文林
(1915–1998)

Our beloved dad played a leading role in the community since the kampong days.

我们父亲对社会的贡献。

Dad was a founding member of the Chung-Lim Community Oversea Association, founded in 1959

爸爸章文林是1959年成立的樟林旅外同乡会的创始人之一。

Prof S.W. Hwang, Adviser of the Association, presenting an educational award to a member's son.

会务顾问黄勖吾教授为会员的孩子颁发了教育奖。

From the 70's, dad was actively involved in steering Chung-Lim Community Oversea Association to scale new heights.

从70年代起爸爸参与领导樟林旅外同乡会。

The members of the Chung-Lim Community Oversea Association visited their compatriots in Thailand in the 80's.

樟林旅外同乡会的成员在80年代拜访了泰国的同乡。

30th anniversary celebrations of Chung-Lim Community Oversea Association — 1989.

*1989*樟林旅外同乡会成立*30*周年庆典。

Dad was a founding member of the Lorong Lew Lian 7th Moon Festival Committee, which was formed in the late 70's to gel the resettled residents and strengthen their bonds.

从70年代起爸爸是罗弄榴梿中元会的创始人之一,目的是加强居民之间的联系。

The Braddell Heights Zone A Residents' Committee Senior Citizens Club was formed in 1984 with dad as the chairman and officiated by MP Goh Choon Kang.

*1984*年，国会议员吴俊刚先生主持布莱德岭A分区居民委员会乐龄俱乐部成立典礼，
爸爸是俱乐部的主席。

Building social cohesion and strengthening the true kampong spirits with the resettled residents of Lorong Lew Lian.

领导罗弄榴梿老年人建立社会凝聚力和增强居民中的甘榜精神。

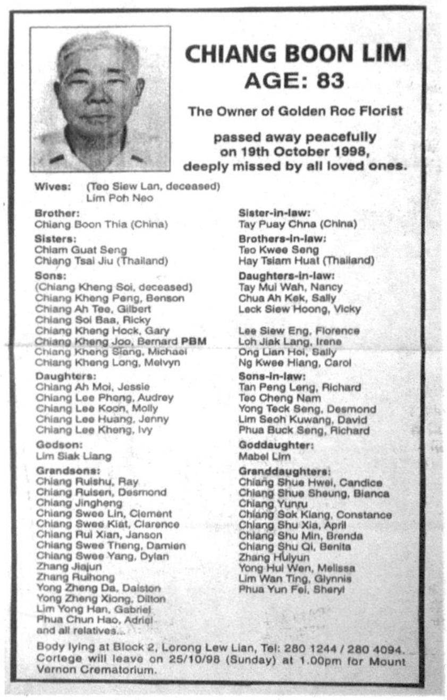

CHIANG BOON LIM
AGE: 83

The Owner of Golden Roc Florist

passed away peacefully
on 19th October 1998,
deeply missed by all loved ones.

Wives: (Teo Siew Lan, deceased)
Lim Poh Neo

Brother:
Chiang Boon Thia (China)

Sisters:
Chiam Guat Seng
Chiang Tsai Jiu (Thailand)

Sons:
(Chiang Kheng Soi, deceased)
Chiang Kheng Peng, Benson
Chiang Ah Tee, Gilbert
Chiang Soi Baa, Ricky
Chiang Kheng Hock, Gary
Chiang Kheng Joo, Bernard **PBM**
Chiang Kheng Siang, Michael
Chiang Kheng Long, Melvyn

Daughters:
Chiang Ah Moi, Jessie
Chiang Lee Pheng, Audrey
Chiang Lee Koon, Molly
Chiang Lee Huang, Jenny
Chiang Lee Kheng, Ivy

Godson:
Lim Siak Liang

Grandsons:
Chiang Ruishu, Ray
Chiang Ruisen, Desmond
Chiang Jingheng
Chiang Swee Lin, Clement
Chiang Swee Kiat, Clarence
Chiang Rui Xian, Janson
Chiang Swee Theng, Damien
Chiang Swee Yang, Dylan
Zhang Jiajun
Zhang Ruihong
Yong Zheng Da, Dalston
Yong Zheng Xiong, Dilton
Lim Yong Han, Gabriel
Phua Chun Hao, Adriel
and all relatives...

Sister-in-law:
Tay Puay Chna (China)

Brothers-in-law:
Teo Kwee Seng
Hay Tsiam Huat (Thailand)

Daughters-in-law:
Tay Mui Wah, Nancy
Chua Ah Kek, Sally
Leck Siew Hoong, Vicky

Lee Siew Eng, Florence
Loh Jiak Lang, Irene
Ong Lian Hoi, Sally
Ng Kwee Hiang, Carol

Sons-in-law:
Tan Peng Leng, Richard
Teo Cheng Nam
Yong Teck Seng, Desmond
Lim Seoh Kuwang, David
Phua Buck Seng, Richard

Goddaughter:
Mabel Lim

Granddaughters:
Chiang Shue Hwei, Candice
Chiang Shue Sheung, Bianca
Chiang Yunru
Chiang Sok Kiang, Constance
Chiang Shu Xia, April
Chiang Shu Min, Brenda
Chiang Shu Qi, Benita
Zhang Huiyun
Yong Hui Wen, Melissa
Lim Wan Ting, Glynnis
Phua Yun Fei, Sheryl

Body lying at Block 2, Lorong Lew Lian, Tel: 280 1244 / 280 4094. Cortege will leave on 25/10/98 (Sunday) at 1.00pm for Mount Vernon Crematorium.

（金鹏生花店　老东主　章文林逝世）

讣　告

哀启者：先严文林章府君恸于1998年10月19日（农历戊寅年八月廿九日）下午四时，寿终正寝，享寿积闰八十有五。孝眷等随侍在侧，亲视含殓即日遵礼成服，订于10月24日（星期六）延请修德善堂设坛礼佛一午连宵，是晚为社团亲朋戚友探丧之期，涓10月25日（星期日）下午一时，由丧居扶柩发引至阿裕尼路翡珑山火化场火化。恭

姻亲族世乡友　谊　哀此讣　闻

妻：张秀兰(已故)
林宝娘

胞弟：章文定(中国)
胞妹：章月枝(中国)(已故)
章月吟(中国)
章月娥(中国)(已故)
章月笙
章月全(中国)(已故)
章赛柔(泰国)

孝男：章庆先(已故)
章庆平 Benson
章庆光 Gilbert
章细峇 Ricky
章庆福 Gary
章庆裕 PBM Bernard
章庆祥 Michael
章庆隆 Melvyn

孝女：章亚妹 Jessie
章丽萍 Audrey
章丽君 Molly
章丽芳 Jenny
章丽卿 Ivy

内孙男：章瑞书
章瑞森
章敬恒

弟媳：郑佩妆(中国)
妹婿：林天敏(中国)
陈进楳(中国)
郑传芳(中国)
张贵成
陈亿秋(中国)
夏森发(泰国)

孝媳：郑美华 Nancy Tay
蔡亚菊 Sally Chua
陆秀凤 Vicky Leck

李秀英 Florence Lee
卢若兰 Irene Loh
王莲花 Sally Ong
黄桂香 Carol Ng

孝婿：陈炳灵 Richard Tan
张振南
杨德成 Desmond Yong
林绍光 David Lim
潘木甡 Richard Phua

内孙男：章瑞麟
章瑞杰
章瑞贤
章瑞颖
章瑞渊

内孙女：章淑慧
章淑娴
章韵茹
章淑娟
章淑霞
章淑敏
章淑齐

外孙男：张加俊
张睿宏
杨政达
杨政雄
林勇翰
潘俊豪

外孙女：张惠云
杨惠雯
林琬婷
潘韵妃

服内尚有亲属众多，恕未尽录。

同泣启

丧居：罗弄榴梿大牌2座 Blk. 2 Lorong Lew Lian　Tel: 2804094, 2801244, 96794094.　Fax: 2812505.

Obituary of our beloved father Chiang Boon Lim, who passed away on 19 October 1998.

Our family members preparing for our beloved father's funeral procession on 25 October 1998.

1998年10月25日我们为父亲的葬礼做准备。

Speaker of Parliament Mr Tan Soo Khoon and Mrs Tan attended the wake of our beloved father in 1998.

国会议长陈树群先生和夫人对父亲表示最后的敬意。

MP Mrs Lim Hwee Hua and former MP Mr Chin Harn Tong attended the wake of our father on 22 October 1998.

1998年10月22日，国会议员陈惠華女士和前国会议员钱翰琮来表示最后的敬意。

MP Dr. Michael Lim attended the wake on 23 October 1998.

*1998*年*10*月*23*日，国会议员林俊龍醫生和基层领导来表示最后的敬意 。

Former MP Mr. Chin Harn Tong and Mrs Chin attended the wake on 25 October 1998.

*1998*年*10*月*25*日，前国会议员钱翰琮先生和夫人对父亲表示最后的敬意。

MP Goh Choon Kang and grassroots leaders attended the wake on 23 October 1998.

*1998*年*10*月*23*日，国会议员吴俊刚先生和基层领导对父亲表示最后的敬意。

Members of the Braddell Heights Zone B RC Senior Citizens' Club and residents paying their last respects to dad on 22 October 1998.

*1998*年*10*月*22*日，基层领导和居民表示敬意。

CHAPTER 5

Beloved Mum, Who is Always in Our Thoughts

Our Mum did not receive a formal education like many other women of her time, as priority was given to the men. Most of the villagers were poor, and traditionally they had the same thinking that once their daughters were married, they would belong to the groom's family. The parents would rather invest more on their son's education as their succeeding generations would bear the same surname.

Mum was a perfect partner for Dad as she was very patient, supportive and understanding, and her tolerance and low-profile character complemented Dad's dominant characteristics. She had to look after the children and supplemented family expenses by sewing and manufacturing joss papers at home. She was talented in sewing, and most of our clothing and school uniforms during our childhood were custom-made by her and passed on to our younger brothers and sisters. Similarly, school textbooks and stationeries were also passed down to the younger siblings. We also exchanged our textbooks among our relatives and friends. She would walk and guide us to the school for couple of days during our first year of education. Subsequently, we had to learn to make our way to the school without her escort as she had to look after the younger siblings.

She would strap and piggyback the young baby brother or sister to her back while doing her daily routine or buying groceries. There were ten of us and one could imagine how many years she had to struggle and persevere to bring us up. With ten mouths to feed, looking after our needs and ensuring we had a good education was a very challenging task. During the rainy season, she had to prepare the charcoal stove covered over with a high bamboo basket so as to place the wet laundry for drying our school uniform and shoes. She could only afford to sew us two pairs of uniforms and buy us a pair of canvas shoes.

"She was very friendly, helpful, approachable and socialised easily with the kampong folks. She inherited her culinary skills from maternal grandma and we were always craving to taste her signature dishes prepared during festive periods".

We were certainly indebted to her for the love and care showered on us and our children. We were blessed to have such a caring and responsible mother/grandmother who sacrificed so much for us. We were happy that she lived a full life, although she had suffered from dementia and poor health towards the end of her life.

She was very friendly, helpful, approachable and socialised easily with the kampong folks. She inherited her culinary skills from maternal grandma and we were always craving to taste her signature dishes prepared during festive periods. Our family members always remembered the tasty curry chicken she prepared for us paired withwhite rice and French loaf. We loved her crabmeat ball cooked with young bamboo shoots soup and buah keluak chicken dishes. Other signature dishes such as pig liver spring rolls and the Peranakan mixed vegetables were always in demand.

We always looked forward to the Dumpling Festival, when she would prepare her signature Peranakan dumplings with blue-coloured rice wrapped with dual meat and sweet-bean paste ingredients. The traditional festival would be celebrated annually by the Chinese all over the world on the fifth day of the fifth lunar month in honour of a patriotic poet Qu Yuan, who drowned himself in the river to protest against injustice and the corrupt court officials. When the commoners came to know about it, they prepared dumplings to offer to the sea creatures, believing that they would not eat his body.

Mum's signature spicy belacan chilli paste and Nonya achar (spicy pickle) were also very tasty and could go well with plain white rice to be taken as dinner. Regretfully, none of us had taken the initiative to record down her recipes and inherited her cooking skills. Even till the present day, the grandchildren and great grandchildren crave for her signature dishes. Nothing could beat her traditional Peranakan food cooked with passion and motherly love. I could recall in the earlier years that sometimes without helping hands she even had to multi-task and carry our younger sibling in piggyback while preparing food for us. When she was operating the sewing machine, she would use one of her legs to swing the baby hammock in order to calm and serenade our little sibling with the famous Teochew lullaby *Ong Ah Ong, Ong King Kong* (啳啊啳, 啳金公). We admired and appreciated her patience and ability to raise the ten of us despite her limitations and financial constraints. We were fortunate to have a mother who could not even write her own name properly to see us through our secondary education. She had good interpersonal skills and could get along very well with relatives and friends. I assume it was this strength that drew support and help from her good friends. With her close contacts, she was also able to influence and encourage her friends to support the formation of the Lorong Lew Lian RC Senior Citizens Club. She also started to gather her group of buddies for daily morning breakfast and enjoyed the four-colour cards game to pass time and strengthen camaraderie.

By the 90's, age had caught up with her, and due to her leg problem, she had to slow down all social activities, keeping her weekends free to cook special Peranakan dishes for the family gatherings. Unfortunately, she was diagnosed with dementia in 2004. The same year, she attended our second paternal auntie's grandson's wedding in Guangzhou. She returned from the trip and was unwell for a couple of months. Initially we speculated that she did not rest well and was probably suffering from jet lag. As time passed on, she started to lose her memory and appetite. She also had difficulty in swallowing solid food, and all her meals had to be ground into soft paste and spoon-fed with the assistance of domestic help.

Over a period of time, she became weaker and frail and had difficulty walking. She required the assistance of domestic help to go to the toilet and take her shower. She also needed a wheelchair to move around, and at times, when the helper wanted to wheel her downstairs to enjoy fresh air and meet her friends, she protested using her body language. This was probably because she had lost her memory and was handicapped by her expressions and disability to communicate with her friends. It was more stressful for her when someone wanted to speak to her, and she felt very frustrated that she could not respond and express herself. She became short-tempered and infuriated as she was unable to communicate with the domestic helper. That was the reason why she refused to socialize and meet her friends at this critical stage. Her health deteriorated and she could not even recognize and remember the names of her own children. Her days were numbered, and in mid-July 2016, she was admitted to Tan Tock Seng Hospital as her condition worsened.

On 17 July 2016, she passed away at the age of 93, with the doctor certifying the cause of death being pneumonia, after a short period of intensive care and close observations in the hospital.

The wake was held at Block 416 Serangoon Central from 17–23 July 2016. The Indonesian domestic helper Lena was saddened to learn of the bad news and rushed back from Indonesia during her Hari Raya break. She was very close to Mum and looked after her needs. She was very upset to part with her, knowing that in the future she would not be able to spend time with our family members anymore. We all were lucky to have her and treated her like our family member. Her last wish was to bid farewell and see our mum off on her final journey. Luckily for her, she found a new employer and took time to visit us during her off days.

Another former domestic helper, Nikon from Udon Tani, Thailand, was also notified of the demise of Mum, and she too rushed over to bid farewell to our beloved Mum. Nikon was with us for quite some time until our dad passed away in 1998. She was also close with our family members and quickly learned to speak Teochew. Later on she also picked up basic conversational Mandarin and returned home to work as a translator. She came back to Singapore to attend my nephew Clarence's wedding in 2019, an occasion not to be missed as she had helped to look after him since he was a baby.

We were also very grateful to have five relatives from Thailand who attended the wake and took part in the religious ceremony and funeral. We were greatly touched by the love and concern showered by many relatives and friends. She was the last surviving member of her Lim family, outliving her three other brothers. Mum was well loved not only by her children, but also grandchildren and great grandchildren, who would make it a point to visit her on most weekends. She had a full life and was fortunate to have four generations of her family members, relatives and friends to see her on the final journey. She is forever in our thoughts and fondly remembered by all the loved ones.

Since the day we moved over to Lorong Lew Lian, about forty years ago, Mum had lost many of her close friends and contemporaries due to old age and sickness. Losing good friends one after another was a devastating and painful experience. Over the decades, while serving as a Residents' Committee member and dealing with many elderly residents, I could feel a sense of great loss each time we had to remove the membership registration of the deceased from the register. At the same time, we had to recruit new members to rejuvenate the Senior Citizens Club committee and membership. With new and younger leaders, we hope to continue to reinforce the kampong spirit for many more years to come.

Our beloved Mum never attended school but she cared and ensured all of us had a good education.

妈妈从来没有机会上学,但她确保我们所有人都受过良好的教育。

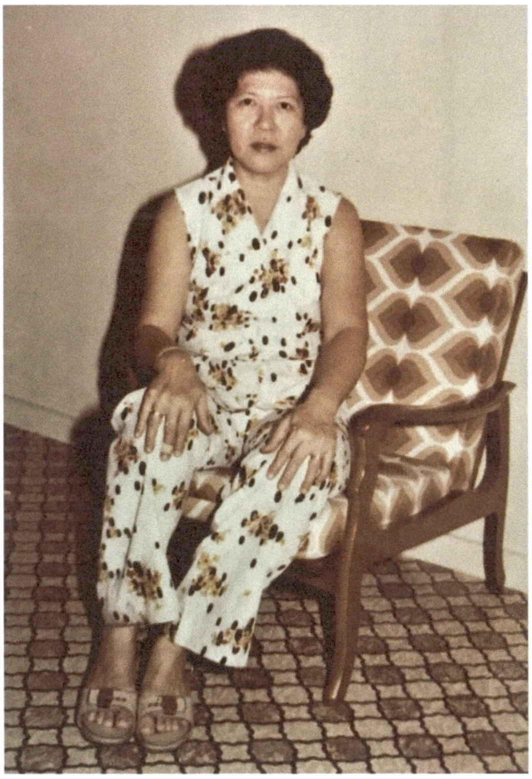

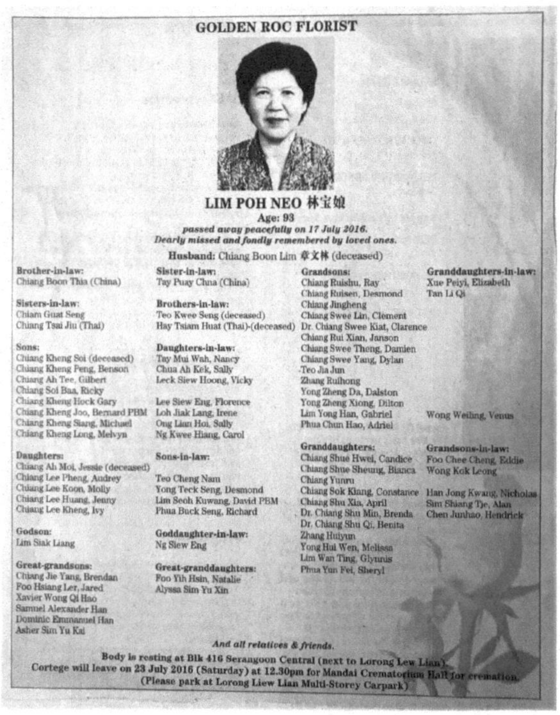

GOLDEN ROC FLORIST

LIM POH NEO 林宝娘
Age: 93
passed away peacefully on 17 July 2016.
Dearly missed and fondly remembered by loved ones.

Husband: Chiang Boon Lim 章文林 (deceased)

Brother-in-law:
Chiang Boon Thia (China)

Sisters-in-law:
Chiam Guat Seng
Chiang Tsai Jiu (Thai)

Sons:
Chiang Kheng Soi (deceased)
Chiang Kheng Peng, Benson
Chiang Ah Tee, Gilbert
Chiang Soi Baa, Ricky
Chiang Kheng Hock Gary
Chiang Kheng Joo, Bernard PBM
Chiang Kheng Siang, Michael
Chiang Kheng Long, Melvyn

Daughters:
Chiang Ah Moi, Jessie (deceased)
Chiang Lee Pheng, Audrey
Chiang Lee Koon, Molly
Chiang Lee Huang, Jenny
Chiang Lee Kheng, Ivy

Godson:
Lim Siak Liang

Great-grandsons:
Chiang Jie Yang, Brendan
Foo Hsiang Ler, Jared
Xavier Wong Qi Hao
Samuel Alexander Han
Dominic Emmanuel Han
Asher Sim Yu Kai

Sister-in-law:
Tay Puay Chna (China)

Brothers-in-law:
Teo Kwee Seng (deceased)
Hay Tsiam Huat (Thai)-(deceased)

Daughters-in-law:
Tay Mui Wah, Nancy
Chua Ah Kek, Sally
Leck Siew Hoong, Vicky

Lee Siew Eng, Florence
Loh Jiak Lang, Irene
Ong Lian Hoi, Sally
Ng Kwee Hiang, Carol

Sons-in-law:

Teo Cheng Nam
Yong Teck Seng, Desmond
Lim Seoh Kuwang, David PBM
Phua Buck Seng, Richard

Goddaughter-in-law:
Ng Siew Eng

Great-granddaughters:
Foo Yih Hsin, Natalie
Alyssa Sim Yu Xin

Grandsons:
Chiang Ruishu, Ray
Chiang Ruisen, Desmond
Chiang Jingheng
Chiang Swee Lin, Clement
Dr. Chiang Swee Kiat, Clarence
Chiang Rui Xian, Janson
Chiang Swee Theng, Damien
Chiang Swee Yang, Dylan
Teo Jia Jun
Zhang Ruihong
Yong Zheng Da, Dalston
Yong Zheng Xiong, Dilton
Lim Yong Han, Gabriel
Phua Chun Hao, Adriel

Granddaughters:
Chiang Shue Hwei, Candice
Chiang Shue Sheung, Bianca
Chiang Yunru
Chiang Sok Kiang, Constance
Chiang Shu Xia, April
Dr. Chiang Shu Min, Brenda
Dr. Chiang Shu Qi, Benita
Zhang Huiyun
Yong Hui Wen, Melissa
Lim Wan Ting, Glynnis
Phua Yun Fei, Sheryl

Granddaughters-in-law:
Xue Peiyi, Elizabeth
Tan Li Qi

Wong Weiling, Venus

Grandsons-in-law:
Foo Chee Cheng, Eddie
Wong Kok Leong

Han Jong Kwang, Nicholas
Sim Shiang Tje, Alan
Chen Junhao, Hendrick

And all relatives & friends.

Body is resting at Blk 416 Serangoon Central (next to Lorong Lew Lian).
Cortege will leave on 23 July 2016 (Saturday) at 12.30pm for Mandai Crematorium Hall for cremation.
(Please park at Lorong Liew Lian Multi-Storey Carpark)

金鹏生花店

讣告

我们的至亲:先慈**章门林氏宝娘太夫人**

恸于2016年7月17日（农历丙申年六月十四日）中午12时50分寿终内寝，享寿九十有三岁。孝眷等随侍在侧，亲视含殓，即日遵礼成服。于7月22日（星期五）恭请修德善堂养心社设坛礼佛一午连宵，每晚为社团亲友探丧之期。涓于7月23日（星期六）中午12时30分出殡，由治丧处扶柩发引至万礼路万礼火化场火化。忝属

姻亲族世友乡　谊　哀此讣　闻

夫:章文林(已故)			
张秀兰(已故)			
夫弟:章文定(中国)	夫弟妇:郑佩妆(中国)(已故)	内孙男:章瑞贤	
夫妹:章月枝(中国)(已故)	夫妹婿:林天敏(中国)(已故)	章瑞颖	
章月吟(中国)(已故)	陈进樑(中国)(已故)	章瑞渊	
章月娥(中国)(已故)	郑传芳(中国)(已故)	内孙女:章淑慧	内孙婿:符致清
章月笙	张贵成(已故)	章淑娴	黄国梁
章月全(中国)(已故)	陈亿秋(中国)(已故)	章韵茹	
章赛柔(泰国)	夏森发(泰国)(已故)	章淑娟	韩荣光
孝男:章庆先(已故)	孝媳:郑美华Nancy	章淑霞	沈湘泽
章庆平Benson	蔡亚菊Sally	章淑敏医生	陈俊豪
章庆光Gilbert	陆秀凤Vicky	章淑齐医生	
章细峇Ricky		外孙男:张加俊	
章庆福Gary	李秀英Florence	张睿宏	
章庆裕PBM Bernard	卢若兰Irene	杨政达	
章庆祥Michael	王莲花Sally	杨证雄	
章庆隆Melvyn	黄桂香Carol	林勇翰	外孙媳:王玮玲
谊男:林锡亮	谊媳:黄秀英	潘俊豪	
孝女:章亚妹Jessie(已故)		外孙女:张惠云	
章丽萍Audrey	孝婿:张振南	杨惠雯	
章丽君Molly	杨德成Desmond	林琬婷	
章丽芳Jenny	林绍光PBM David	潘韵妃	
章丽卿Ivy	潘木生Richard	内曾孙男:章杰扬	
内孙男:章瑞书律师	内孙媳:薛佩宜律师	外曾孙男:符祥乐	外曾孙女:符铭欣
章瑞森	陈莉倚	黄啟豪	沈羽馨
章敬恒		韩淞畴	
章瑞麟		韩烨畴	
章瑞杰医生		沈羽凯	

服内尚有亲属众多，恕不尽录。　同泣启

治丧处：Blk 416 Serangoon Central (next to Lorong Lew Lian)　实龙岗中心大牌416 (罗弄榴梿隔邻)
注：本辆请停泊在罗弄榴梿多层停车场

In loving memory of our beloved mother, who passed away on 17 July 2016.

Mr Seah Kian Peng, MP for Braddell Heights, and Ms Tin Pei Ling, MP for Macpherson, and grassroots leaders attended the wake of our mother on 19 and 20 July 2016, respectively.

2016年7月19和20日，国会议员谢健平先生，陈佩玲女士和社区领袖对妈妈表示最后的敬意。

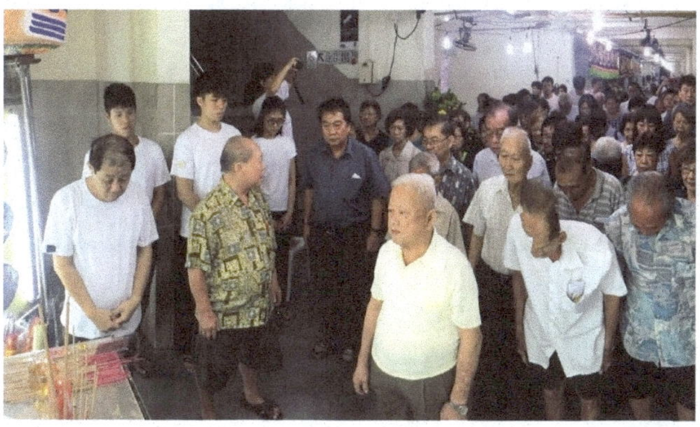

Braddell Heights Zone B Residents' Committee grassroots leaders and residents paying their last respects.

基层领导人和居民表示敬意。

Mum's final journey, leaving Lorong Lew Lian for cremation at Mandai.

家人，亲戚和朋友陪伴母亲到她最后的安息之地。

The Indonesian and former Thai domestic helpers paying their last respects to Mum.

现任和前任家庭女佣专程从印尼和泰国分别回来向妈妈告别。

Three generations of Thailand relatives came to send Mum off on her final journey.

泰国三代亲戚参加妈妈葬礼。

The fifth-and sixth-generation descendants warming up for the funeral procession.

第五代和第六代后裔为葬礼做准备。

Maternal relatives at the wake to pay their last respect to mum.

母亲亲戚们对我们挚爱的妈妈表示最后的敬意。

Three generations of family members will miss Mum, but she will never be forgotten (23 July 2016).

三代家庭成员会想念妈妈,但她永远不会被遗忘。

CHAPTER 6

致奶奶
Farewell to our Beloved Grandmother

Grand-daughter Dr Benita Chiang
(Singapore 5th Gen, China 23rd Gen)

I received a text from Dad that you weren't well; he rushed down to your place and then we received the reassuring text: 'Nai Nai is better now'. But within hours, they rushed you down to the hospital, and I found myself at the backseat of my speeding brother-in-law's van, fervently praying. To be honest, I was in shock when I arrived at the ED. I found out that you have been strong, holding on even though you were very very sick, with your BP not even half the normal value. Fast forward one week later, I was on the dreary Sunday call. I was in your ward, rounding one of my patients. I popped by into ACA and suddenly realised I was now the one who had to send the dreaded text to my parents: to get everyone down ASAP.

I sat beside you, typing the horrible message to my extended family. I saw you slipping away in front of my eyes. I saw your breathing getting shallower and slower... The screen of my phone became blurrier by the second. And I remembered begging my sister to hurry down. I was alone and afraid. What followed was an onslaught of questions. Questions that weren't easy to answer or that carried answers that might bring heartbreak or guilt.

And then in the next week, I learnt so much more about you. Little bits of information that slowly became treasures that I yearned to uncover. Everyone had their own fond memories of you. Mine wasn't that fanciful but I am glad I had that one year with you. I may or may not have tasted the French toast you used to make for my sister, or learned your many many origami crafts or stole a tip or two of your delicious Peranakan dishes, but I will always remember you peeping over my head while I did my homework or sitting at the dining table, trying to wake me up for lunch before school. I was a horrible piggy, I didn't like waking up, but you had so many tricks and antics up your sleeves that I had no choice but to crawl out of my slumber.

My name is a mouthful even for friends in school, and you definitely had a hard time with it. You endeared yourself to me and started calling me 'tata'. I'm not sure if you knew it then, but I really hated it. But if you can hear me now, please forgive the mischievous ignorant young girl I was. I would do anything to hear you call me 'tata' again.

And thank God for giving me the chance to have travelled with you, to know that you snore really loudly at night (that's probably where Daddy got his snoring from… haha), to know that you are made of layers of warmth; enjoying ice cream while I was wrapped up in my many jackets and daddy's arms and to know that you are always up for an adventure.

In that week of mourning, it hurt to go to work and it hurt to be even on level 7; it was so painful that I had to run and hide in the toilet. I couldn't face the patients, I couldn't face my friends and I couldn't stop crying. All I could think of was the night before your last moments, you must have felt so scared when the on-call team hovered around you, with big fat machines trying to take a CXR, young tired doctors trying to get an ABG, as bigger and bigger face masks started appearing in front of you... This must be the feeling that my friend was talking about when said she hated hospitals because her father passed away in one.

In this last week, I came across so many different scenarios that kept replaying in my mind. (1) My reg and I had the EOL discussion with the family of our patient. We had to tell them it was time, time to withdraw treatment and it was time to be with her and to keep her company. (2) I was now the MO of my friend's granny and the bearer of bad news. I was now on the giving end when I was on the receiving end just a few months back, the irony of life. (3) Performing CPR over and over again on the same patient and telling her son her heart may stop over and over again despite all our efforts. (4) Getting called for a code blue in the wee hours, down time unknown, no family at bedside. Starting CPR and intubating her but to no avail.

Nobody likes death and this might be slightly morbid. It was difficult to say goodbye, the hardest I ever had to say. But I was glad you passed away peacefully, with everyone around you and holding your small fragile hands for the last time. And I thank God for that. I was thankful that your last moments weren't spent alone behind closed curtains with multiple hands forcefully pumping your chest, or someone shoving a plastic tube down your throat. You were with us.

"You left behind so many of us,

那么多分的爱，那么多对你的思念。你一生给予我们每个人的爱远远超过了海的能量，天空的无限。而这都在我们的泪水，在我们的不舍，在我们不停的悼念反映着你的伟大。

奶奶，谢谢你。"

It wasn't easy. Not easy for you, not easy for everyone. I saw how everyone broke down, from the eldest of your children to the youngest of your great grandchildren. Nobody left without a red teary and screwed up ugly face. But what impacted me the most was I saw how my many uncles, who were usually jovial, cheery and sturdy, and some always serious, broke down. It pained them so much that tears flowed freely from them, it pained them so much their knees buckled, it pained them so much that it pained me to see them that way. But thank you Nai Nai, thank you for holding on, thank you for letting each and every one of us say goodbye. Although you are gone now, you are in a better place. A place with no dementia, a place with no NG tubes, a place with no nasal cannulas, a place with no needles or IV plugs, a place with no dopamine, a place with no beeping machines.

Finally, you are in a place of peace.

Enjoy the fluffy clouds and the shining stars, you are probably the brightest one up there. This took really long to come together, too many emotions that I couldn't find the words for, too many what-ifs that got me off-track. Some things are hard to write about; it becomes easy to dramatise or underplay it, and the wrong parts get exaggerated and the really important ones are ignored. Anyhow, you never really write it the way you want it, but I am glad this is finally completed, my own little memory of you.

CHAPTER 7

Strengthening our bonds with Relatives in China

After my first visit to our ancestral village at Chung Lim with my Dad and fourth aunt in 1988, we tried to keep in touch with and strengthen our relationship with the relatives in China. Whenever we had the opportunity to travel to places near Shantou or Chung Lim Village, we would make an effort to catch up with them. In the 60's and 70's, we used to hear from unconfirmed sources that many people feared returning to their ancestral home as their hungry relatives would strip them of their personal belongings and leave them empty handed before their departure. Over time, many things had changed since I went on my first trip with my dad, when our relatives requested the sponsorship of television sets and sewing machines from my dad; others would prefer to have motorcycles as part of their changing lifestyle and personal comfort.

Over the years, I could see the tremendous transformations in the village and was very happy to see my relatives getting affluent and having better lifestyles and comfortable living conditions. I went with my two childhood friends to visit my young uncle in 2009 and my cousin Choon Tiang offered us two air-conditioned rooms for our stay in their four-storey home cum factory. In the following couple of years, I would catch up with them for lunch or dinner whenever we had short tours passing Shantou. Similarly, my older brothers would catch up with the relatives when they travelled to Guangzhou and Shantou. With advances in technology, communications through this cyber age had certainly further cemented our ties with the overseas relatives. I remembered my first trip to China when making an overseas call for a few minutes could cost between forty and fifty Singapore dollars. With social media, the world is well connected and getting smaller and smaller as we can call and send messages anytime with instant photos attached.

In preparation for writing this book, I was blessed to receive much information and input from my paternal cousin through social media. I regretted not starting to trace my paternal roots earlier when all the older relatives were younger and mentally alert. I could have extracted more information about their past histories and been connected to the missing link of our earlier ancestors. By the time I developed an interest in researching the family history, some members of the older generations were too old to recall the past and some even had hearing problems. Over the years, many aged relatives had already passed away and I was disappointed not to learn and hear their personal experiences and stories.

Our paternal uncle from Chung Lim Village, with an entourage comprising his family members and friends numbering more than ten, surprised us with a visit to Singapore in the year 2011. Many of them were first-time visitors. It was certainly a breakthrough and big reunion for the Chiang families as many of our brothers and sisters had not seen our relatives from China in person before. Over the years, many of the earlier generations of relatives in China had passed away due to advanced age and sickness. The recent relatives who had passed away were our young uncle's wife Tay Puay Chuan who passed away in 2013 and our second aunt who passed away in 2014. The more shocking one was the passing of my cousin Choon Teng's young wife who succumbed to cancer. I managed to catch up with our late aunty Tay Puay Chuan for the last time when I was on a short tour with friends to Putien and Shantou in 2013. When I visited her at her youngest son's shophouse, she was weak and frail-looking, but still alert enough to have a short conversation with me. Since my first visit to China in 1988, I witnessed that the numbers of our elderly relatives from my father's generation were diminishing.

The latest was the passing of my fourth aunt on 30 January 2022. She was 93 years old and I was fortunate to interview her several times despite her deteriorating health. I regret that she missed the launch of this book.

On January 8, 2018, my elder brothers, Benson and Gilbert, and I were invited to attend my cousin Choon Tiang's son's wedding at Chung Lim Village. It was also a rare occasion to catch up with many other relatives during the wedding dinner. The following year, I revisited Chung Lim Village again with some childhood friends to explore some ancient and historical sites in Shantou. This was an opportunity for us to try out the traditional Teochew cuisines, especially at the porridge restaurant that prepared a selection of more than one hundred dishes every day for their regular customers.

Our hope is that the younger generations will continue to maintain good relationships with our relatives in China and continue to grow and nurture the family tree. We have paved the path for them and we hope they can build on the current bond to link and strengthen the ties with the younger generations in China and Thailand.
With advances in technologies and communications, I am confident that this dream can be realized and the ties improved further as soon as the next generation of young leaders can be established. We need live wires to spark the fire and keep the flame of the Chiang family glowing for future generations.

Inaugural reunion with China uncle Boon Thia and his family members held in Singapore on 5 Feb 2011.

2011年2月5日,我们第一次与中国叔叔章文定及其家人在新加坡团圆。

Visit by uncle Boon Thia and family members to our shophouse at Lorong Lew Lian. This was the maiden trip to Singapore for many of them.

叔叔章文定和他的家人在花店团圆快乐, 许多人是第一次来新加坡。

A Lunar New Year toss for a better future and prosperity which amazed the relatives from China as they experienced it for the first time.

来自中国的亲戚在新加坡享受他们的第一道鱼生菜。

We made many trips over the years to our ancestral village to reinforce our ties with our relatives.

我们多次拜访祖籍地加强我们的关系。

Building family bridges through our regular visits to the ancestral village.

其他兄弟和亲戚也轮流拜访我们的中国亲戚。

Meeting with uncle Boon Thia and family in Chung Lim Village with the arrival of his first great-grandson in 2019.

2019年会见我们的叔叔章文定和他的家人，很高兴看到他的第一个曾孙子。

Gathering with relatives at the wedding of Lau Chiap, uncle Boon Thia's Grandson at Chung Lim Village in 2018.

2018-我们三个兄弟参加了叔叔孙子刘捷的婚礼。

Bridging Our Family Ties With Thailand Relatives

加强我们与泰国亲戚的家庭联系

A Branch Of The Chiang Family Tree In Thailand
章氏家族的泰国分支

CHAPTER 8

Paternal Grandpa's Journey to Thailand

Grandpa Chiang Sia Hua was very entrepreneurial and forward looking. Foreseeing opportunities of a better future for his family, he decided to migrate to Thailand, along with millions of Teochew migrants from Chaosan. He began his humble beginnings as a street hawker in Bangkok. He was in his late 40s and had to move on fast before his age caught up. With his experience in rice business, soon he set up a shop in Bangkok, and not long after he settled down with his business, he started a second family there. He needed a life partner in Thailand to help in his shop and married a Thai Chinese citizen known as Tang Ngoa Jue and thereon had a daughter named Chiang Sai Jieu. Sai Jieu, known as Saijai in the Thai language, became his eighth and the youngest child.

Living in a country with different language and culture, he naturally had to learn to communicate with the local people in the Thai language and embrace their culture and practices.

We all were too young and never had the opportunity to meet our paternal grandpa and grandma. Poverty and restrictions meant many people took a long time to be reunited with their loved ones back in their ancestral homes. Our dad and grandpa had not seen each other since the day they left Chung Lim Village. They never saw each other for more than thirty years from the day they arrived in South East Asia. Grandpa passed away in 1966 at the age of 72, and his remains were placed in a columbarium housed in a temple in Bangkok. In Singapore, a memorial service was conducted in Chia Keng Village. Dad was unaware of Grandpa's passing till our fourth aunt Chiang Guet Seng broke the bad news to him. He was not in the position to fly to Bangkok to attend the wake and funeral as there were many personal commitments and financial constraints. Most of us were still too young, and facing hardship, and the idea of going to Bangkok to bid Grandpa farewell was unfortunately not possible.

Poverty and restrictions meant many people took a long time to be reunited with their loved ones back in their ancestral homes. Our dad and grandpa had not seen each other since the day they left Chung Lim Village. They never saw each other for more than thirty years from the day they arrived in South East Asia.

Twenty years on, in 1986, the same year of the Hotel New World collapse, I had the opportunity to travel with Dad on his first trip to meet Grandpa's second family in Thailand. We met our youngest aunty Sai Jieu for the first time, and she brought us to the temple where Grandpa's ashes were located. Along with my younger brother Michael and Thailand cousin Pacharee, we paid our tribute to grandpa. Grandpa and Dad had not returned to their ancestral home in China to be united with our grandma in Chung Lim village ever since they migrated overseas. Dad only managed to visit the final resting place of Grandma, who passed away in 1977 at the age of 83 years.

Aunty Sai Jieu (Saijai) was married to a Thai Chinese citizen called Uncle Hay Siam Huat (Somchai Prayadrat) and the family moved out from Bangkok to Buriram, northern Thailand, after the passing of Grandpa in 1966. Fortunately, Dad and his stepsister were able to communicate in Teochew, otherwise they would have had to overcome the language barrier. Uncle Somchai was also a Teochew, and they had many things in common. Over time we developed a strong bond with their five children, Rewat, Wanna, Nipa, Pacharee and Thanyatorn, and visited each other regularly, including their extended families. Initially we had communication problems with the Thailand third-generation relatives as most of them could not speak Teochew or English. Luckily the third daughter, Pacharee, could speak English and helped with interpreting. On the contrary, none of our family members could speak the Thai language, and we had to rely on aunty Saijai and Pacharee to do the translations. With the advance in technology and availability of social media, we are transcending the language barrier with the help of the fourth generation led by Saksit Prayadrat and his cousins. The younger ones are more versatile and better educated in higher institutions. The future is bright, with economical air travel and the convenience of online bookings for air tickets and easily available hotels. Inter-visits by family members could be intensified and family bonds could be strengthened among the younger generations.

Another advantage was that most of the younger generations were better educated and could communicate in English and Mandarin. In the past, we took years to contact and visit each other as flights and telephone calls were too expensive. Now we can send text messages through social media and receive updates and photos almost every day. With the demise of our Thailand grandma in 1999 and uncle Somchai Prayadrat in 2015, we hope the third and fourth generations of our Thailand relatives would continue to strengthen the good relationships with the succeeding generations.

The last time I met uncle Somchai was in the year 2001, where he spent his retirement days with his third daughter Pacharee and family at Loei, northern Thailand. My brother Gilbert and his wife Vicky, sister Jenny and husband David, and I with a group of friends made a trip to northern Thailand and Laos and stopped over at Loei. We had our reunion dinner with uncle Somchai, Aunty Saijai and family members near the Mekong River. He was still active despite his health condition and helped in the chicken farms belonging to his daughter Pacharee and son-in-law Chukiert. The roots of the Chiang Family ancestors must be deepened and the new branches of the family tree must continue to grow. I am looking forward to the day when we have a big reunion with all the relatives from China and Thailand. This will pave the way to strengthen our family ties in the future generations.

After the passing of Thailand Grandma and uncle Somchai, Aunty Saijai and her children decided to relocate the remains of Grandpa from the Temple in Bangkok to be housed together within the same Temple in Buriram. It made sense to reunite Grandpa with other family members after 33 years in his final resting place in the Bangkok temple. It would be convenient for the family members to visit and pay their respects at the temple called Wat Ban Nong Prong during festive occasions. After all, the majority of the family members were living in the northern region.

Paternal grandpa Chiang Sia Hua passed away at the age of 72 years in Bangkok (1894 to 1966). His memorial service was held in Singapore for friends and relatives.

爷爷于1966年在曼谷去世,享年72岁。他的追悼会在新加坡进行。

Our first meeting with Thailand aunty and the visit to grandpa's niche in a temple near Bangkok in 1986.

1986年, 泰国姑姑章赛柔和她的女儿带我们去一座寺庙,向祖父表示敬意。

CHAPTER 9

Bonding With Grandpa's Second Family in Thailand

Over the years, our family members made regular visits to meet our Thailand relatives in Bangkok, Buriram and Loei. Likewise, our Thailand relatives, especially the fourth and fifth generations, also travelled frequently to catch up with us in Singapore. Their latest visit was in 2019, when they attended the wedding of my fifth brother's son. Aunty Saijai was accompanied by her two grandsons, grand daughters-in-law and their children to witness the wedding ceremony.

Through the inter-visits, we hope to strengthen our relationships and pave the way for the fifth generation to strengthen family bonding. Our earlier obstacles were communication problems, as most of our cousins could not speak Teochew or English and we could not understand Thai. Fortunately, our aunty and uncle helped us with Teochew translations. Our worries were that, in future, if the interpreters were unavailable, the communication gap would be widened. Some of us may have to be prepared to learn Thai to counter this problem.

I believe that our Thailand cousins also felt the same way and decided to send some of their children overseas for further studies in English. It turned out to be a blessing that some of cousins' children were more versatile and could speak English and Mandarin. Progressively, we tried to overcome the language barrier, and now we have the advantage of communicating in English through social media. We are confident that the future generations could build on this strength and scale new heights to reinforce our family relationships.

Our next challenge is to cement the relationships between the relatives from China and Thailand, who need to overcome the language barrier. I am praying hard and looking forward to the day of a big reunion when the Thailand aunty with her children and grandchildren could visit our ancestral home in Chung Lim Village. This learning journey would give the younger generations a better understanding of their roots and appreciate the values passed on by our ancestors. There is a Chinese proverb that reminds us to understand and know our ancestors. "To forget one's ancestors is like a brook without a source or a tree without roots."

Once we are able to pave the way for the future generations to strengthen their bonds and deepen the roots of the family tree, I am confident that the tree will start to mature and bear fruits for many more generations to come.

My father and I undertook our maiden visit to Buriram to meet grandpa's second family in 1986.

*1986*年,我和父亲拜访了武里喃府的祖父第二家庭 。

Our paternal grandfather's shophouse in Bangkok, most likely in the late 40's.

这是在曼谷爷爷的商店,很可能40年代租下的。

Inaugural reunion with Uncle Somchai, Aunty Saijai and their daughters in Singapore in the early 80's. They happened to stay at the fateful Hotel New World before it collapsed in 1986.

泰国亲戚第一次来新加坡。他们住在新世界酒店几个月后倒塌。

Thailand relatives undertook their maiden visit to our shop at Lorong Lew Lian in the 80's.

在80年代泰国的亲戚第一次访问我们新加坡的花店。

Uncle Somchai Prayadrat and Aunty Saijai with three generations of Thailand relatives at the wedding ceremony of Nikky and Notty in 2013.

*2013*年- 泰国亲戚在武里喃府的婚礼上聚会。

Eldest daughter Wanna Prayadrat and husband Somchai Chuenpakorn with their son Phanuwat; daughters Pariya, Preeyala and Phattaraporn; sons-in law and grandchildren.

章赛柔姑姑的长女
(Wanna Prayadrat)
和她的家人。

Only son Rewat Prayadrat and wife Jintana Sawangnomchit with sons Saksit, Noppadol, Phonlawat, daughters-in-law and grandchildren.

章赛柔姑姑儿子 *(Rewat)* 和她的家人。

Second daughter Nipa Prayadrat and husband Krisada Manorat with daughter Napattamol.

章赛柔姑姑第二女儿 *(Nipa)* 和她的家人。

Third daughter Pacharee and husband Chukiert Tangchewinsirikul with son Kittipong and daughters Sirikam, Nuanrat and Ariyaporn 章赛柔姑姑第三女儿 *(Pacharee)* 和她的家人。

Youngest daughter Thanyatorn and daughters Woranan, Suwapee and Natcharee

章赛柔姑姑最小的女儿 *(Thanyatorn)* 和她的家人。

CHAPTER 10

Our Memorable Moments with Singapore Relatives
与新加坡亲戚一起度过的难忘时光

Sasit Prayadrat, Ornusa and daughters Atom and Neutron

WHAT I REMEMBERED

I remember the old days when my grandmother told me that we have a big family in Singapore, before giving me a Merlion T-shirt in 1990. This was my first memory of Singapore. Having heard some great stories about our relatives, whom I had never met before, I grew up wondering what would I discover there. As time went by, I grew up from being a little boy to a teenager and then a father of two daughters. Finally, I did meet some of my family members from Singapore in Bangkok.

WHAT I EXPERIENCED

It was late 2004 at Narai Hotel, Silom Road, where I met Uncle Gilbert. It was my first experience with the Singaporean relatives. That first meeting broadened my mind on how amazing it is to be connected to people of different ages who share the same ancestral origin.

Before long, Uncle Bernard and some of his friends visited me in Buriram in summer 2005. Soon, Uncle Gilbert and his friend arrived in Nakon Ratchasima in 2006, where we managed to meet to celebrate at a Thai-style barbeque restaurant.

After that, I and my family hosted Uncle Michael on his visit to Buriram in late 2008. The greatest surprise came in the form of an unimaginable solo visit by Clement in 2009. He rode his motorcycle all the way from Singapore to northern Thailand to catch up with our family.

Again, I had an opportunity to meet with some of my relatives, namely Uncle Benson, Uncle Gary, Uncle Gilbert and Uncle Michael, when we held my grandfather's funeral in June 2015. After my grandfather passed away, I knew that my grandmother's life would never be the same. It's tough to lose one's love, but it is tougher to spend the rest of one's life alone.

I managed to take my grandmother for a trip to Singapore for the first time despite the huge generation gap. From the moment I got my Merlion T-shirt to when I saw it with my own eyes, it took 26 years. It was very late at night in the middle of May 2015, when our flight landed at Changi Airport. To be truthful, I was stunned to see my relatives standing outside the passenger's arrival hall, waiting for us at 1.00 A.M. At that moment, I realized the importance of having a family. Every time I reminisce, the 2015 Singapore trip was certainly my best overseas trip ever.

My second trip to Singapore followed before long, when I, my grandmother, Uncle Somchai, Aunt Tim and Ar Bee attended the funeral of grand aunty Mdm Lim Poh Neo in July 2016. As all Chiang family members gathered together, I needed to have a piece of paper with the list of everybody's names because I could never remember everyone at once. What a big family!

We did share some precious memories outside Thailand and Singapore too. In November 2016, I and my family in Buriram hosted a memorable visit from Aunty Audrey, Aunty Ivy, Aunty Jenny and Uncle David, Uncle Michael and Aunty Sally, Uncle Melvyn and Aunty Carol. We spent a night in Siem Reap, Cambodia, and had a great experience at Angkor Wat.

To accept a long-time invitation to Singapore, my father and mother came with me and my grandmother to visit our relatives in December 2018. At that time, it seemed that I had accomplished a plan to link the third generation of the family from two countries.

The mission had not been accomplished yet! I took my wife, my brother, my sister-in-law (fourth generation) along with the fifth generation (my daughters) to Singapore in October 2019 to attend Clement's wedding, where the family members from the two countries began building the never-ending bridge of familial ties.

WHAT I DISCOVERED

On every visit to Singapore, I have always experienced great hospitality and the warmest welcome from everyone, which made me realize how important and precious it is to be a part of this great big family.

From one generation to another, the Chiang family has steadily expanded. We share love and care and wish well to each other. The valuable legacy will surely be passed on through future generations.

Sasit Prayadrat
(Fourth Generation)
Grandson of Aunty Chiang Saijai

We visited Loei, northern Thailand, to catch up with Uncle Somchai and their family members in 2011.

*2011*年我们拜访泰国北部六姑妈第三女儿的家。

Reunion with the extended families of Thailand relatives at Sentosa Island.

泰国亲戚在圣淘沙岛重聚。

Inter-visits were held regularly as the younger generations were conversant in English.

泰国的年轻亲戚经常和我们相互访问，他们精通英语，没有语言问题。

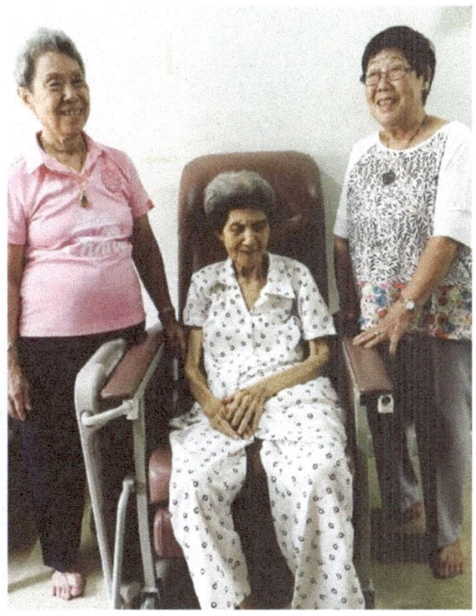

Fourth aunt from Singapore and sixth aunt from Thailand visited our aged mum before she passed away in 2016.

四姑和泰国六姑在妈妈于2016年去世前拜访她。

Meeting with Thailand relatives in Bangkok during the mourning period of King Bhumibol Adulyadej in 2016, followed by a short tour to Cambodia.

2016年-我们的家人在泰国国王哀悼期间拜访了泰国亲戚，随后访问了柬埔寨。

A surprise birthday celebration for our Thailand nephew Nack (centre) who accompanied his grandmother and parents to visit Singapore in 2018.

2018年, 泰国的年轻亲戚Nack, 他祖母和父母亲访问新加坡, 我们为他庆生。

Farewell to Uncle Somchai

告别姑丈颂猜

Uncle Somchai's funeral was held in Buriram on 26 June 2015.

2015年6月26日泰国夏森发姑丈在武里喃府的葬礼。

Four Chiang brothers from Singapore attended the wake to pay respect to uncle Somchai in Buriram.

我们四兄弟在武里喃府参加了颂猜 (Somchai) 姑丈的葬礼。

CHAPTER 11

Maternal Roots

Our maternal great grandmother Lee Cheng Keow (李清娇), grandmother Tan Mui Luang (陈美鸾), granduncle Tann Kim Hai (陳金海) and their families lived under one roof. Grandmother and granduncle's families were closely knit and had a strong filial bond. Grandmother was married to Lim Mong Sim (林茂森) and they had four children — three boys and one girl. Our Mum, Lim Poh Neo (林宝娘) was the only girl in the family. Granduncle Tann Kim Hai married his sweetheart Seah Siew Eng (余秀英) and they had six sons. Our house originally was uncemented with an attap roof located a few hundred metres away from grandma's house. The house was in very bad condition, with a leaking roof and no electricity and running water. During rains, we had to use portable basins and pails to contain the dripping water and used old calendar zinc sheets to patch up the leakage. My fond memory of great grandmother Lee Cheng Keow was short as she left us in 1958 when I was about seven years old. I could only remember that she loved to eat durians together with white rice and other Peranakan dishes. Her personality and character resembled grandma's, who was very patient and never raised her voice even when she was disturbed and stressed.

I remembered that our second uncle was very close to her and looked after her needs, especially when durians were available. She was very hygienic and would remove her false teeth to wash after every meal. She would wash her hair every day and tie it up with a bun held by a big golden pin. She was particular with her Nonya Baju Panjang and matching batik sarong dress. To complement the dress, she would pick some artistically crafted brooches to button up and belted the sarong with a hand-made silver accessory. To complete her attire, she would choose a pair of matching beaded slippers for outings. Occasionally she would also engage the service of a traditional facial beautician to freshen up her face using white powder and sewing string. I remember that her funeral was very grand, attended by a few generations of mourners and a couple of hundred friends and neighbours to send her off to her final resting place. Our great grandfather Tan Huan Hng (陳煥勳) left us long ago before we were born. Unfortunately, I couldn't even get a picture of him.

In hierarchy, we have to address our granduncle's six children as uncles although we were contemporaries. Granduncle's children were young due to his late marriage. All our older brothers and relatives were born in the 40's, with many more born between the 50's and 60's. Life was hard and difficult, with many mouths to feed and take care. The most unfortunate event was the passing of our maternal grandfather Lim Mong Sim at the young age of fifty-seven. With his departure, the responsibility of raising the family fell on our maternal grandmother; her three sons, uncles Seng Kiat (林成吉), Seng Chua (林成泉), Seng Chye (林成财); and daughter Poh Neo (林宝娘).

According to a former neighbour, during the Japanese occupation, Grandpa was very helpful and was appointed as a guide to thirty families to ensure their safety and protect them from capture by the Japanese soldiers.

However, we were blessed to have a strong and caring maternal grandmother, Tan Mui Luan, who helped to look after the big family. She was soft spoken but her iron-hearted personality and leadership helped to keep the families together. Grandma and all the uncles started a small provision shop along Yio Chu Kang Road opposite the Chia Keng Market. The shop was named Lim Hup Seng and was helmed by the youngest uncle Lim Seng Chye, as the two older uncles worked full-time jobs. There were several provision shops around the vicinity, and to stay competitive, our grandma and young uncle worked long hours, from 6.30 AM to 10.00 PM daily.

When our older brothers and cousins were mature enough, they chipped in to help as in those days the shop had to provide delivery services to households as far as in Serangoon Gardens. All the groceries were packed and mounted on the back of the only heavy-duty bicycle and delivered to the customers' houses. The younger relatives were assigned to look after the shop and replenish fresh water supply for the shop from the common stand-pipe about 100 metres away. Some of us who were not able to cycle would help look after the shop and bundle up all empty soft drink and beer bottles by the dozens. The emptied bottles would be returned to the wholesalers when they were scheduled to replenish the stocks.

When new stocks of groceries arrived, we had to help arrange and stack them up on the display shelves under the supervision of grandma. Every afternoon, when we had our tea break, she would assign one of us to buy coffee from the nearby coffee shop, which cost ten cents per container without sugar added. We would also take the opportunity to ask the coffee shop boss for the unwanted shaven layers of the bread to go with the freshly brewed coffee. She would also offer us broken pieces of biscuits that were not suitable for sale to the customers.

In those days it was customary for the provision shops to offer free gifts to their loyal customers during the festive seasons. Our uncle would assign us to deliver the free gifts such as F&N soft drinks, calendars, glass wares and other provisions to the loyal customers and supporters to appreciate their support and strengthen the bonding.

It was here that many of us took the opportunity to learn to ride the adult bicycle, which was too big for most of us as we were teenagers. During our free time, we used the shop bicycle for practice with coaching from the older brothers and cousins. The cycling lessons would be useful as more people could help in the delivery services. As such many of us would volunteer to take up the delivery job with the intention to use the bicycle to improve our cycling skills.

Running a small business was not easy as thefts and break-ins in the shops and dwellings were rampant, not to forget the organised gangs and extortionists who sought protection money. There were cases where some customers could only afford to pay their provisions at the end of the month when they received their pay packet. As such, these individual customer orders were placed on credit term and recorded in a pocket-size '555' brand notebook, based on mutual trust. Late payments and bad debts were other problems that the shopkeepers had to bear with. Some dishonourable customers would suddenly disappear and move to other places without honoring their payments.

From a young age, we were influenced and nurtured by the village elders to help the underprivileged, the aged and the poor people.

It was at this shop that all our cousins helped and worked together as a team under the supervision of our youngest uncle. We developed a strong bonding and were cohesive when coming to serve the villagers as volunteers under the Yio Chu Kang Villagers Mutual Help Association. This association was responsible for strengthening bonds between the villagers and looked after their welfare, security and safety. From a young age, we were influenced and nurtured by the village elders to help the underprivileged, the aged and the poor people.

A life-threatening experience I remember was when my second brother Benson was struggling for his life when a thief broke into my uncle's shop and tried to strangle him in his sleep. He put up a fierce fight with the perpetrator and luckily was able to overpower and get rid of him; the thief then escaped through the small opening between the plank shutters. In those days, burglars were very desperate and could do anything to kill anyone who resisted. There was another occasion when our family members were woken up by the shouts of two villagers who were stabbed and robbed while on their way to operate their stall at a nearby market. The robbers made off with their cash and escaped into the darkness. The two villagers were left bleeding and we attended to them while waiting for the police and ambulance to arrive.

A neighbour's son was having family disputes and wanted to end his life. He tried to commit suicide by hanging himself in the house. Luckily a family member discovered him struggling on the noose, while his mother was shouting for help. My dad was awakened by her loud wailing and immediately rushed over to their house to help lower the unconscious victim down and take him by ambulance to the hospital. He was very lucky to be saved in time.

Gang fights were common as different gang groups would try to dominate their areas of influence. Trouble could arise over the collection of protection money. The clandestine societies would control swill collection, newspaper distribution, tontine operations and chap ji kee betting. There were opium smoking dens everywhere, and fighting among the operators and smokers was common. On one occasion, we were told that there had been a fight between two smokers and one of them used a hammer to smash the head of another person. Whenever there was a gang clash, our uncle would order us to close the shop as there would be opportunists taking advantage of the chaotic situation to carry out looting. Other gang members would be going around to demand protection money, and if their demands were not met, they would make life difficult for the shop owners. Street beggars and desperate buskers would also prowl around the shopping areas to beg for money and food.

House break-ins and kidnappings of business tycoons for huge ransom were organized by big-time gangsters. The boss of a famous biscuit company was kidnapped and murdered in the 60's. His body was tied up and dumped in the graveyard at Plantation Avenue. We happened to be around the vicinity to catch spiders when we saw policemen cordoning the cemetery area.

We were young and very inquisitive and wanted to know what was happening and managed to find our way to have a peek at the deceased body. It was very scary when we came face to face with the gruesome murder. The sight of the victim`s body been tied up with wires was frightening, and on that night, we were mentally stressed and had unpleasant nightmares. This was part of growing up with exposure to good and bad experiences in the kampong during the 60's. In 1968, the police were involved in a gun battle with a group of notorious kidnappers whose hideout was in a bungalow house at St Heliers Avenue, a few hundred metres away from the graveyard. I had been studying for my O Level examination during that time.

While burning the midnight oil, my eyes suddenly teared up as the wind blew in the direction of our house. Later we learned that it was due to the heavy tear gas used by the police to flush out the kidnappers. Being inquisitive and naïve, some of us rushed to watch the stand-off, but were chased away by the police. True enough we were told that some of the bullets ended up piercing a passing taxi along Yio Chu Kang road. About 300 police officers, led by then Deputy Superintendent Goh Yong Hong and the Gurkhas, and backed up by the army tank, were engaged in the stand-off with the heavily armed kidnappers. The stand-off started early in the morning, with two of the kidnappers, including the notorious chief Loh Ngut Fong, being shot dead. We learned that these elusive gang members underwent arms training and purchased their weapons from a nearby Indonesian island.

Great grandmother Lee Cheng Keow and family members (1883 to 1958).

外曾祖母李清娇 *(1883—1958)* 和她的家人 (老舅,祖母和老姨)。

Maternal Family Tree

母亲家谱

Group picture of maternal grandmother, combined family members of our three uncles together with our family members taken in the 60's.

*1960*年代- 外祖母与4个家庭成员合影。

Maternal grandmother with our family members.

外祖母和我们的家人。

Maternal grandmother with second uncle Lim Seng Chua and family members.

外祖母和二舅林成泉及其家庭成员合影。

Gathering of four generations of relatives at the wedding of our youngest brother Melvyn and Carol on 6 April 1991.

*1991*年4月6日,四代亲戚参加了我们最小的弟弟庆隆和柱香的婚礼 。

Chinese New Year gatherings with relatives during our kampong days and in the current HDB flat.

在车宫村和住宅区举行新年聚会。

Kampong days gatherings with relatives and friends in the 60's.

1960年代甘榜时代与亲朋好友聚会。

Gathering of Kampong childhood friends and former schoolmates in the 70's.

70年代甘榜童年时代的朋友和同学合影。

CHAPTER 12

The Values Imparted by Maternal Grandmother

Our beloved Peranakan maternal grandmother would always remind us to study hard and be frugal while she gave a small token of twenty cents as allowance for helping in the provision shop. She also taught us valuable lessons to recycle the wooden boxes and nails that were used to pack the canned condensed milk. The pieces of wood from the boxes would be dismantled and used as firewood or fabricated into low stools and toy guns. All paper wrappers and jute strings used by the wholesalers for packaging would be salvaged and recycled. She even taught us to make paper bags from old newspapers for packing rice, sugar and red and green beans ordered by customers.

These valuable lessons and values she imparted to us helped us to build character and be better people. What we learned from her was not taught in school, and we always treasured her advice to be wise in our spending and kind to others. Beggars who approached her for alms were never turned away as she would usually save all the square and round Straits Settlement one-cent coins to give them. Some beggars would even ask for cigarettes, and she would oblige them with a stick or two. In those days, with ten one-cent coins, they could have a decent meal of mee siam or kway teow soup.

She was very skillful in Peranakan cooking, and our mum and aunties inherited her culinary skills. During our childhood days, we used to help her prepare her signature vegetarian dishes to be offered to the Tian Kong Deity on the ninth day of Lunar New Year. She was a devout Taoist, and every night she would use her favourite jade beads for her prayers before bedtime. Just like great grandmother, she was a durian lover and always paired it with white rice for dinner. The younger generations discontinued this practice as doctors had advised that excessive consumption of durian would result in high cholesterol and diabetes due to the high sugar content.

Beggars who approached her for alms were never turned away as she would usually save all the square and round Straits Settlement one-cent coins to give them

As I was close to her, she taught me how to save water when washing dishes and cups as potable water was very precious during the kampong days. She would spend almost the whole day at the shop as our youngest uncle had to run errands every now and then. Life was not easy for her as she lost her second son Lim Seng Chua in 1971 and first son Lim Seng Kiat in 1982. She did not show any signs of depression and persevered with her daily routine. In the mid 80's, she was diagnosed with colon cancer and part of her intestine was removed. Even after her operation, she did not show any signs of weaknesses or fatigue. Life went on as usual, and as far as I know, she never complained of any post-operative pain or side effects.

I remembered that at that time I had just passed my driving test and I would take her to Toa Payoh Hospital for her routine check-ups. After her operation, she continued to help in the shop till the resettlement of the village. Being an active octogenarian, she was back to her working routine and could even climb up the ladder to stack up and display the canned food. She had a strong conviction and fighting spirit as age was just a number to her. We salute her for her resoluteness and never-say-die attitude. With more than thirty grandchildren, she never raised her voice at anyone even at times when some turned boisterous and mischievous.

During the 60's, sanitation workers often went on strike, and the toilet waste were not cleared for weeks and overflowed to the ground. I remember witnessing her taking advantage of the heavy rains to flush away the human waste which were infested with maggots. During that period many of us were afraid to visit the toilet as the sight of the moving maggots below the squatting pan was very scary. I admired her for her bravery and loving care for the family members. She survived the operation and outlived her two older sons for many years before she passed away at the age of 91 on 24 November 1991.Grandma was very fortunate to have four generations of mourners to send her off to her final resting place. She left behind an outstanding legacy for all the descendants, and we hope we could emulate all her exemplary qualities

Our beloved maternal grandmother Tan Mui Luan (1900–1991) celebrating her birthday with grandchildren and great grandchildren.

三代亲戚庆祝外祖母的生日。

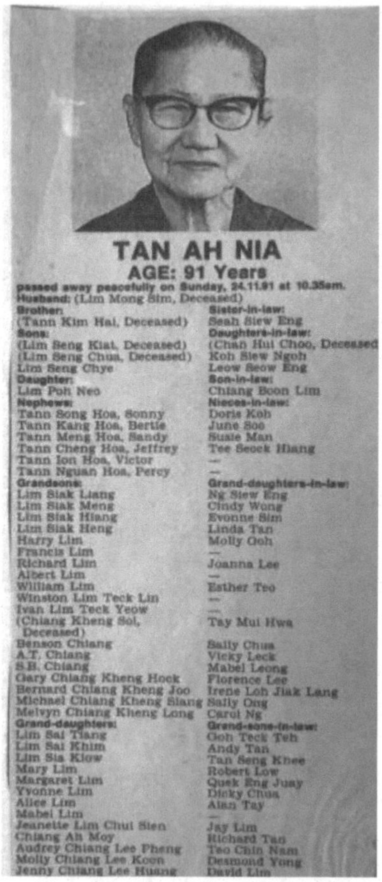

TAN AH NIA

AGE: 91 Years

passed away peacefully on Sunday, 24.11.91 at 10.35am.

Husband: (Lim Mong Sim, Deceased)

Brother:
(Tann Kim Hai, Deceased)

Sons:
(Lim Beng Kiat, Deceased)
(Lim Seng Chua, Deceased)
Lim Seng Chye

Daughter:
Lim Poh Neo

Nephews:
Tann Song Hoa, Sonny
Tann Kang Hoa, Bertie
Tann Meng Hoa, Sandy
Tann Cheng Hoa, Jeffrey
Tann Ion Hoa, Victor
Tann Nguan Hoa, Percy

Grandsons:
Lim Siak Liang
Lim Siak Meng
Lim Siak Hiang
Lim Siak Heng
Harry Lim
Francis Lim
Richard Lim
Albert Lim
William Lim
Winston Lim Teck Lin
Ivan Lim Teck Yeow
(Chiang Kheng Soi, Deceased)
Benson Chiang
A.T. Chiang
S.B. Chiang
Gary Chiang Kheng Hock
Bernard Chiang Kheng Joo
Michael Chiang Kheng Siang
Melvyn Chiang Kheng Long

Grand-daughters:
Lim Sai Tiang
Lim Sai Khim
Lim Sia Kiow
Mary Lim
Margaret Lim
Yvonne Lim
Alice Lim
Mabel Lim
Jeanette Lim Chui Sien
Chiang Ah Moy
Audrey Chiang Lee Pheng
Molly Chiang Lee Koon
Jenny Chiang Lee Huang

Sister-in-law:
Seah Siew Eng

Daughters-in-law:
(Chan Hui Choo, Deceased
Koh Siew Ngoh
Leow Seow Eng

Son-in-law:
Chiang Boon Lim

Nieces-in-law:
Doris Koh
June Soo
Susie Man
Tee Seock Hiang
—
—

Grand-daughters-in-law:
Ng Siew Eng
Cindy Wong
Evonne Sim
Linda Tan
Molly Ooh
—
Joanna Lee
—
Esther Teo
—
—
Tay Mui Hwa
Sally Chua
Vicky Leck
Mabel Leong
Florence Lee
Irene Loh Jiak Lang
Sally Ong
Carol Ng

Grand-sons-in-law:
Goh Teck Teh
Andy Tan
Tan Seng Khee
Robert Low
Quek Eng Juay
Dicky Chua
Alan Tay
—
Jay Lim
Richard Tan
Teo Chin Nam
Desmond Yong
David Lim

Three generations of mourners at the funeral of our beloved maternal grandmother Tan Mui Luang on 24 November 1991.

我们心爱的外祖母于1991年去世。
葬礼上有3代亲戚送葬。

CHAPTER 13

Grandduncle Mr Tann Kim Hai, Our Role Model

The other person that we most respected was our grandmother's younger brother, Tann Kim Hai. We called him Low Koo (老舅) or granduncle. He was our role model and was probably responsible for influencing our father to send most of us to schools with English-medium education. My father was a typical and traditional Teochew-speaking immigrant from Shantou Prefecture. He was not well educated, and during his time, lessons were taught in Teochew dialect only. It was very challenging for him as he was not able to converse in Mandarin and English and couldn't help us in our studies.

Our granduncle was very proficient in English and had a very good education background. He was also an avid sportsman and a good badminton buddy of former President Wee Kim Wee. President Wee was one of his guests at his wedding in the late 40's. They lost touch with each other for a long period as Mr Wee was a very busy person before he became the fourth president of Singapore. He was the Ambassador to the Republic of South Korea from 1981 to 1984 and concurrently the Ambassador to Japan from 1980 to 1984. He was also appointed as High Commissioner to Malaysia from 1973 to 1980. Unfortunately, granduncle was very sick and unable to meet up with President Wee when he was invited to visit the Istana on a few occasions. At that time, granduncle Tann Kim Hai had been hospitalised and was undergoing chemotherapy treatment. Instead, it was his third son Sandy who visited Istana to update the President on granduncle's condition and took his heart-warming get well message back to his father.

At that time, our granduncle had been diagnosed with cancer and was too weak to move around. However, he managed to speak with President Wee over the phone for about half an hour. The inspiring call from the President certainly lifted up his spirits to fight on for a quick recovery. He was under treatment at the hospital, and unfortunately after a year, he passed away in 1990 at the age of 78 years.

News of my granduncle's demise was disseminated to President Wee and his former badminton buddies. As an old friend and badminton buddy, President Wee attended the wake on 17 May 1990 held at Blk 238, Hougang Avenue 1. It was certainly an extremely high honour and great surprise for our grandaunty Seah Siew Eng and her family, who were humbled by President Wee's visit.

During the kampong days, many villagers would enlist granduncle's help to provide verbal translations when they received letters or circulars written only in English. He was privileged to be one of the earliest owners of a black and white TV, which was introduced by Television Singapura in 1963. Many of us, including the neighbours' children, would gather at his house, which turned into a mini theatre when the then most popular series *The Man from UNCLE*, starring Robert Vaughn and David McCullum, was televised. Apart from these long episodes, many of us also liked to watch the Disneyland Cartoon shows. Granduncle was very hospitable and would try to accommodate all the neighbours' children who turned up early to reserve a seat to watch their favourite shows.

He was also a very generous person, and many of us would prioritise our visits to his house during Chinese New Year as he would treat us with his sumptuous signature dishes. Apart from the food and goodies that he served, he also prepared red packets for all the relatives, young and old. He was a very generous person who would cook his signature dishes to share with his friends and host them for daily beer-drinking sessions held at the nearby fruit stall. At the end of the day, he would give away the empty beer bottles which could be exchanged for ten cents each.

I remembered that he invested in and maintained a huge collection of encyclopaedias for his children. There were many bookshelves with neat display of different series of encyclopaedias and books. He treasured his collections and was very particular about people using his books. He would remind us to take good care and to ensure the corner of the pages were not folded up like dog's ears.

He was very entrepreneurial as he started his printing business in the house catered to the banking sector. His good reputation and close contacts with the bank staff gave him the opportunity to service the banking requirements on printing matters. At one stage, he also ventured into fabrication of welded iron window grills, gates and children's swings for shops and houses even though he was not familiar with the trade. We admired him for his remarkable acumen in business matters and his diplomacy in interpersonal relations.

Granduncle Tann Kim Hai (1912–1990) visited relatives in Chung Lim village in 1988.

陳金海老舅(于*1912—1990*)于1988年在樟林村拜访他的亲戚。

Mr Wee Kim Wee (centre) at the wedding dinner of our granduncle Tann Kim Hai (standing).

黄金辉总统(中间)是陳金海老舅的婚宴嘉宾。

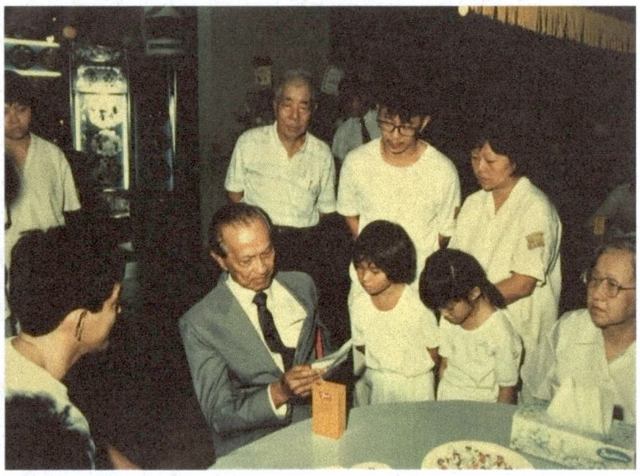

President Wee Kim Wee paid his last respects to granduncle Tann Kim Hai and chatted with his family members.

总统黄金辉向好友陳金海老舅致最后的敬意。

President Wee Kim Wee offered his condolences to grandma at the wake of granduncle Tann Kim Hai, who passed away in 1990.

总统黄金辉慰问外祖母陈美鸾。

President Wee accompanied by granduncle's children, daughters-in-law and grandchildren.

陈金海老舅的家人陪同总统黄金辉。

Granduncle's sons, Sunny, Bertie, Sandy, Jeffrey, Victor and Percy, with their wives Doris, June, Susie, Tee Seock Heong, Zhang Xian Man and Rosie, respectively, and their children.

老舅的子孙们在他的灵前留念。

CHAPTER 14

Our Parents and the Succeeding Generations

Our father Chiang Boon Lim married his first wife Teo Siew Lan in the 30's in China at Chung Lim village. They had their first child named Kheng Soy before he migrated to Singapore. He came to Singapore in 1936 and struggled hard to make a living in order to support his family and younger brother and sisters back in China. He started to work as a janitor and shop assistant for a couple of years at Boat Quay and later at Upper Serangoon Road before he ventured to set up his own business at Chia Keng village. It was around this time that he met my mother Lim Poh Neo and decided to settle down with her after a short courtship. As a life partner and assistant, she was of great help to him in running the business.

Not long after they settled down, Singapore was invaded by the Japanese and the business was on hold for a couple of years. The Second World War reached Singapore shores in 1942, and the British surrendered Singapore to the Japanese and the latter renamed it Syonan-to. After the Japanese surrendered in 1945, life went back to normal and peace prevailed. Dad was able to carry on with his business and spend more time with mum. It was time for him to start a family, and the first Singapore-born child arrived and was named Kheng Peng (Benson), translated as a "Celebration for Peace" in English.

A few years later, when business picked up, dad was in a better financial position to arrange for his first wife and eldest son from China to be reunited in Singapore. Not long after they settled down in Singapore, the first wife was expecting and gave birth to a pair of twins named Ah Moy (Jessie) and Soy Bah (Ricky). The twins were born after the birth of the second wife's second son Kheng Kwang (Gilbert).

Thereafter followed by the birth of another eight children by the second wife at an interval of two to three years. The fifth son Kheng Hock (Gary) was born in the late 40's. From the sixth son, Kheng Joo (Bernard) and the rest of the siblings, all were born in the 50's and 60's. Bernard was followed by second daughter Lee Peng (Audrey), third daughter Lee Koon (Molly), fourth daughter Lee Huang (Jenny), and subsequently the seventh son Kheng Siang (Michael), youngest son Kheng Long (Melvyn) and youngest daughter Lee Kheng (Ivy).

The first and second families were housed separately nearby each other. Our relationships were close and cordial, with no distinction of different mothers. We grew up together as one big family, and with dad's guidance and leadership, we were motivated to contribute our services to the community to help those less privileged and needy in the kampong. All our brothers and sisters were happily married and have our own families with a total of twenty-five fifth-generation children. The fifth generation had done us proud with their academic success as among them are lawyers, doctors, engineers and other professionals. The fifth generation in turn produced thirteen sixth-generation children, including the latest three additions during the difficult year of 2020. I am sure there would be many more in years to come, beating the fifth generation's record.

The fifth generation was fortunate as they had more comfortable living conditions and opportunities for higher education. They were brought up in the Information and Technology (IT) age and were better informed and connected with international affairs. With the growing need to depend on IT for our daily working routine, our lifestyles had to change. As such the gap between our parents and our children was getting wider, with communication in our Teochew dialect becoming obsolete. Our parent's generation also had difficulties catching up with the IT age, and many of them were unable to pronounce the names of their grandchildren correctly. We are at crossroads and living in a cosmopolitan society, with many of us using social media and performing digital transactions, making it even harder for our parents to catch up.

As years pass by, I believe our ancestral Teochew dialect will slowly disappear and die a natural death. From our generation to the fifth generation, the education system was revamped, focusing on speaking Mandarin only.

This had resulted in the shift of using dialects among the Chinese families, and the concern was whether our family values, cultures and traditions would suffer the same fate as our dialect. The younger generations are resorting to online food delivery for their lunch and dinner, and soon traditional home-cooked food would also be phased out. There would be lesser face-to-face conversation between family members as many of us are using social media and Zoom for communication. There is always a price to pay to adapt to the fast-changing world and the new normal.

The Chiang Family Tree

章氏家族

Our family members and the succeeding generations.

我们的家庭成员和后代

Mum, Lim Poh Neo, and Dad, Chiang Boon Lim.
母亲 林宝娘, 父亲章文林

Eldest Brother Kheng Soy & Nancy Tay.
大哥庆先, 大嫂郑美华

Right: Second brother Benson and Sally Chua with daughters Candice and Bianca.
右图: 二哥庆平, 二嫂蔡亜菊
, 侄女淑慧和淑娴

Left to Right: Third brother Gilbert and Vicky Leck with sons Ray and Desmond.
左起: 三哥庆光, 三嫂陆秀风, 侄儿瑞书, 瑞森

Eldest sister Jessie and Richard Tan.
大姐亚妹, 大姐夫陈炳灵

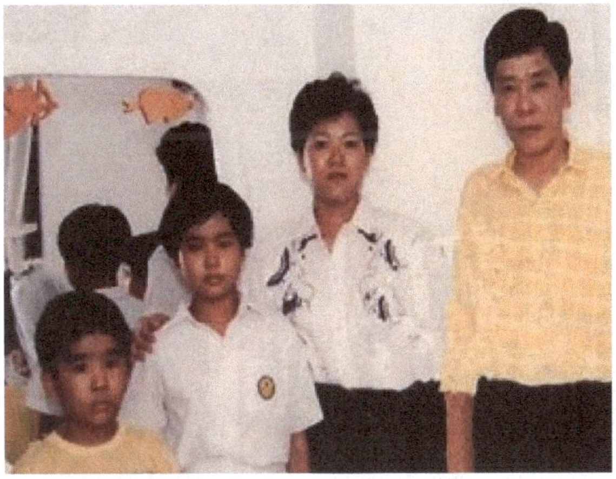

Top Left to Right: Fourth Brother Ricky and Mabel with daughter Yunru and son Jingheng.
上图左起: 四哥细咨, 四嫂梁月娇, 侄女韵茹, 侄儿敬恒

Fifth brother Gary and Florence Lee with daughter Constance and sons Clement and Clarence.
五哥庆福, 五嫂李秀英, 侄女淑娟, 侄儿瑞麟, 瑞杰

Sixth brother Bernard and Irene Loh with daughter April and son Janson.
六哥庆裕, 六嫂卢若兰, 女儿淑霞, 儿子瑞贤

Left to Right: Second sister Audrey and Teo Cheng Nam with son Jiajun, daughter Huiyun and youngest son Ruihong.
左起: 二妹章丽萍, 二妹夫张振南, 侄儿张加俊, 侄女张惠云, 侄儿張睿宏

Third sister Molly and Desmond Yong with daughter Melissa and sons Dalston and Dilton.
三妹丽君, 三妹夫杨德成, 侄女杨惠雯, 侄儿杨政达和杨政雄

Fourth sister Jenny and David Lim with son Gabriel and daughter Glynnis.
右图: 四妹丽芳, 四妹夫林绍光, 侄儿林勇翰, 侄女林琬婷

Left to Right: Seventh brother Michael and Sally Ong with daughters Brenda and Benita.
左起: 七弟庆祥, 七弟妹王莲花, 侄女淑敏和淑齐

Youngest brother Melvin and Carol Ng, with sons Damien and Dylan.
小弟庆隆, 小弟妹黄柱香， 侄儿瑞颖和瑞渊

Youngest sister Ivy and Richard Phua with son Adriel and daughter Sheryl.
小妹丽卿, 妹夫潘木甡， 侄儿潘後豪, 侄女潘韵妃

Weddings of the fifth generation (China 23rd Gen).

Top Left to Right: Candice & Eddie 淑慧& 符致清, *Constance & Nicholas* 淑娟& 韩荣光, *Ray & Elizabeth* 瑞书& 薛佩宜, *April & Alan* 淑霞& 沈湘泽 *and Bianca & Danny* 淑娴& 黄国梁。

1st row Left to Right: Top — Brenda & Hendrick 淑敏& 陈俊豪, *Desmond & Li Qi,* 瑞森& 陈莉锜

2nd Row — Gabriel & Venus 林勇翰& 王玮玲, *Clement & Ivy* 瑞麟& 陈奕姿

Right: Clarence & Jane 瑞杰& 萧清晶

The sixth generation (China 24th Gen)

Top Left to Right: Jared & Natalie 符祥乐 & 符懿欣 (children of Candice & Eddie), Brendan & Sara 章杰扬 & 章莉恩 (children of Elizabeth & Ray), Samuel & Dominic 韩淞畴 & 韩烨畴 (children of Constance & Nicholas), Asher & Alyssa 沈羽凯 & 沈羽馨 (children of April & Allan).

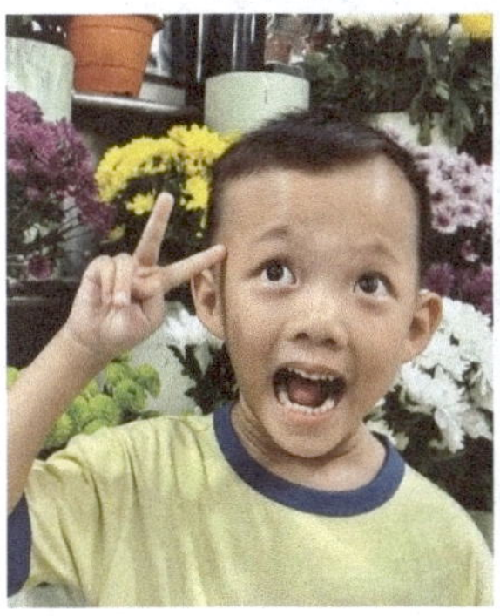

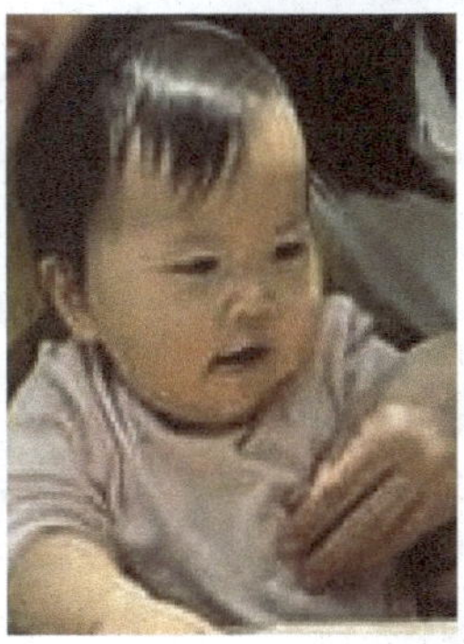

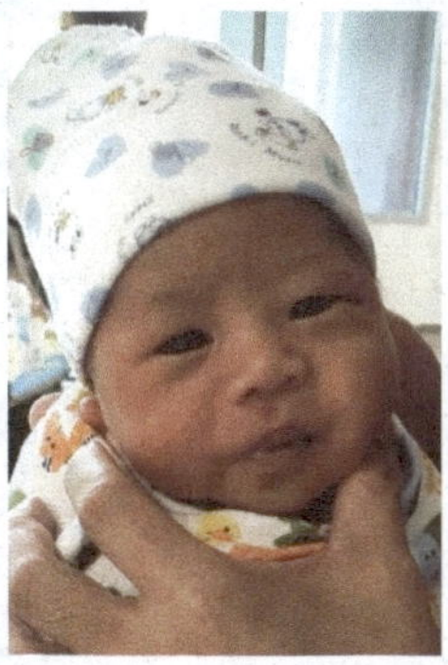

Left to Right: Xavier 黄啟豪 (son of Bianca & Danny), Carys 陈玥涵 and Caden 陈圣喆 (daughter and son of Brenda & Hendrick) Julian 章楷正 (son of Clarence & Jane), Emmeline Lim Xin En 林歆恩 (daughter of Gabriel and Venus), Matthew 章雯傑 (son of Desmond & Li Qi).

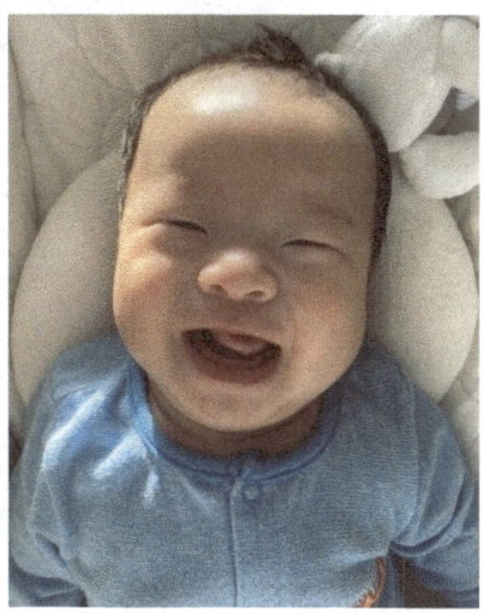

The gathering of four generations at the wedding dinner of Clarence and Jane — 10 March 2019.

2019年3月4日四代家人在章瑞杰和萧清晶的结婚晚宴欢聚。

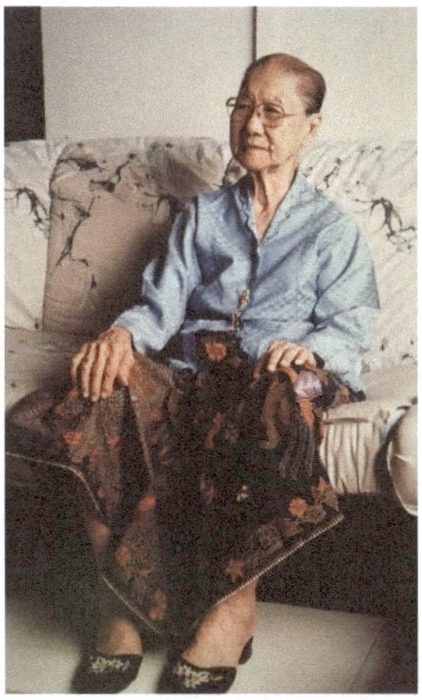
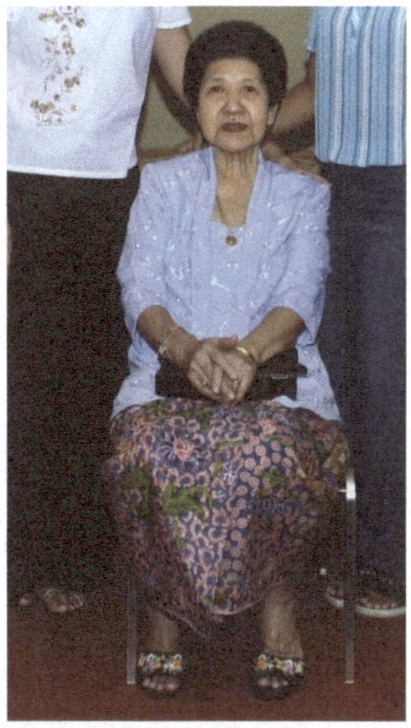

Keeping up with the Peranakan traditional attire for six generations.

保留了6世代娘惹的传统服饰。

Preserving our diverse family cultures and traditional Peranakan and Thai outfits.

保留我们多样化的家庭文化以及传统的土生华人和泰国服装。

A Peranakan-style wedding for Clement and Ivy.

土生华人风格的章瑞麟和陈奕姿婚礼。

Adapting to new cyber-bonding with overseas relatives.

适应与海外亲友的新网络交流。

CHAPTER 15

Our School Days

Most of the fourth-generation relatives and our family members were brought up in Kampong Chia Keng since the 40's until the village was affected by resettlement in the 80's. We experienced the Japanese occupation and faced hardships and poverty together. During that era, the only recreation we enjoyed was listening to the Rediffusion, which was inaugurated in the late 40's. By the 60's, many households and coffee shops were serviced by the first cable-transmitted radio station, which broadcast multilingual programmes. To cater to the older generations, there were news, songs and folk tales programmes in different Chinese dialects. Many villagers would gather at the coffee shops to read the newspaper and listen to their favourite dialect stories narrated in Cantonese, Teochew and Hokkien by the three anchor storytellers, Lee Dai Sor, Ng Chia Kheng and Ong Toh, respectively. While the adults were engrossed with listening to their Rediffusion stories and songs, the children would be playing marbles, fighting spiders and played hopscotch games. Boys preferred catching fish in the open drains and swimming in muddy ponds. During that period, we were also crazy over borrowing miniature comics of Chinese Kung Fu stories from the roadside vendors. Other younger villagers in upper primary schools would prefer to borrow storybooks by Enid Blyton and other popular detective storybooks of Sherlock Holmes from the school libraries. Occasionally, some of the more adventurous youth would walk all the way from Kampong to Farrer Park and Mount Emily swimming pools to learn swimming and soak in the pools. As such they could save up to thirty cents to pay for admission charges and refreshment.

Almost all our family members attended English-medium schools except our eldest and fifth brothers, who studied in Chinese-medium schools. Our second and fourth brothers studied at Yio Chu Kang School. The third brother and three younger brothers studied at St Gabriel's School. The eldest brother studied in China and the fifth brother studied at Chong Hwa Public School. We had to walk to St Gabriel's School at Upper Serangoon Road and would take about 20 minutes. Our fifth brother took about 10 minutes to reach his school. The second and fourth brothers and all the sisters would travel to their schools by public transport. The eldest sister studied at Paya Lebar Methodist Girls' School and all the youngest sisters studied at Serangoon Garden South Primary School. They received their secondary education at Serangoon Secondary School. School textbooks and uniforms were passed down from the older to the younger brothers and sisters. We were given twenty cents per day for our school allowances. Usually, the four brothers who studied at St Gabriel's would prefer to walk to school to save on bus fares in order to enjoy a wholesome meal for our lunch.

What puzzled me was my second brother Benson, third brother Gilbert and fourth brother Ricky were admitted to English-medium schools but my fifth brother Gary studied in a Chinese-medium school. My two younger brothers Michael and Melvyn and I followed my third brother to study at St Gabriel's School. My guess was probably there was not any vacancy for my fifth brother as priority was given to Catholic students so he ended up in a neighbourhood Chinese school. Another possibility was that this was dad's strategy to have another brother beside the eldest China-born brother to study in the Chinese medium to ensure we follow our Teochew traditions and values and touch base and communicate with our China relatives.

We experienced the Japanese occupation and faced hardships and poverty together. During that era, the only recreation we enjoyed was listening to the Rediffusion, which was inaugurated in the late 40's

We were brought up near a Taoist Temple and our grandparents and parents were staunch Taoists, but they were opened to the religious teachings by the Catholic missionary school. They had no objections when we followed our friends to pray in the school chapel or churches. In the school we just had to follow the practice of praying three times a day, before and after class and during recess time. Perhaps my dad's involvement with the Franciscan Missionaries of Mary in operating a free clinic in the kampong had cemented his relationship with the Catholic community.

We respected each other's religions and practices and even went to pray at Immaculate of Heart Church while on the way to school. Next to our school was the Haji Yusoff Mosque and those classes that were close to the Mosque had to halt the lessons when the Religious Leader started to call for prayer in the afternoon. During this period the teacher would allow us to rest or copy notes from the blackboard. In the earlier years, outdoor amplifying loudspeakers were allowed during the sermons and praying sessions. This was a routine practice since day one of my admission to St Gabriel's School, and we were accustomed to and respected each other's religious traditions and practices. Our school management was also very accommodating and understanding.

When I was at the upper primary level, I would prefer to stay back in the school library or play basketball after dismissal time. Occasionally we would play until late evening till the caretaker chased us out. When we reached secondary level, we were very enthusiastic to participate in tournaments and began a private team known as "The Falcons" to compete with other teams. Our team members were very closely knit, and some of us enrolled together in the newly formed school brass band inaugurated in 1965. The band practiced twice a week and we had to carry back home the bulky instrument to practice at our own time. The training was intensified under the instructions from the British army officer Mr Colin Hunter. Drills and formations were also part of the training as we prepared for the first National Day Parade the following year to mark our Independence Day. From the start we practiced rigorously along with Cedar Girls' School and Kong Yong School as a combined contingent.

CHAPTER 16

1968 National Day Parade

To prepare for the Third National Day Parade and ensure we were not late, many of us slept overnight in the school classrooms. It was generally a good idea but bad for the light sleepers as when a group of growing up boys got together, they tend to be boisterous and mischievous. Most of us ended up with no proper rest and were very tired the following morning as we had to wake up very early to reach the assembly point at Merdeka Bridge by 5 AM. Shortly after that we had to march all the way to Padang to assemble by contingent order to have final rehearsals and get ready for the parade.

This was our most memorable parade as the weather turned stormy and rained heavily at the time when all the contingents formally assembled to wait for the arrival of Singapore's first President Yusof Ishak. Everyone in the open areas were drenched and shivering under the heavy storm, including the Prime Minister, the Cabinet Ministers and Members of Parliament. Even the Prime Minister's son Lee Hsien Loong was not spared as he was with the Catholic High School band contingent. The colours from our uniform started to bleach, and rain water filled up the field and created a pond around us. Our band instruments became cold and we had to hold them in an inverted position to prevent rainwater from filling up. It was a shower of blessings as the splashes from the rainwater kept us awake and recharged after lack of sleep the previous night at school. Many of us stayed in a crouched position to keep warm as the merciless strong winds swept across Padang. Most of us were around 17 years old and were energetic and able to withstand the dire weather conditions.

To paraphrase, no matter what happens the parade must go on, and so we waited impatiently for the march past in front of the Supreme Court Building. We had to live up to our national slogan — "Building a Rugged Society" — as Singapore became independent and had to show our neighbours we could make it. We felt a sense of relief when the band started to march off as our body became warmer, with the spectators on both sides of the routes applauded and encouraged us to march on. As we marched through the streets reaching the halfway mark, our uniforms started to dry up when the weather turned sunny and bright. We had no idea of the parade routes or how long it would take to reach the ending point. We just prayed that it would be over soon as the weather became very hot. We marched from the Padang all the way to Queenstown, and everyone was feeling thirsty and hungry by the time we reached the end point. By then, we were exhausted and our uniforms were fully drenched again due to the heavy perspiration. It was certainly the most unforgettable day in our lives and we were very proud to be there at that historical moment.

School days at St Gabriel's from 1959 to 1968.
We were pioneers of the School Brass Band and Basketball Team.

从*1959*至*1968*年，我们是学校首批篮球和铜乐队队员。

The St Gabriel's Secondary School Brass Band was formed in 1965 to prepare for Singapore first National Day Celebrations in 1966.

圣加伸尔中学铜乐队成立于1965年，参加1966年的国庆庆典做准备。

CHAPTER 17

The School Old Boys' Association

Our strong bonds with the school band members and school mates has been perpetually sustained as we still keep in touch with one another after more than fifty years. We met frequently at the school and the alumni anniversary celebrations. Apart from the celebrations, we also gathered occasionally in smaller groups to catch up with one another. In 2018, we organized a trip to Perth to catch up with our former teacher John Grosse and some other former schoolmates we had not seen for a long time. We were very blessed to foster this camaraderie and received strong support from the majority who spent time to support a retired teacher who was undergoing chemotherapy. Through our chat group, we also kept in contact with other former schoolmates who migrated to other countries such as US, England and Australia. Whenever there was any event or opportunity, we would update and catch up with them. Maintaining a big chat group was also challenging as from time to time there would be disagreements and arguments between members over trivial matters and spamming of irrelevant subjects. To counter this problem, another sub-group was initiated for those who wished to discuss other matters and have regular chats not related to the alumni.

I joined the Old Boys' Association 30 years ago and have been actively involved in the Executive Committee, presided by a pioneer and patriotic supporter Mr Henry Pang. He was the big pillar of the association with the strong support from our Advisor, the late Brother Emmanuel and some other veterans. I was roped in to help organize many school and Old Boys' anniversary dinners since 1992. This was the year we had our last dinner gathering at the old school field located at Upper Serangoon Road. The dinner was to commemorate the relocation of the school to Serangoon Ave 1 near Bartley Road. Our first dinner gathering at the new secondary school was held in 1996 followed by the New Millennium dinner in 2000. With this successful large-scale farewell dinner, we were motivated and confident to organise more gatherings for future occasions rotated between the Secondary and Primary schools. The most memorable grand celebrations was for the school fiftieth anniversary in 2003 held at Neptune Theatre.

The dinner was originally planned in the month of April 2003, but due to the Severe Acute Respiratory Syndrome (SARS) outbreak, it was almost called off but fortunately we managed to postpone to September. It took us many months to plan and coordinate with both the Secondary and Primary schools together with the Old Boys' Association. After all the hard work, we managed to secure more than one hundred tables. It was the biggest gathering we ever had with the current and former principals, staff, students and Gabrielite Brothers. Representatives from the Ministry of Education; Priests who were old boys; and representatives of the Montfortian, Boys' Town and Assumption Alumni Associations were also invited.

Apart from anniversary celebrations, the Old Boys' Association also organized golf tournaments to raise funds for the new schools and sports halls. Bursary awards were given out to hardship cases and commendation awards for students who did well in their studies and excelled in sports. We were very blessed and fortunate that the Old Boys' Association managed to recruit more younger members to take on responsible roles for future challenges. The new team had initiated sports activities such as soccer, softball and badminton games to reinforce bonding with the Old Boys. Overseas trips and wine appreciation nights were also introduced recently.

The old boys met frequently and helped the alumni to organise many anniversary dinners. Our special guests included Archbishop Gregory Yong, Archbishop Nicholas Chia and Mr Ee Peng Liang.

校友帮助校友会举办许多周年晚宴。我们的贵宾包括杨瑞元大主教谢益裕大主教和余炳亮生先。

The Alumni helped raise funds for the school through dinners and golf tournaments. I also presented my painting to the Guest-of Honour Minister George Yeo on the opening of the new school. We also had many small gatherings every year as far as Australia.

校友会举办晚宴和高尔夫比赛为学校筹款。我也献一副我的画作给新校园开幕典礼嘉宾杨荣文部长。多年来我们也举办校友聚会包括和移民澳洲的校友。

CHAPTER 18

National Service

In 1967, when Britain announced the withdrawal of their troops from Singapore, our political leaders were worried about the future of our country's defence and security. The sudden exodus of the British Army would cause serious problems not only with regard to defence but also have economic consequences as many of our citizens would be rendered jobless. By 1971, most of the British soldiers had moved out of Singapore, and there was a need to form our own defence forces, thus leading to the establishment of National Service (NS). All male Singapore citizens and second-generation permanent residents were conscripted to serve a period of compulsory NS in the various uniformed groups. All our cousins and brothers born in the late 40's and 50's were called up to serve in the armed forces and police force for two years. We served in different vocations and uniformed groups such as infantry, air force, navy and commando units. As most of us were very involved in the kampong firefighting training and had undergone some physical and endurance exercises, we were more or less prepared for our NS obligations. I was enlisted in 1970 and underwent my basic military training at Holland Road Camp. After three months of basic training, I was posted to Singapore Armed Forces Training Institute (SAFTI) for Section Leader course. The training at SAFTI was very tough and regimental to prepare those with potential for qualification in the Officer Cadet Training courses (OCT). Trainees were also trained to handle different types of heavy firearms and weapons apart from the rigorous exercises, physical endurance, obstacle courses and jungle survival training.

At the end of the Non-Commissioned Officer Course, I was selected to be an instructor for basic military training and posted to Tampines Camp. There we trained recruits from scratch starting from day one when most of them had to completely shave off their hairdo for the first time in their life. Military discipline was of utmost importance as they have to listen and take orders given by their leaders and instructors and maintain their code of conduct. Apart from physical training, the importance of teamwork and comradeship was also instilled in them as one lacklustre soldier would affect the whole platoon. During my tenure as an instructor, I trained a few batches of recruits before my NS obligations were completed on 19 July 1972.

I became a Reservist and was called up again to take part in the National Day Parade in 1974. The first round of training started on 28 April 1974 and lasted more than 2 hours. The subsequent period of training lasted almost three months, averaging about four hours per session till the actual day of the parade. These drills and practices were very regimental as we would be marching under the watchful eyes of the President, Parliamentarians, Foreign Dignitaries and other VIPs during the National Day Parade. Apart from the National Day Parade, we had to make periodical routine reporting and underwent personal physical training test and in-camp training. My Reservist obligations ended on 20 March 1984.

The two most memorable incidents that I encountered during my two years in the army were preparing for the funeral ceremony of an officer who was killed by a live hand grenade while trying to save two soldiers. The highly respectable 2LT Tay died at a very young age of about 21 years old during a live grenade throwing exercise on 26 August 1970. He sacrificed his life to grab the hand grenade from an incompetent recruit who fumbled during the training. Unfortunately, the grenade exploded and killed him on the spot as he shielded the two other soldiers. This happened during my second month as a recruit at Holland Road Camp. We had to put in extra efforts and time to practice these unprecedented funeral drills and learned the commands in Malay language within two days. As all of us were still young and fresh from our school days, we were chosen to perform the ceremonial funeral send-off with full military honours to 2LT Tay.

The other incident happened in January 1974 when we had our first reservist in-camp training. I was was picked to be the bearer of a shotgun loaded with live bullets to protect the trainees at the time when a black panther escaped from the Singapore Zoo in March 1973. I had to stay alert at all times to keep a look out for any sign and movement of this elusive panther in the jungle. I would always be the last person in the file while doing road march or other exercises. As such I could be the most vulnerable person if I was attacked from the back so I had to turn my head back every now and then. The panther was on the run for almost a year, and on 2 February 1974, it was spotted taking cover in a monsoon drain near the former Singapore Turf Club at Bukit Timah. Many policemen and zoo officials tried to flush out the animal with flames ignited by petrol. This marked the end of the national efforts to search for the escaped panther, and it was a big relief for all fellow Singaporeans when the carcass was found inside the covered monsoon drain.

National Service Days as recruit at Holland Road Camp to SAFTI for Section Leader course and as Instructor at Tampines Camp (20 July 1970 to 19 July 1972).

*1970*年至*1972*我接受国民服役。

CHAPTER 19

Fine Arts Study At NAFA

Since my childhood days in the kampong, I have had great interest in drawings and paintings. Arts was my favourite subject in school and this was the only subject in which I scored a distinction in my O Level examination. In secondary school, I was handpicked to design the cover for the school magazine and our class graduation portrait pages. Some of my poster designs were also selected for school campaign promotions and exhibitions.

During my childhood days, I was also interested in the appreciation of performing arts, and I volunteered to help in the kampong's Teochew Opera Troupe. I was given the chance to play supporting roles in several opera performances, which I performed with much enthusiasm, and also learned to master some of the percussion instruments. When the troupe decided to fabricate its own backdrop, I was approached by the artist Mr Yeo Piang, a close friend of my dad, to help in the painting and designing of the artwork. I was also involved in designing some of the covers for the anniversary celebration magazines.

With a passion for fine arts, my ambition was to study at the renowned Nanyang Academy of Fine Arts (NAFA), which produced many famous artists in Singapore and Malaysia. When I completed my National Service, I decided to pursue a three-year Fine Arts course at NAFA, which was located at St Thomas Walk. I enrolled in 1972 and was fortunate to learn from some of the top, distinguished, first-generation Nanyang artists in Singapore. At that time, my school principal was Lim Yew Kuan, the son of NAFA founder Mr Lim Hak Tai, who also taught us watercolour painting and sculpture. The strictest and most serious teacher was Mdm Georgette Chen, also known as Zhang Liying. She was a perfectionist and would not hesitate to erase the charcoal sketches that were near completion if she was not satisfied with the perspective. I was very fortunate to learn from a strict teacher who taught us

NAFA Academy was very prestigious, and many of the students came from overseas such as Australia, Taiwan, Malaysia and even Thailand.

with passion and earnestness. Oil paintings was taught by Mr Ng Yat Chuan and Ms Lai Foong Moi and our Chinese painting and calligraphy teacher was Mr See Hiang To, who specialized in the traditional Chinese style. Mr Chen Chong Swee specialized in his Nanyang-style Chinese painting and water colour. Pencil sketching was taught by Mr Tan Tee Chie, who guided us in using simple lines and strokes for portraitures and anatomy studies.

The Academy was very prestigious, and many of the students came from overseas such as Australia, Taiwan, Malaysia and even Thailand. The former school premises was an extraordinary huge villa with ancient architecture. The ambience of the school was very rustic, and many full-time students would spend most of their time in class even after dismissal time. Some of us even stayed back till late evening to attend commercial art lessons that were introduced by Tan Ping Chiang and Sim Kok Huoy in the mid-70's.

I graduated in 1975 as part of the thirty-fifth batch of graduates, and we held our graduation exhibition at the Chinese Chamber of Commerce from 14–17 November. In the following year, I joined three other friends from the thirty-fourth and thirty-fifth batches to hold our inaugural private exhibitions at the same venue from 18–21 November 1976. I started work as a designer at a publishing firm for several months before I was approached by dad to help out the family flower shop. What I learned from NAFA, I applied to my floral arrangements in terms of colour combinations, compositions and the choice of flowers for different occasions. The study of fine arts ran in our family blood as my daughter and son also pursued art courses at NAFA. Currently my two grandchildren are taking part-time courses on weekends at the Middle Road Campus. With my training in fine arts, I was able to contribute my skills to promote arts in the community. I also represented my Residents' Committee in the National Mural painting competitions organised by the Ministry of Community Development in 1988 and 1989.

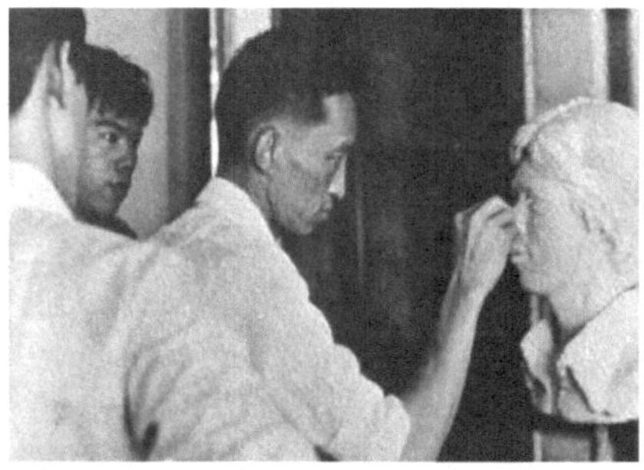

I studied at Nanyang Academy of Fine Arts at St Thomas Walk from 1973 to 1975. As part of our learning journey, we were privileged to visit the house of Mr Yeo Khee Lim, a renowned art collector.

我在南洋美术专科学校学习了三年从*1973*至*1975*年，其间很荣幸参观了大收藏家杨启霖先生的珍藏。

Four Friends Arts exhibition — Peter Khang, Bernard Chiang, Chew Choon and Leong Chun Hong.

四友聯展 - 唐輝傑,章慶裕,周俊,梁振康。

18–21 November 1976 at the Chinese Chamber of Commerce Building.

*1971*年*11*月*18–21*日, 在中华总商会举行。

Three generations studying at Nanyang Academy of Fine Arts.

三代在南洋美术专科学校习美术。

I represented Aljunied Zone E Residents' Committee in the National Mural Painting Contest organised by Ministry of Community Development in 1988.

我代表阿裕尼E分区居民委员会参加了由社区发展部于1988年组织的全国壁画竞赛。

The second round of the mural painting contest was held in 1989. The paintings were done at Blk 6 and Blk 7 Lor Lew Lian.

第二轮比赛于1989年举办。壁画坐落在罗弄榴莲第六和第七座。

Achievements and Recognition

成就与认可

Pingat Bakti Masyarakat Award (PBM)
Public Service Award conferred by President Ong Teng Cheong in 1998.

公共服务奖由1998年获王鼎昌总统颁发。

Brother-in-law David Lim, standing next to PM Lee Hsien Loong, was conferred the Public Service Award (PBM) by President Tony Tan in 2012.

2012年，林绍光获陈庆炎总统颁发公共服务奖章。

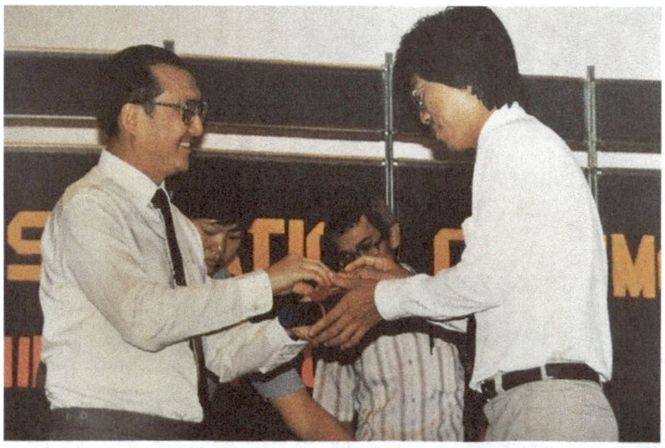

Hotel New World Rescue Badge Award presented by Mr Chin Harn Tong, Senior Parliamentary Secretary, Ministry of Home Affairs (1986).

1986年，高級政务次长钱翰琮先生颁发新世界酒店救援徽。

Ministry of Home Affairs Commendation Awards presented by DPM Wong Kang Seng in 2008.

2008年副总理黄根成颁发内政部表彰奖。

Peoples` Association 30-Year Long Service Award presented by Minister Tan Chuan Jin in 2011.

2011年陈川仁部长颁发人民协会30年服务奖。

People's Association 40-years Long Service Award presented by Prime Minister Lee Hsien Loong - 2021

总理李显龙颁发人民协会40年长期服务奖 – 2021。

People's Association Long Service Award Medals.

人民协会长期服务奖。

Ministry of Culture Community and Youth IRCC Colour Award.

文化社区及青年部IRCC表彰奖。

MCCY Colour Award presented by Minister Lawrence Wong to three IRCC Chairmen: Bernard Chiang, Mr Sarjit Singh and Mr Chia Keng Hian in 2015.

2015年，黄循财部长颁发文化社区及青年部族群与宗教互信圈表彰奖予三位主席。

Singapore Civil Defence Force Commendation Award.

新加坡民防部队表彰奖1986。

Mr Heng Chee Yong and I received the Letter of Commendation from the Civil Defence Force for helping to stop the raging fire at Blk 2 Lorong Lew Lian in 1986.

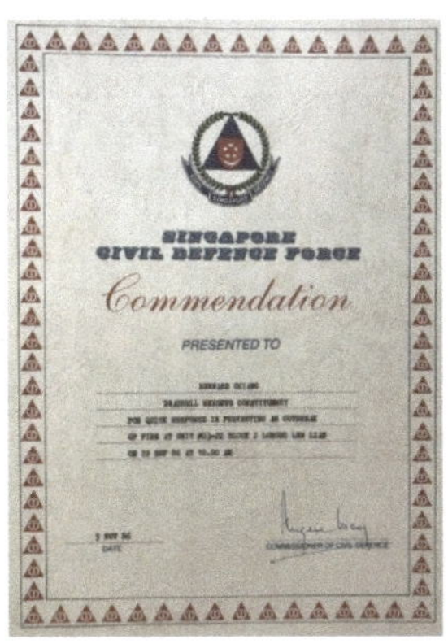

Teo Shun Xie, 2014 Commonwealth Game Gold Medalist.

2014年，表弟张志浩女儿顺惜赢得英联邦运动会射击项目金牌。

Our late cousin Teo Chee How's daughter Shun Xie won the silver medal in the women's 10m air pistol at the Southeast Asian Games held in Myanmar in 2013. In 2014, Shun Xie clinched the first gold medal for Singapore in the Commonwealth Game Women's 10 M air pistol competition held in Glasgow. In 2015, she added another feather to her cap when she clinched another gold medal by beating Thailand's competitor in the Southeast Asian Games hosted by Singapore.

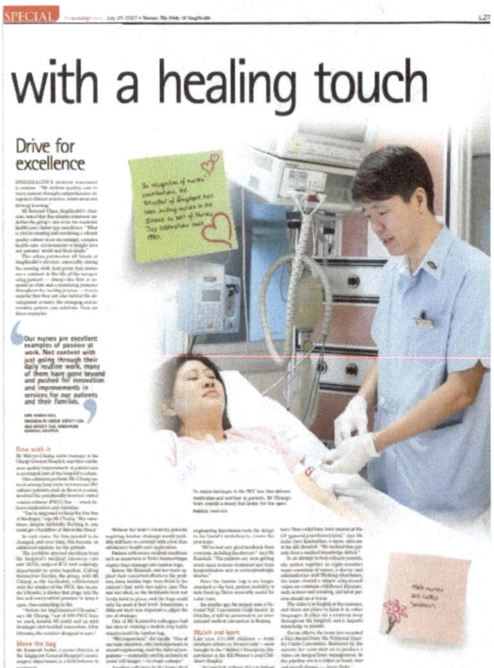

SPECIAL

with a healing touch

Drive for excellence

Our nurses are excellent examples of passion at work. Not content with just going through their daily routine work, many of them have gone beyond and pushed for innovation and improvements in services for our patients and their families.

Youngest brother Melvyn awarded the Professional Nurse Award.

小弟庆隆获颁专业护士奖。

CHAPTER 20

My Passion for Professional Nursing

The valuable lessons I learned from my mentors at the St Anthony Free Clinic

It is indeed an honour to be appointed to participate in the voluntary led by the Franciscan Missionaries Sisters at the St Anthony Free Clinic. It brings back sweet memories of life at Yio Chu Kang Road Villagers Mutual Help Association in the 60's to early 70's. The St Anthony Free Clinic, under the umbrella of Yio Chu Kang Mutual Help Association, was a collaboration with the Franciscan Missionaries of Mary. This Roman Catholic organisation was founded by Mother Mary of the Passion for the international religious congregation of women in over 74 countries. It provided free consultation and treatment to the villagers for common cough and cold. The clinic also provided treatment of wounds and health education for the villagers.

The clinic was helmed by Rev. Sister Leonora Pau and Rev. Sister Maria Kiang from Franciscan Missionaries of the Mary. The villagers were also blessed and fortunate to have a volunteer doctor known as Dr. Wee Sip Leong, a General Practitioner, to be the medical consultant at the clinic. He helped to review cases that needed doctor's advice and prescriptions. If there was a need, he would write referral letter to the polyclinic for the patient to be followed up and receive further in-depth treatment by a professional healthcare team.

Life at that time was simple and less stressful. The villagers got along happily with each other, and free healthcare services were provided. I was young and inquisitive about the operations of St Anthony Free Clinic, and therefore volunteered to help in the clinic twice a week. The clinic workers taught me a lot, and I was fortunate to learn the operational aspects of running the clinic from them. After many years, as good things inevitably come to an end, the Singapore Government announced plans of nation-building and industrialization in the early

70's. It was inevitable that the Yio Chu Kang Road Mutual Help Association finally had to close its doors and stop operations. By then, many villagers had started relocating to the new Housing & Development Board (HDB) estates, and the clinic had obviously outlived its usefulness and served only as a reminder of the past.

It was also the beginning of the next chapter of my life as I served two years of National Service in the Armed Forces. After the completion of my National Service in April 1981, I continued to spend time as a volunteer at the Yio Chu Kang Road Village Mutual Help Association. However, the experience I gained from the free clinic was only very basic and superficial. I had great passion to be a professional nurse and wanted to learn more and help people. When an opportunity came by, I made up my mind to take up nursing as my lifelong career. I successfully completed three years' training at the School of Nursing and graduated as a Registered Nurse. Few years later, I continued to enhance my nursing knowledge and skills by pursuing Advance Critical Care Nursing course and followed by Bachelor of Nursing. For many years, I have been providing patient care in the Surgical Intensive Care setting.

As a professional nurse, I strongly believe that, apart from my roles and duties, I should support the Singapore Nurses Association (SNA). Therefore, I joined as a committee member of the SNA in 1992. It was an exclusive association for nurses, and through this platform, members gathered to exchange ideas and shared their experiences in the core of duties to further improve the standards. It was through this transition that the profile of professional nurses was raised and better appreciated by the community for being capable and having the foresight to think out of the box. During the Annual Nurses Day, nurses from various healthcare institutions were recognized and invited by the First Lady to visit the Istana. In the year 1996, the Nurses Association was honored to invite the First Lady Mrs Ong Teng Cheong to grace the opening of the Singapore Nurses Association House located at Maude Road. I was privileged to be in the working committee to organize the official opening and welcome her to this historic event.

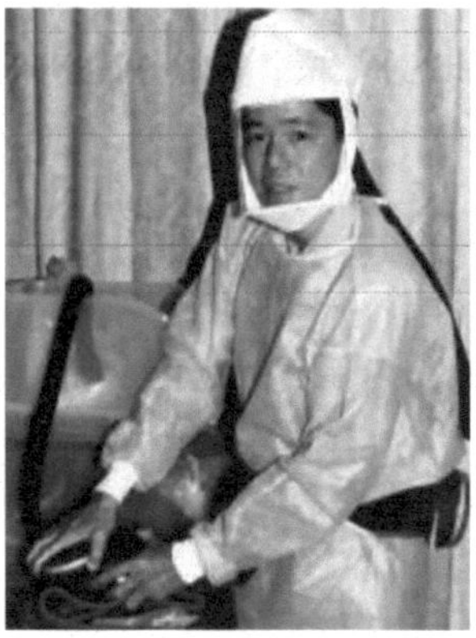

Melvyn Chiang Kheng Long

Youngest Brother
Singapore Fourth Generation
(China 22nd Generation)
Former Administrator, Health Science Authority, Blood Services Group

Former President Ong Teng Cheong and Melvyn were delegates to the Australian Universities International Alumni Convention held in Sarawak in 2000.

2000年前总统王鼎昌和小弟庆隆出席在砂拉越举行的澳洲大学国际校友大会。

Youngest brother Melvyn and colleagues were invited by President and Mrs S R Nathan to the Istana reception in 2003.

2003年纳丹总统和夫人邀请庆隆和同事出席总统府招待会。

Official opening of the Singapore Nurses Association officiated by the First Lady Mrs Ong Teng Cheong on 6 July 1996.

1996年第一夫人王鼎昌夫人主持新加坡护士协会开幕。

Melvyn and fellow Council Members were guests of Mrs S R Nathan at the Istana tea reception on 10 September 2000.

2000年庆隆和护协委员应总统*S R Nathan*夫人 的邀请出席总统府茶会。

A Concise History of Chia Keng Village

车宫村的传说

176

Our nieces Constance and Candice (fifth generation) pose in front of our maternal ancestor's home at Yio Chu Kang Road built in the 40's.

建于1940年代父母亲在杨厝港路车宫村的房子。

Youngest brother Melvyn poses in front of our renovated house in the 60's.

这是我们1960年代装修后一家人住的房子。

In the 50's, there were a few hundred houses mainly built with combustible materials such as timber and attap. Most houses had no proper sanitation, running water and electricity. A common toilet was shared by a few families.

这是1950年代建造的甘榜木屋, 没有水电, 和适当的卫生设施。

The remaining old shophouses and wet market from the 40's at Kampong Chia Keng.

40年代保留至今的甘榜车宫市场的建筑物和商店。

CHAPTER 21

Our Village in the 50's

Our maternal granduncle's children, maternal cousins and our family members from the fourth generation were all brought up in Kampong Chia Keng, which was the central area surrounded by Upper Yio Chu Kang Road, Jalan Teck Kee, Plantation Avenue, St Helier's Avenue, Lorong Chuan, Boundary Road and Lim Tua Tow Road.

This central location of the Chia Keng village was unique as we had a good balance of merchants dealing in different trades. To cater to the needs of the villagers, there were a wet market, shops dealing with Chinese traditional medicine, laundry shops, coffee shops and provision shops. There were also other shops that catered to diverse needs such as tailors, frame makers, Chinese cake shops, beauty salons, barbers, wooden clog makers, iron mongers and a bakery.

Complementing the various trades, there was a book store, signboard manufacturer, fruit stall, motor vehicle and bicycle shop and a Taoist paraphernalia shop.

The nearest public water standpipe was near the market, so many villagers from the opposite side of the road had to make many trips to collect water and for washing. When we were teenagers, all our older brothers had to help collect water from the standpipe for our household. We also had to help top up the water supply of the house of our maternal great grandmother. Topping up of water supply was also needed for grandma and the uncles, who operated a small provision shop opposite the market. In those days, there were no plastic pails, and we had to use recycled oil or kerosene tin containers fitted with a wooden handle to carry water. I started carrying half a tin as it was too heavy and increased the amount I carried gradually when I grew up.

There were also some villagers who provided home delivery of water at a cost; for example, I remember a woman who provided potable water supply services to the weaker folks and those who could afford to pay her. Initially, she would charge two tins for ten cents, which was equivalent to the price of a packet of nasi lemak. She was very hardworking and strong, making many trips around the neighbourhood to supply water to the villagers. Her house was a few hundred metres away from ours, and her husband dealt with scrap metal. To supplement their income, the couple also planted vegetables in a small plot of land in front of their house.

Our family members were brought up in this kampong, which had mostly wooden houses and attap roofs cluttered back to back. There was no supply of treated water, electricity or proper sanitation. Clean water was collected from a central standpipe, where villagers took turn to wash their utensils and laundry. Others patiently queued up to collect water for their homes while some inconsiderate villagers would occupy the water collection point for washing their laundry and household items.

The roads and alleys were narrow with no street lights. Villagers had to use candles or torchlights when they moved around at night. All households were equipped with wall-mounted kerosene lamps or pressured kerosene lamps. Those who could not afford lamps or were thrifty used candles to light up their homes. Over the passage of time, some better-off and entrepreneurial villagers invested in the supply of generator-operated electricity to the village from 7 AM to 7 PM. This was the beginning of a new era when electric bulbs were used.

As far as sanitation was concerned, a few households shared the use of the common toilets. Old newspapers and used fruit wrappers were collected and used as toilet papers. Some villagers would store home-made cigarettes in the toilet for those who could not bear with the stench. All the human waste would be deposited in a metal bucket and cleared by the sanitation workers the following morning. At times, when the workers went on strike, some kind souls would help to drag the fully filled buckets of human waste to be buried somewhere and use them as manure for their vegetable farms.

Usually the villagers would take baths at the common water standpipe either late at night or early in the morning to avoid the long queue and take advantage of the cover of darkness. The same bar of soap cut into several pieces was used for washing laundry, as shampoo and as body soap. The Packet Kao brand shampoo powder, which cost ten cents per packet, was introduced later, and to extract maximum value for money, we only used half a packet per shower.

The village life was very tough and difficult as many struggled to make a living by earning extra income to feed the family members. During those days, family planning was not enforced, and many villagers generally had an average of six to ten children per family. To provide regular meals for the family members and make ends meet, many planted their own vegetables and reared poultry. Others resorted to selling opium and providing opium-smoking services. Illegal gambling and betting were common among the villagers.

Our family members were brought up in this kampong, which had mostly wooden houses and attap roofs cluttered back to back. There was no supply of treated water, electricity or proper sanitation.

All households had to store enough firewood picked up from forest areas or chopped from mature trees to be used us fuel for cooking. The ashes collected from the burnt wood were used to clean oily utensils and cutlery. Those who could not afford to buy proper toothpaste would use the ash to brush their teeth. At times the ash was also used as a remedy to stop bleeding if no medicated ointment was available.

With regard to recreational activities, most of the adults played mahjong, card games and Chinese chess. Others would gather over beer and Chinese tea-drinking sessions while waiting to listen to their favourite dialect stories and songs of yesteryears broadcasted by Rediffusion Singapore.

The children and youth would be busy playing with marbles, five stones and kuti kuti or fighting spiders. The more adventurous ones would go swimming and fishing in the streams and stagnant water ponds. Others would go hunting for fruits and fish and catch wild birds in the wooded areas.

In the evenings, most villagers, young and old, would visit the night markets and travel to the nearby constituencies such as Serangoon Gardens and Upper Serangoon Road, which scheduled events on different dates. Open-air cinema theatres, which charged 10 cents per person, were also available for movie lovers and courting couples. Many youngsters would wait for free shows screened monthly by the former Paya Lebar Police Station. To keep the youth away from juvenile delinquency, the Ministry of Culture would also screen free film shows occasionally at the open area at Jalan Teck Kee.

This was the same spot where political parties held their rallies in the 60's and 70's. I could still remember that, at one of the rallies, the former Minister of Foreign Affairs Mr S Rajaratnam was angered and reprimanded a member from the audience who sarcastically passed racist remarks. I was still young but could understand that such uncalled-for racial remarks could undermine our racial harmony and also spark a race riot. Hawkers appeared in the afternoons and evenings to sell their home-made snacks and cooked food to the villagers. The Teochew fishball kway teow seller would instruct his assistant to use a bamboo instrument to create a continuous tick-tock sound to alert and take orders from the villagers. Other hawkers would be promoting different products such as satay, rojak, bread, carrot cake and lotus seed paste to compliment the kway teow stall.

There were some popular permanent stalls selling their signature dishes along Yio Chu Kang Road. They catered mainly for lunch and dinner to the villagers, whereas those who catered for breakfast would ply their trade around the Chia Keng market vicinity. My favourite stalls were the nasi lemak and the kway chap sellers. In the late evenings, we would patronise our favourite char kway teow stall and usually used our own eggs as additional ingredients. This stall headed by the father, named Ah Luar, also had a fish porridge stall next to his son's char kway teow stall. Their business was prosperous, and they had sharp business acumen to venture into bridal car rental service with their newly acquired Mercedes Benz. The other popular stall was the Teochew kway shop operated by a husband-and-wife team known as Mr and Mrs Soh. Next to their stall was a sugarcane juice vendor known as Ah Aow, who had a distinct cleft on his upper lip.

The neigbourhood was polluted by the pungent smell from the opium-processing dens, as in those days there were many opium addicts in the kampong. They believed that smoking opium would revitalise their energy and used it as a relaxant after a hard day's work. The pungent odour from the opium-smoking den did not escape the anti-opium enforcement officers' attention and helped them narrow down the houses of the addicted smokers.

During the Lantern Festival, the young villagers were joyous and happy to soak in the festive celebrations. Some mischievous teenage villagers would take advantage of the celebrations to practice their shooting skills using the skin of the Duku fruits and rubber bands. In the act of gaining self-satisfaction and cheap thrills, they would aim at the lighted lanterns held by the children and cause it to catch fire. This would cause the children to panic and disperse. Firecrackers were also lighted indiscriminately by the bullies to irritate and disperse those involved in the procession.

CHAPTER 22

Founding of the Village Mutual Help Association

The precious record book of the Yio Chu Kang Road Villagers' Mutual Help Association was compiled by my dad, who saved it just in time before it was completely destroyed by rats. Most of the historical events and activities were recorded and reported in the newspapers and filed since 1957, thanks to the founders who had the foresight to archive for the future generations. With the incredible kampong spirit and remarkable track records of the leaders and villagers, it is my privilege to share with all fellow Singaporeans the legacy of our Kampong Chia Keng volunteers.

The elders of the Chia Keng village Taoist Temple management committee, formed in the early 50's, decided to start an association to look after the welfare and security of the villagers. The temple, whose main deity was the Heavenly Jade Emperor, was started by a group of villagers and housed in a wooden hut. The temple was founded by the early settlers as a place of worship for the Hokkien and Teochew immigrants from China. It also served as a focal point for the villagers to meet and socialise, apart from commemorating religious events.

My father was recruited to help in the association, and the aim of the committee was to make him take on a leading and more responsible role. With the growing population and the changing roles of the temple management committee to lead and represent the villagers, it was officially registered with the Registrar of Societies in 1951. The society was under the purview of the Chia Keng Temple management committee, and the name was changed to Yio Chu Kang Tian Kong Tua.

Thereafter, as the population grew, along with the needs of the villagers and the arrival of other ethnic and religious groups, there was request to change the name of the association to reflect its actual role as a community self-help organisation. In 1954, the name of the association was changed again to Yio Chu Kang Road Villagers' Mutual Help Association. What was founded as a religious organisation gradually evolved into a community-based, self-help organisation, reaching out to other races and villagers of different faiths. This widened its scope and objectives, which was not restricted to just religious activities. The association was officially inaugurated by the area Assemblyman Mr Lim Choon Mong in 1957.

Village elders held regular meetings to look after the welfare and security of the villagers since the 50's.

1950年代,村领导定期开会照顾村民的福利和安全。

Meeting with government officials followed by appointment of committee members and dinner celebrations.

与政府官员会面和村委会委任典礼及晚宴。

The founding of Yio Chu Kang Villagers' Mutual Help Association in 1954 with the premises behind the temple and the formation of the Kampong Fire Prevention Unit.

1954成立楊厝港律村民互助社和消防队。

The village committee also started the St Anthony Free Clinic and collaborated with the Ministry of Health to provide medical assistance for Maternal and Child clinic.

1950年代开设聖安东尼免费诊所和政府母婴诊所。

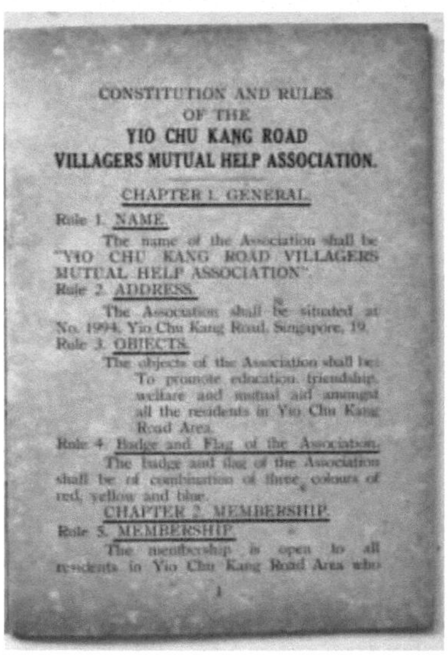

CONSTITUTION AND RULES
OF THE
YIO CHU KANG ROAD
VILLAGERS MUTUAL HELP ASSOCIATION.

CHAPTER 1. GENERAL.

Rule 1. NAME.
The name of the Association shall be "YIO CHU KANG ROAD VILLAGERS MUTUAL HELP ASSOCIATION".

Rule 2. ADDRESS.
The Association shall be situated at No. 1994, Yio Chu Kang Road, Singapore, 19.

Rule 3. OBJECTS.
The objects of the Association shall be:
To promote education, friendship, welfare and mutual aid amongst all the residents in Yio Chu Kang Road Area.

Rule 4. Badge and Flag of the Association.
The badge and flag of the Association shall be of combination of three colours of red, yellow and blue.

CHAPTER 2. MEMBERSHIP.

Rule 5. MEMBERSHIP.
The membership is open to all residents in Yio Chu Kang Road Area who

1

Badges and booklet on constitutions and rules were presented to appointed committee members.

村委会成员的任命和规章制度。

CHAPTER 23

Roles of the Association

In order to create a sense of unity among the kampong folks and foster a cohesive community, the village community required able and committed members to take on leadership roles. Volunteers had to prove their sincerity and be committed to lead by example. A committee was officially formed to look into the welfare, safety and security of the kampong dwellers. The welfare sub-committee looked after villagers who lived alone and faced financial hardship. To raise funds for the needy families, villagers were encouraged to join as official members on a nominal monthly subscription fee. The fees collected, together with donations from better-off villagers, were channelled to the welfare fund for mutual benefit. The security and safety sub-committee was in charge of fire and crime prevention. The education and recreation sub-committees were formed later when the association was ready to recruit better-educated volunteers to run tuition classes for the children of the kampong.

The welfare committee also helped those who had lost their loved ones by going around the kampong to distribute a pair of red candles tied with red thread to spread the unpleasant news. It was a practice then to use this gesture to encourage the neighbours and friends to provide donations and moral support to the bereaved family. In this way the villagers could strengthen the kampong spirit and forge camaraderie. For registered members, the association would arrange a wake visit and a funeral send-off ceremony. Attendance would be recorded for those participating in the wake and funeral to ensure a good turnout. At the wake, usually the bereaved family would offer the iconic Green Spot orange drink with home-cooked curry chicken and bread to show their appreciation, whereas fragrant porridge, cooked with a variety of ingredients, and drinks would be served before the funeral commenced. A donation would be given by the association executive committee to help the bereaved family defray the funeral expenses.

The cohesive kampong folks normally turned up in full force to pay their last respects and comfort the bereaved family. Family members and friends would take turns to be pallbearers, as in those days the coffins were made of very heavy and lasting wood. Strong and tough villagers were selected to carry the coffin from the house of the deceased to the hearse, which was stationed at quite a distance away on the main road. The footpaths and alleys were too narrow to carry out the funeral procession. Villagers and relatives of the deceased would volunteer as outriders and traffic controllers to ensure a smooth flow of the procession. At that time, burial was preferred over cremation, and the task of the pallbearers to climb up the steep and slippery slopes for the burial was very challenging. Strong and experienced villagers were tasked to be pallbearers at the final stage when lowering down the coffin into the pit for burial.

Villagers were encouraged to be registered members to enjoy the perks devised by the committee members. The registered members had the added benefit of including their parents and parents-in-law as beneficiaries even if they were not from the same village. Help was also rendered to those who couldn't afford to join as members on a case-by-case basis.

Apart from welfare and financial assistance, the village elders presided over disputes among neighbours. Petty quarrels and misunderstandings were very common as many lived in close proximity. Excessive barking from neighbour's dogs could spark off a quarrel. Tree foliage overgrown into another family's compound could be an eyesore to the immediate neighbour. Jumping queue at the standpipe for water collection and prolonged usage of the laundry washing areas could also spark off arguments.

Juvenile delinquency was another area the association committee had to deal with. The committee had to find ways to provide education and sports activities for the youth to draw them away from committing crimes and mixing with the wrong company. There were many poor families who couldn't afford to pay for their children's education, who could end up being manipulated by gangsters to commit crimes for a living. As such, the welfare sub-committee was responsible for looking into these issues as well.

CHAPTER 24

Recreational Activities, Festive Celebrations and Anniversaries

Occasionally, the association would organise open-air cinemas that screened black-and-white movies, such as *Tarzan*, *Three Stooges* and *Three Musketeers*, that usually attracted a large crowd. The villagers would be charged ten cents per person. These events also helped create opportunities for courting couples to strengthen their romantic relationships. The more agile and surreptitious youngsters would wait for an opportunity to sneak into the cinemas for free shows. Other youngsters would wait for free shows, which were screened monthly at the former Paya Lebar Police Station and by the Ministry of Culture at the Jalan Teck Kee open ground.

Occasionally, villagers were also entertained by Teochew and Hokkien operas held by the various temple management committees in conjunction with the various festive celebrations. During this period, illegal hawkers would appear, and this would be the best time to make money from the kampong folks. Children would be enticed to try their luck with the tikam tikam game for free ice-cream and kacang puteh. Villagers would turn up early and bring their own chairs to reserve vantage viewing positions for their family members.

Perpetrators would take advantage of the crowded areas to prey on their victims and try their luck in pickpocketing. Aggressive secret society members would be on the prowl to demand protection money from the shop owners and stall operators, failing which they would cause trouble and disrupt their businesses. The Safety and Security sub-committee would be deployed to ensure peace and security prevailed during this period. These security personnel also doubled as fire prevention officers to stand by for any eventual outbreak of fire.

Festive celebrations were part of the villagers' way of strengthening the social fabric, graced by Dato Tay Kia Hong.

通过节日庆典将村民联系在一起。拿督郑鏡鴻是这次庆典嘉宾。

Religious festive celebrations were one of the main activities in the 50's.

从50年代开始, 宗教节日庆祝活动是该村的主要活动。

Yio Chu Kang Road Villagers' Mutual Help Association's 15th anniversary celebrations cum Wushu performances.

楊厝港律村民互助社15周年庆典和武术表演。

Yio Chu Kang Road Villagers' Mutual Help Association's 19th anniversary celebrations.

楊厝港律村民互助社19周年庆典。

VIPs Mr Lee Khoon Choy and Mr Lee Kim Tah were invited to grace the occasion.

李炯才部长和李金塔先生是贵宾。

Celebrating the successful re-election of the Association's Honorary Advisers Mr Lee Khoon Choy and Mr Sia Kia Hui as parliamentarians and re-appointment of the Association Executive Committee.

庆祝李炯才和谢嘉惠成功当选国会议员，再次任命村民互助社执行委员会。

CHAPTER 25

Formation of the Volunteer Firefighting Unit

The most worrying and life-threatening issues were the safety and security issues in the village. Most of the houses were built with combustible materials, such as wood and attap. Once a fire broke out, all the village folks would be engaged to help contain the fire and prevent it from spreading as the inferno could possibly wipe out the whole kampong.

Everyone was living in fear and had sleepless nights most of the time due to the threat of a fire outbreak. At all times, they had to be prepared to be evacuated, leaving behind their possessions and possibly separated from their loved ones should a disaster happen. Old folks and children might not even escape from a big fire, should there be a stampede at the narrow alleys and footpaths in between the cluttered houses.

These unfavourable premonitions of disasters prompted the village elders, including my dad Chiang Boon Lim, to take the matter seriously and prioritise the formation of the village volunteer firefighting unit.

Coincidentally, the first person in Singapore to own a private fire brigade was Mr Cheang Hong Lim (not related). He was a renowned philanthropist and businessman who donated generously to create a public garden which was named after him as Hong Lim Green. In the 60's, the garden, along with a clubhouse for the Straits Chinese, was redeveloped and renamed as Hong Lim Park. The firefighting unit headed by Mr Bay Ah Hian, a Rural Board member, was officially formed in November 1954 with strong support from the government and generous donations from well-to-do citizens. Firefighting skills and trainings were conducted by the Singapore Fire Brigade.

An inauguration ceremony was held at the Sing Hwa School basketball court with the unit flag presentation by the then Singapore

Rural Board Acting Chairman Mr S T Stewart to the unit Sergeant Harry Tan.

One week after its formation, the volunteer firefighters were tested to handle their first case of a real kitchen fire. Luckily, the fire was brought under control by the volunteers before the arrival of the fire engines. It would have been disastrous if the fire had started to spread to the other neighbouring houses in the midst of the attap kampong. Fortunately, the only victim was a young girl with slight burns, whose mother was shopping at the nearby market.

Outbreak of fire was not the only concern, as the village elders had to rally the support of the villagers and the government to widen the roads and footpaths for emergency vehicles' access. Speed and timely arrival by helpers and rescue personnel to reach the disaster areas was crucial. The roads and footpaths had to be accessible and free from obstruction. Water supply points had to be increased as the fire engines' water storage capacity was limited, and certain areas were difficult to access by the fire engines. Living conditions were unsanitary as the drains and gullies were used as refuse dumping grounds. The refuse accumulation was not only a fire hazard, but also turned into a breeding ground for mosquitoes and houseflies, which were carriers of contagious diseases.

Enforcement and education had to be carried out as changing the bad habits and mindset of the illiterate villagers was challenging. Improving the living environment would take a long time as funds were needed and education and enforcement had to be carried out. It was a very difficult task to handle the recalcitrant and stubborn villagers to seek their co-operation and give them more responsibility as stakeholders in improving the living conditions of the kampong. The safety of the kampong folks was of

The village leaders appointed Mr Bay Ah Hian (extreme right), a Rural Board Member to head the formation of the volunteer firefighting unit.

村执行委员会委任乡村局委员马亚贤先生（最右边）统筹建立村义务消防队。

utmost importance as the falling coconuts from surrounding coconut trees posed a danger. In a freak accident, a child was killed by a fallen coconut tree in 1961, and the elders of the kampong had to mediate the disputing parties. With the assistance of the association elders, a token sum of five hundred dollars was donated to help the bereaved family. Many trees had to be sacrificed to make way for improvement works and road-widening purposes.

While preparation and improvement works were in progress, the village leaders had to go around the village to rally the support and recruit more villagers to serve as volunteer firefighters. Gang members who turned over a new leaf were accepted as part of rehabilitative education. These were the tough and daring villagers likely needed to lead the frontlines in case of a disaster.

The initial response was tremendous as 50 villagers, including some of our elder brothers and cousins, signed up for the basic training provided by the Singapore Fire Brigade. Training later intensified, with mocked-up fire drills to simulate the inferno scene, to test the volunteers' acquired skills and knowledge. Quick reactions and preparedness of the volunteer firefighters were also an important factor. Fire drills were also conducted along with professionals from the Singapore Fire Brigade to sharpen their skills. On 29 June 1958, the volunteers were invited to the Singapore Airport at Paya Lebar to study and witness a fire drill conducted by the professional Airport Fire Brigade.

For physical and endurance training, the volunteers would undertake vigorous jogging around the forested circuit of the eerie cemetery ground at Plantation Avenue. The evening jog would start from the association to Plantation Avenue and Lorong Chuan areas with no street lightings and muddy tracks. Those days there were rumours of ghost sightings in the cemetery areas, coupled with the unpleasant howling of wild dogs in those wooded areas. Along the jogging track, we had to pass through an abandoned open coffin hidden in the bushes, and every runner would speed up and try to get past it as fast as possible. Under such eerie and unpleasant scenarios, members toughened mentally and physically. As such, they were better prepared and became gutsier in their approach to fight big fires and evacuate victims under extremely dangerous conditions.

The volunteers put their acquired skills and experience into good use when they were recalled in the mid 50's to help evacuate the flood victims at the Potong Pasir and Lorong Chuan areas. These flood-prone areas experienced one of the worst disasters that destroyed the crops, livestock and possessions of the entire village after several days of incessant rains. The sudden surge in the water level was also aggravated by the high tide of the Kallang River that cut across the village. There were also many sand quarries in Potong Pasir that created ponds of water and added on to the flooded water levels. Rescuers had a hard time persuading the flood victims to leave their homes and move to safer areas. Some had to be taken away by force as saving lives was of paramount importance. The villager's main concern was whether their belongings would be safe and their houses intact. Some even climbed on their rooftops to evade the rising flood waters, but they never considered that the roof could give way at any time. Others were too engrossed with saving their poultry, pigs and other domestic animals.

The volunteers managed to save a young boy from drowning using an abandoned sampan that drifted near a bridge. The boy was shivering and frightened, and one of the volunteers took off his jacket to cover and keep him warm. An elderly man was also saved from the heavy flood, along with some other victims. They were brought to the hospital for treatment and temporarily housed at the Association premises. The volunteers stayed there for a couple of days, and when the flood subsided, accompanied the folks back to their homes to help clear up the mess.

The next problem to solve was providing the flood victims with three meals, clothing and medication. The immediate task of the volunteers was to rally the support of the villagers and donors to donate money and food for the victims. Through the efforts of the volunteer firefighters and the Association committee, they managed to raise enough funds, and each affected household were given one hundred dollars.

The signage of the Kampong Chia Keng Firefighting Unit and the personal fireman identity that was issued to all trained personnel.

消防单位的招牌和会员的个人身份证。

CHAPTER 26

Building of Concrete Water Storage Tanks

Beginning in the early 60's, the village Association Committee decided to build concrete water storage tanks all over the village. This was to ensure that enough water supply was available during the dry season and in areas without fire hydrants. Initially there were objections as the storage tanks would be a cause of concern as mischievous children might swim inside the tanks and drown. Mosquito breeding was also another problem the village elders anticipated. Obtaining funding for the project was also a headache, and the elders had to raise enough money to engage a contractor to do the job. Lastly, maintenance and treating the storage of water regularly was also challenging.

Despite the setbacks, the Association management committee made a firm decision to go ahead with the construction of the concrete tanks. Their primary concern was to be prepared for a fire disaster that might wipe out the whole village. With concerted efforts and support from the sponsors and residents, about ten concrete water storage tanks were built around the village within two years. The size of the tanks was about half size of the living room in a standard Housing & Development Board (HDB) flat. With the support and collaboration from the Singapore Fire Brigade and permission from the Public Utility Board, water was drawn from the nearest hydrants to fill up the tanks. The water had to be periodically treated with anti-mosquito chemicals.

To ensure the water was not kept too long and to prevent the discharge system from being clogged up by algae, firefighting exercises were conducted regularly, thereby draining the water and maintaining the tank properly. During emergencies, the villagers were very cooperative and would permit the kampong firefighters to siphon water from their household wells and fishing ponds in case the water supplies were exhausted. With many sources of water supply as the frontline defence and the united kampong spirit, the villagers could have peace of mind and be more assured of the safety of their loved ones when they were at work or away.

I joined the Volunteer Firefighting Unit as a junior member in 1963 when I was 12 years old. The same year, the former Prime Minister Lee Kuan Yew made his constituency visit to Chia Keng village. Those days whether young or old, we had to be self-sufficient and stay alert at all times to prepare for and prevent fire from spreading across the villages. It would be disastrous, with the possibility of complete destruction like Bukit Ho Swee, if we were not prepared and remained complacent. Everyone in the kampong were tuned to stay alert and united at all time to nip the problem in the bud.

The worst outbreak of fire near the kampong was an inferno in early 1980 at the warehouse near Sirat Road, where about 200 villagers took turns to prevent the fire from spreading to nearby thatched attap-roof squatters. The fire was intense and beyond the capability of our volunteer firefighters as the burning materials were highly combustible, comprising huge piles of plastic, rubber and paper. This major task was left to the professional firefighters who were better equipped. Luckily, the spread of fire was stopped in time as there were other adjoining warehouses stocked with more combustible materials near the private residential estates at Lange Road. The residents panicked and the situation was chaotic as they started to move important belongings out of their houses.

In contrast, the villagers helping at the attap houses near the kampong market were very co-operative and, in an act of quick thinking, helped to drench the nearby wooden houses to lessen the combustibility and slow down the spread instead of fighting the big fire at the warehouses. Importantly, their job was to calm down the residents and help them to evacuate and house them in a safe holding area. This was not an easy task too as the situation was chaotic, and many households were worried about their properties and their family members. Some stubborn and hardcore residents insisted on staying behind to watch over their houses as looting always occurred in this type of situation.

Fire was not the only concern — the welfare of the fire disaster victims had to be taken care of. They had to be counselled for the devastation and disruption to their daily routine and loss of property. They also needed temporary shelter, food, clothing and financial assistance.

In the 50's and 60's, the living conditions in Singapore were very basic, and houses were haphazardly built. There were no considerations for fire safety and hygiene. Many residents were immigrants, and as long as there was a place to live, they considered themselves to be lucky. Those without friends and relatives had to depend on charitable institutions and government for immediate assistance. As relief volunteers, we were in a better position to understand the moment of anguish and suffering when there was a disaster, especially the loss of loved ones. We tried our best to help in whatever way we could.

We would be similarly heartbroken when a disaster strikes. As such, the association committee and the firefighting volunteers would try to help in whatever way possible and raise funds to help the victims even in other parts of the island. A substantial amount was raised and donated to the victims of the fire disaster at Geylang Avenue 3 in 1958. The following year, another disaster struck at Tiong Bahru, where about one thousand attap houses were gutted. However, the worst and biggest fire was at Bukit Ho Swee in 1961, with more than 15,000 kampong dwellers rendered homeless. It was a national disaster as the government had to provide alternative housing and cash donations for all those who were affected. New flats were built in the shortest time to rehouse the victims, and they were provided with basic needs and financial assistance to prepare them to start a new journey in life.

Kampong fire station and volunteer firefighters dressed in ceremonial uniform to celebrate the Association's anniversary in the early 60's.

60年代志愿消防队成员庆祝村民互助社周年纪念。

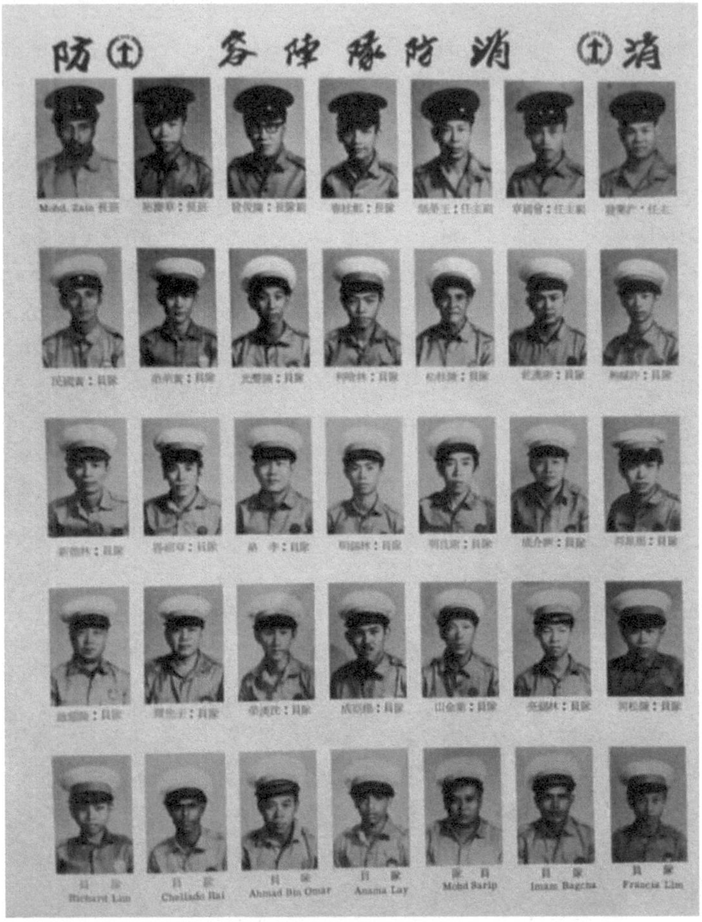

Rank and file of volunteer firefighters in official attire and firefighting training outfit used in the 60's.

楊厝港律村民互助社志愿消防员礼仪制服和训练服装。

楊厝港消防隊搶救水災的經過

圖：楊厝港消防隊隊員與災民合影

一得小言

由搶救水災而談人性

My dad led the rescue team to help the flood victims at Potong Pasir and Lorong Chuan in the 50's and 60's.

50及60年代父亲领导的消防队员练习救火。

Source: Lianhe Wanbao, Singapore Press Holdings Limited.

The observatory tower, the Singapore Fire Brigade vehicle and the kampong-style firefighting engines.

消防瞭望塔，新加坡消防队救火车辆和甘榜版本灭火器材。

Senior firefighters in ceremonial attire were deployed for duty during the kampong events. Mr Lee Khoon Choy inspecting the Guards of Honour formed by the firefighters at the National Theatre.

村委会在国家剧场演出潮剧为慈善筹款, 李炯才先生检阅村高级消防队员组成的仪仗队。

P6 2015年11月17日 星期二 WB NEWS 晚报新闻

光阴的故事

"光阴的故事"温情系列再度登场，邀读者在建国50周年之际，回顾小小岛国在风雨飘摇的大历史中，所经历的冷暖人情及往昔风貌。

▶笔者的父亲章文林是救火队的发起人之一。

▶60年代的消防车，大家都叫它铁皮车，当时民防部队派出消防车配合甘榜的志愿救火队演习。

口述：章庆裕（65岁，花店老板）
笔录：黄志发
图片：受访者提供

12岁参加防灾队 200人轮流救火24小时

章庆裕还保留着当年救火队的徽章等物品。（黄志发摄）

我12岁就参加防灾青年队，学习如何救火灭火，当年甘榜有一场大火患，两个篮球场大的货仓付诸一炬，我们和村民近200人轮流救火24小时，到现在还记忆犹新。

50年代，我父亲章文林和几个乡亲在甘榜内组织一个志愿救火队，叫做"实龙岗花园区（车间）防灾委员会办事处"。

当年成立这个防灾小队，是因为有200多户人家的甘榜，每当火灾发生，消防车都无法驶进来，因为甘榜路面狭窄，只能靠村民们守望相助。

我受父亲影响和鼓励，1963年也加入青年队，是当中20多名队员里年龄最小的，只有12岁，那个年代也没有所谓年龄限制，有人愿意参加就可以了。

加入后需要接受几个星期的训练，学习如何操作水泵车和灭火工具。我们还进行演习，拿水泵枪朝起火的亚答屋灌救。

用作演习的亚答屋，都是一些废弃的屋子，或者由队员临时搭建一个屋架，铺上棕榈叶和木板做成的。

当时民防部队人员也偶尔会过来指导我们，有时甚至开着"铁皮车"（消防车）停在村口，配合演习。

但我的毕竟年龄太小，所以当时每当真的有火灾发生，我只能帮忙搬工具和收拾东西。

▲资深的队员用水泵车边进行演习，边向年轻的队员讲解水泵车使用方法。

水泵车是红犀牛的前身

观火台上敲钟

讲起水泵车，其实它是现在民防部队所使用的红犀牛（Red Rhino）的前身，那时的甘榜的路很窄，路面的宽度只能允许两三辆脚踏车并行，所以铁皮车没法开进来，所以就有了水泵车的出现。

水泵车很小辆，水泵的四面各自有一个踏板，当要用水救火时，就需要把连接水泵车的抽水水管，放进甘榜旁的大沟渠，跟着4个人脚踩踏板泵水上来，另一个人就拿着连接水泵车的水枪去灭火。

在救火队的办事处旁边，还有一个约四层楼高的观火台，因为那时没有通讯设备，什么扩音器、麦克风、电话和手机都没有，只能靠眼睛去看。

我们的甘榜范围有两个足球场范围那么大，每当发生火灾，只要村民来到办事处投报，值班的队员就需要爬上观火台敲钟通知，同时在高处观察火势在甘榜里的哪个方向，并指出前往火场最快捷的路线。

志愿救火队进行演习，队员们往临时搭建的失火亚答屋上灌水。

一场难忘的火灾

记得我16岁那年，参与过甘榜附近一场火患的救火工作，那也是我参加志愿队所经历过最大的一场火患。

当时是一家货仓起火，货仓有两个篮球场那么大，里面囤积着很多轮胎，一箱箱的卫生棉和裁缝机。

这种大火的级别，我们甘榜救火队无法应付，惊动民防部队派出多辆铁皮车参与行动。

但货仓的四周紧挨着五六十间的亚答屋，两者只距离三四十米，我们担心火势蔓延到屋子，于是发动起全村村民，往紧挨火场的亚答屋洒水，弄湿屋子的外部来隔火。

那场火烧了24小时，货仓被烧到清光，而我们和村民就轮班守着亚答屋一整天，看着旁边火场的火势肆虐，这是一辈子都不会忘记的经历。

欢迎来稿：（约800字）
电邮：wanbao@sph.com.sg
地址：SPH News Centre，Lianhe Wanbao，1000 Toa Payoh North，Singapore318994
传真：63198133 （请注明"光阴的故事"负责人收，并附上名字及联络号码）
（逢星期二及星期五刊登）

The biggest fire occurred in the 80's at the warehouse near the kampong, with about 200 villagers taking turns to prevent the fire from spreading.

最大的一场火灾发生在1980年代的甘榜附近的仓库，大约200名村民轮流来防止大火蔓延。

Source: Lianhe Wanbao,
Singapore Press Holdings Limited.

CHAPTER 27

Formation of the Vigilante Corps

With the good track record and trust forged by the kampong firefighters, many villagers came forward to volunteer their services. The bonding of the villagers was further strengthened with the recruitment of villagers of other racial groups such as Indian, Malay and Eurasian into the firefighting unit. The presence of a united and multi-racial force served as a deterrent for troublemakers who harboured ill-intentions to stir racial tensions in the village dominated by the Chinese.

When Singapore joined the Federation of Malaysia in 1963, our country was sabotaged by the Indonesian militant infiltrators due to the leadership, political differences and the British decolonisation in South East Asia. There was a need to form a voluntary force to protect the village and keep a look out for suspicious characters who might be hiding and planning attacks to destabilise our country and divide our united community. The situation was obviously very tense and disturbing when the saboteurs bombed several key installations in Singapore. The worst hit was the bombing of the MacDonald House at Orchard Road that killed two Singaporeans. When I was serving my National Service, I was told that, in 1964, eight soldiers from Singapore based at Kota Tinggi were ambushed and massacred by the armed Indonesian infiltrators. An urgent meeting was called to recruit the firefighters to join the formation of the Vigilante Corps initiated by the government. Without hesitation, many dedicated and selfless villagers came forward to volunteer their services in keeping the village and their families safe.

Trainings were customised and conducted in order not to risk the lives of the volunteers as the militants were heavily armed and skilfully trained with a killer instinct. The kampong folks too were engaged and given the task to keep a lookout for suspicious

With the uniformed group fronting the security line, crime rates were naturally eliminated. They might not have the full authority like the police but still commanded the respect of the members of public.

---

characters and report to the peacekeeping forces.

The formation of the Vigilante Corps was formalised and officiated by former MP for Serangoon Gardens Mr R A Gonzales in 1964. All appointed Vigilante Corps members were issued custom-made white shirts and blue long pants, torchlights, whistles and a meter-long wooden baton. Members would be rostered to patrol the village on different shifts from 7 PM to 7 AM.

Night snacks and beverages were prepared by women volunteers for those who were performing night duties. The reporting and resting stations would be at the Yio Chu Kang Road Villagers' Mutual Help Association and Jalan Teck Kee Community Centre.

With the formation of the Vigilante Corps, the village's security and safety were further enhanced. The village was well protected by all these unsung heroes led by my father, Chiang Boon Lim. The additional layer of security came from the household pet dogs, which would alert the villagers when strangers sneaked into the village. The villagers were so closely knit and alert that any strangers who loitered in the village were easily spotted and closely monitored by the duty personnel.

With the formation of these organised multiracial Vigilante Corps, the notorious perpetrators in the village and the militant infiltrators would think twice before they made their advances into the kampong. Whenever there was an event in the village, such as festive celebrations and wayang performances, members of the Vigilante Corps would be on patrol. Their public presence would be a deterrent to troublemakers and criminals.

With the uniformed group fronting the security line, crime rates were naturally eliminated. They might not have had the full authority of the police but they still commanded the respect of the members of public. This government-backed movement boosted the confidence of the villagers and resulted in a peaceful and united community in this kampong. The most commendable job of the Vigilante Corps was when they managed to prevent a group of arsonists from trying to burn down the community centre at Jalan Teck Kee due to political differences.

The formation of the Vigilante Corps led by my father (with armband) was officiated by MP Mr Gonzales in 1964.

我父亲领导的警卫队成立于1964年,由国会议员 *Gonzales*先生主持成立典礼。

CHAPTER 28

Racial Riots in the 60's

With the close collaboration between the Vigilante Corps and the Firefighting Unit, the villagers were in a better position to enjoy peace and foster the kampong spirit. With their concerted strength, they were in better control to further the course in improving the security, living standards and education of the villagers.

Unfortunately, peace and harmony was short-circuited as Singapore faced the worst racial riots stirred up by irresponsible foreign politicians to destroy the social fabric of Singapore in June and September 1964. This was caused by political and racial tensions between the Chinese and the Malays. The riot sparked off during a religious procession to celebrate Prophet Muhammad's birthday, which ended in bloody fighting between the two ethnic groups. A recurrence took place in 1969, with the spillover of racial riots from our neighbouring country.

An island-wide curfew was imposed, and all villagers were restricted in their movements, while there was a mad rush to stock up on food and household necessities. Prices of food and essential provisions shot up due to high demand. Schools were closed, and businesses and daily working routines were disrupted. Tensions built up and everyone was living in fear and extreme anxiety. Villagers and all Singaporeans felt extremely miserable, having to face uncertainties and insecurities. Many worried villagers in our kampong were restless and endured sleepless nights for several months as a fear of impending attack and sabotage was etched in their minds. Malay villagers within the same kampong also feared for their lives and had to move out temporarily to safer places or stay with their relatives. Despite the strong bonds of the few Malay families shared with their Chinese neighbours, there was fear that troublemakers from elsewhere might sow discord among the villagers and harass them. We all treated the Malay families like our own as we used to roam the kampong and catch spiders with their family members. Most of the kampong folks never forgot the Malay family who catered breakfast with their signature nasi lemak packet and kuih lopes at their makeshift stall. There was also a bigger cluster of Malay families living deep inside Jalan Teck Kee, with their houses cordoned off with barbwire fencing and given protection by the police force.

On the whole, the kampong folks were harmonious and peaceful but there was worry that unscrupulous people might politicise and take advantage of the tense and chaotic situation to destroy our social fabric. It will be difficult for our country to progress if the citizens were not united and living in suspicion of each other.

Rumour-mongering was common and spread like wildfire. Speculations and fake news popped up often that our village was targeted for a showdown. Orders were given to be prepared, and all villagers were kept posted on the latest news and were alert at all time. Tensions ran high and wild imagination crept into the minds of many restless and frightened villagers.

The more they feared, the more they succumbed to rumours. True enough, on a fateful evening, a deranged villager rashly triggered the panic button and turned the whole kampong into disarray. He spread fake news that our village would be attacked by an organised racial group at any time. The worried villagers became frantic and drew out their weapons to prepare and defend themselves. In a moment of confusion and anxiety, many villagers had forgotten about the rules on curfew and rushed out from their houses to defend themselves and their family members against the impending attackers.

After a few hours, with no sign of approaching enemies, the situation slowly cooled off. To the great relief of the frightened villagers, it turned out to be a false alarm triggered by the mentally challenged villager. The police force was alerted and misinformed with the impression that the villagers were rioting and breaking the curfew. The village elders' clarifications were not accepted as everyone was armed to the teeth with offensive weapons. Those who carried weapons were rounded up and led to the police vehicles. The unfortunate confusion and misunderstanding resulted in difficulty to convince the police of the villagers' innocence and led to their arrest.

With the arrest of over ten villagers, their family members were hysterical and started pointing fingers at the village committee. They demanded their loved ones be released from the prison immediately as there had been no fighting or clashes involving the villagers and the weapons had been used for self-defence and protection only. However, with the intervention from the member of parliament and village elders, the police investigators were convinced that the villagers' impulsive reaction was due to the circumstances relating to the fake news.

Due to high tensions and suspicion, the villagers were inclined to be very sensitive and protective as they and their loved ones' lives were at stake. After several days of full investigations by the police, the true reasons were established, and the detained innocent villagers were released immediately.

For a couple of weeks, we were confined indoors, occupying our time with all sorts of indoor games and reading storybooks. Life was miserable and tense, with no television or other forms of entertainment. We just whiled away our time, watching people play mahjong and Chinese chess. Rediffusion was the only news source that provided updates in four languages. Others were enjoying songs in Chinese, English and other Chinese dialects. We sadly missed the good old days of the broadcasts as the radio company decided to withdraw from the entertainment sector after 63 years. During my school days, we could not afford to buy watches to keep track of the time. All we relied on was the timing of the broadcast programs to alert us as all programmes were time-bound.

From the news, we learned that about twenty people had been killed and more than four hundred people had been severely injured in the riots. In the aftermath of this racial conflict, the government initiated the Goodwill Committees to maintain calm and normalise community bonding among different races. This was followed by the then Prime Minister Lee Kuan Yew setting up the Citizens' Consultative Committees (CCC) in 1965. The immediate task was to restore racial harmony and social cohesion and form goodwill committees involving all races to keep calm and allay suspicions. At the onset, most of the recruited members were Chinese-educated businessmen, shopkeepers, teachers, hawkers and Malay village leaders. Over a period of time, the formation of CCC was successful, with more volunteers being recruited, including representatives from different racial and religious groups to promote racial harmony and social cohesion. It also helped to bridge the gap between ordinary citizens and the government by providing feedback from the ground and disseminating government policies.

CHAPTER 29

Opening of St Anthony Free Clinic

After experiencing turbulent years of the 50's and 60's, and with better political stability, the next objective was to help the villagers combat contagious diseases and provide healthcare services, especially for the needy families. During that period, the Asian Flu, Hong Kong Flu, tuberculosis and leprosy were life-threatening diseases that raged beyond control. There was a need to educate the villagers and prevent the spread of the diseases.

In collaboration with the sisters from the Franciscan Missionaries of Mary located at Holland Road and Singapore General Hospital, and with full support of the late tycoon Mr Lee Kim Tah, a free clinic was set up. It was officially opened on 29 September 1957, officiated by Mrs Lee Kim Tah, who ceremoniously unveiled the signboard of the free clinic. The opening of the clinic, which was located behind the Tian Kong Tua Temple, was graced by a couple of renowned politicians, philanthropists and blessed by a Catholic priest, Father Moses Koh from Immaculate Heart of Mary Church. With mutual respect for interfaith collaboration and practices of the nuns, the temple committee gave their blessings and approval for the display of the Crucifix in the consultation and dressing rooms. A perfect display of religious harmony and co-operation of religious leaders from different faiths existed in this kampong a long time ago.

The Catholic nuns were trained in medical schools, led by Sister Superior Dr Benezit as the medical officer and consultant. Assisted by Sister Maria Kiang from Shanghai and Sister Leonora Pau from Hong Kong, they teamed up to serve the poor villagers in this rural area. The free clinic was open every Monday and attended to about one hundred patients daily from 8.30 AM to 12 noon. Dr Benezit was very well-liked and popular with the kampong folks and was not surprised that the patients who came for consultations were of different races and religious backgrounds. They came from far and wide, even as far as Jalan Kayu and Punggol areas.

As the operation of the free clinic progressed extremely well, with increasing number of patients, the management committee was fortunate to engage a young volunteer doctor, Dr Wee Sip Leong, to advise and improve the consultations. Dr Wee was a full-time doctor at his own private clinic, who had kindly consented to succeed Dr Benezit, who was needed to serve the Franciscan Missionaries of Mary. Dr Wee completed his MBBS from University of Singapore in 1967 and MCFP (Family Med) from College of Family Physicians, Singapore, in 1973. He practised for more than fifty years at Kin Mun Clinic in Toa Payoh area.

With the replacement of a young professional doctor, the number of patients multiplied tremendously. It was inevitable that the consultation hours had to be stretched further till lunch time, and it became too taxing for the volunteer medical staff. The Association management committee had to come up with a solution to solve this problem and at the same time source for more financial support to defray the expenses.

To cope with the high demand, a decision was proposed to open up another day of free consultation. With approval and support from the Association management committee and the invaluable sponsorship of Mr Lee Kim Tah, the clinic operations on every Monday was extended to twice a week, every Monday and Thursday from 8.30 AM to 12 PM.

The sisters from Franciscan Missionaries of Mary and the volunteer medical team welcomed Mr and Mrs Lee Kim Tah to the opening of the St Anthony Free Clinic in 1957.

1957年聖安多尼診所迎接李金塔先生和夫人出席诊所开幕典礼。

Going forward, the management committee also needed to look into the increasing expenses and operational costs to run the clinic. Bearing in mind not to overstretch the sponsorship of Mr Lee Kim Tah and to ensure sustainability, donation boxes were set up, and at the same time the Association committee looked to recruit more honorary patrons and philanthropists to help finance the operation costs. The Association opera troupe also chipped in to raise funds through their charity performances.

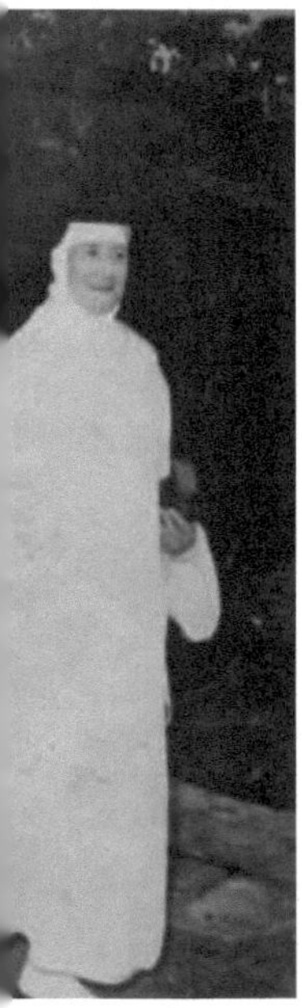

Opening of the free clinic by Mrs Lee Kim Tah and blessing by Father Moses Koh from Immaculate Heart of Mary Church.

Witnessed by Assemblyman Mr Lim Choon Mong and the sponsors Mr Lee Kim Tah and Mr Ng See Tong.

李金塔夫人主持诊所开幕教区神父为诊所祝福。

Guest-of-Honour Assemblyman Mr Lim Choon Mong at the opening address after the inauguration of the free clinic.

主宾议员林春茂致开幕词。

Patron Mr Lee Kim Tah addressing the guests at the opening of the St Anthony Free Clinic in 1957.

赞助人李金塔先生致辞。

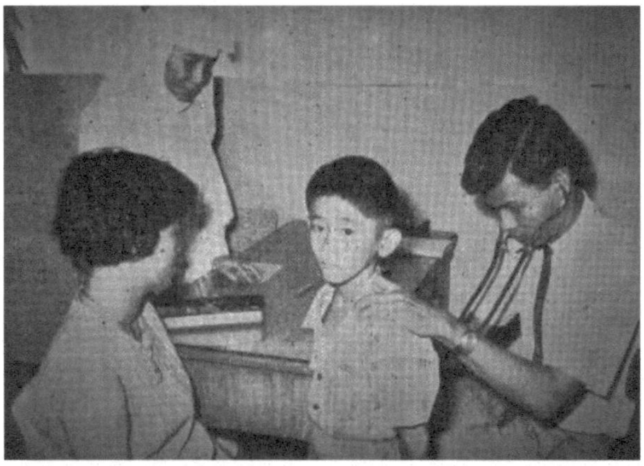

Dr Wee Sip Leong was appointed the Medical Officer and Advisor to the free clinic as Dr. Benezit was recalled for other duties.

黄习良医生受委诊所义务医生及顾问，他接替了*Benezit* 医生的职务。

CHAPTER 30

Successor of the Free Clinic Patronage

In 1974, Mr Lee Kim Tah decided to relinquish his portfolio as the main sponsor of the free clinic. He had helped establish the free clinic from the formative years and wished to find a successor to carry on his legacy. He was succeeded by the Association's Honorary Chairman, Dato Tay Kia Hong, who was a very successful magnate in the reptile skin industry. Dato Tay was also a generous philanthropist and came from a humble background. He was a hawker for a couple of years before he found a job working in a company dealing with leather products. He learned the trade rapidly and later on started his own leather business at Sungei Road. His company, known as Chye Seng Tannery, was doing very well, and he ventured into the Japanese market and built a tannery there. At the peak of his business, he also ventured into property developments in Johore.

The operation of the free clinic continued for the next decade until most of the kampong folks were resettled in the mid-80's. The clinic outlived its usefulness as the large numbers of patients made their exodus from this village. Most of the villagers were relocated to various Housing & Development Board (HDB) heartlands such as Tampines, Hougang, Ang Mo Kio, Bedok Reservoir and Lorong Lew Lian. By then, most of the HDB heartlands also had private clinics and Chinese traditional medical shops. Obviously it would not make sense and be convenient for those resettled to the new towns to return to the kampong for consultations.

Over the years, we had lost contact with many old kampong friends and the people that we used to work with during the kampong days. Many had already passed away, and others were advanced in age and untraceable. Closing down the clinic was inevitable, but the good work of all the volunteers must not be forgotten. Fortunately, we managed to catch up with two highly respectable old friends and unsung heroes who had operated the free clinic. We managed to meet up with Sister Maria Kiang and celebrated her 90th birthday on 10 October 2018. The other person that we were longing to catch up was Dr Victor Wee Sip Leong. Our surprise reunion with Dr Wee was kindly arranged by my former schoolmate Cyprian Lim on 21 July 2019. What a small world it was, as after nearly 40 years, through sheer coincidence, I discovered that Cyprian was Dr Wee's son-in-law!

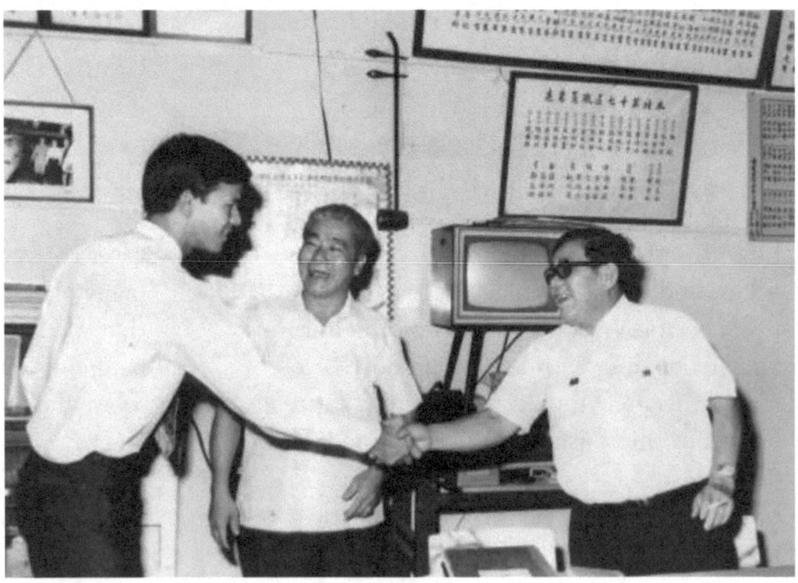

In 1974, the sponsor of the free clinic Mr Lee Kim Tah BBML requested to relinquish his appointment. He was succeeded by Dato Tay Kia Hong

*1974*年诊所赞助人李金塔先生引退，由拿督郑镜鴻接任。。

The handling over ceremony of the sponsorship from Mr Lee Kim Tah to Dato Tay Kia Hong was witnessed by Dr Wee Sip Leong.

黄习良医生见证李金塔先生移交诊所赞助人身份给拿督郑鏡鴻。

CHAPTER 31

Our Family's Involvement in the Free Clinic

The operation of the free clinic required strong financial and logistics support and a long-term commitment with adequate manpower support for its daily operations. Our father was assigned to oversee the operational task during that period. He recruited our family members and other villagers to help provide support to the administration and in logistics matters. Every Monday and Thursday, we would clean and sanitise the multi-purpose hall as these two days were specially reserved for the clinic use only. Routinely we arrived at the clinic before 8 AM. This was to ensure the clinic registration and dispensing counters were ready by 8.45 AM before the medical team arrived to start the clinic service. Importantly, requisites that were needed to be prepared and kept ready for use at the waiting areas were urinals for the babies and sputum mugs for the adults.

Most of the villagers were illiterate and not aware of personal hygiene. They spat indiscriminately on the floor, and much effort was expended to educate them to spit into the sputum mugs that were provided to them within easy reach. As for the smokers, they were advised to discard their cigarettes butts into the ash tray and wrappers into the waste bins.

Our family members and other village volunteers helped to issue queue numbers, perform registrations and prepare medical records for the patients. The patient and their caregiver were subsequently ushered to the consultation room when called. Post-consultation, the patients were adjourned to the dispensing counter to collect their medication prescribed by the medical team led by a group of medically trained Catholic nuns. Our teenage brother, Melvyn, who was passionate and always been interested in patient care, volunteered himself as an apprentice to be trained by the medical team to assist in dispensing basic medication to the patient.

With his strong passion for patient care, he decided to enroll himself at the School of Nursing and graduated as a Registered Nurse in the year 1990. He followed it up by pursuing his professional Post Basic Nursing Knowledge and Skills in Critical Care Nursing Course and graduated in the year 1992. Subsequently, he continued to pursue his Bachelor of Nursing Course through distance learning at La Trobe University and graduated in the year 1999.

Melvyn's great passion for nursing and his hard work earned him many Gold and Star Awards from the Ministry of Health and various public health institutions. In 1996, he was conferred the Professional Nurse Award by the Rotary Club Garden City and Singapore Nurses Association. Apart from his nursing career, he actively served in the Singapore Nurses Association Executive Council from 1996 to 2014. During his term, he represented the council to attend various overseas international conventions to learn and exchange knowledge and skills with overseas delegates. In 2004–2005, he was the organising chairman for the SingHealth Nursing Debates, and in 2006, he chaired the 6th Asian and Pacific Nurses Convention. From 2012 to present, he is an active Board Member of the Parkinson Society Singapore, contributing his time fruitfully to provide support to members with Parkinson's disease in the society.

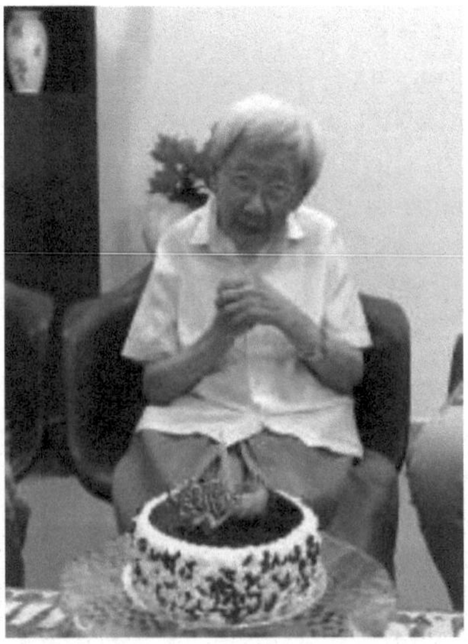

On 1 May 2018, we managed to catch up with Sister Maria Kiang after more than 40 years. On 10 October 2018, my brothers, sisters and sister-in-law surprised her with her 90th birthday celebration.

40年后我们会见了江姑娘。我们很高兴在2018年10月10日庆祝她的90岁生日。

We also had a reunion with Dr Wee Sip Leong at his son-in-law Cyprian Lim's house on 21 July 2019.

2019年7月21日,我们很高兴在40年后由他的女婿林世平安排与黄习良医生重逢。

CHAPTER 32

Formation of the Amateur Teochew Opera Troupe

Before the advent of television in Singapore in 1963, the only form of entertainment in the village was watching the traditional Teochew and Hokkien operas showcased occasionally during festive events. The other was watching the free black-and-white movies in the open area screened by the Ministry of Culture and the former Paya Lebar Police Station.

It was around this period that the Yio Chu Kang Road Villagers' Mutual Help Association decided to form an amateur Teochew opera troupe. The objective was to allow the villagers to appreciate the traditional performing arts and reinforce social bonding among the villagers, while at the same time making these activities as a source of entertainment for the villagers during the routine practice sessions and the actual anniversary celebrations.

It was an uphill task as the organisers had to search for experienced instructors and suitable performers to fill in the different acting roles. Initially, there was a lack of female cast members, and some of the male artistes had to be trained to perform as female characters. The other problems were finding a group of musicians and percussionists. More importantly, a group director was needed to assemble the performers, instrumentalists and percussionists to synchronise and harmonise at the performing stage. Regular practice sessions were necessary to ensure that the performers and musicians were in tune and memorised the scripts. Their health had to be closely monitored, especially that of the performing artistes, whose vocal cords must be in prime condition.

Everyone had to be passionate and responsible to ensure an excellent performance. Their welfare and good teamwork had to be reinforced as it took just one lacklustre artiste to affect the morale of the entire team. Although this was a voluntary organisation, everyone had to be highly committed as the show could not go on with the absence of a key instrumentalist or percussionist. As such, a contingency plan was necessary as the show had to go on no matter what happened.

The Association managed to engage an experienced amateur opera actor, Mr Koh Chiang, who worked in a law firm, to assist as an instructor and director. The musical instrumental section was headed by a former custom officer Mr Tan Hoo Pong and the percussion coach Mr Cheng Kum was formerly working for a professional opera troupe. With the three leading partners, the troupe was able to move on to recruit and train volunteers to fill in the different acting roles.

The experienced percussion coach had leprosy and was unable to commit long hours to training. My older brother Benson was under his tutelage and was roped in to helm the percussion group, supported by another brother Gary and me. Other players were also recruited, and there was one outstanding villager with a big deformed skull, who was trained to play the small bell instrument. The percussion group trainer was a perfectionist and very rigid with the practices compared with other instructors. We had to be focused at all times to watch his body language and tune in attentively to synchronise with the songs and music.

Using different percussion instruments to soothe the rhythm of the artistes would set the mood of the occasions. The rhythm and tone of the instruments could enhance the artiste singing for either a happy and solemn occasion. Similarly the use of a battery of drums of different sizes could set the mood for a fighting scene and, when the octave was lowered, for sombre scenes as well.

It was an amazing yet challenging experience for some of the English-educated artistes who had to translate their scripts into English and memorise them. They depended on the tape recorder to practise their singing in order to master their pronunciation. This was also to ensure that their singing pitch would harmonise and be in tune with the instrumentalists. Unfortunately, the progress of technology came too late for the convenience of our potential artistes; it would have been much easier to practise their singing using a karaoke system with built-in transliterated lyrics.

Not all the volunteer artistes and instrumentalists lived near the association. Some were from different parts of Singapore and came from as far as Havelock Road and Bukit Timah areas. To ensure they arrived on time and returned home safely late at night, the Association management committee bought a second-hand car to ferry some of them to attend the routine practice sessions. It was a very difficult task to ensure the smooth running of the troupe as at times there were personal differences and family problems among the members.

Volunteer female artistes were recruited island-wide to support the opera group. The association management purchased a second-hand car as transportation to facilitate the artistes who lived far away.

全岛招募潮州女戏剧艺人。

委员会购买了一辆二手车作为交通工具接送表演艺人。

The amateur Teochew opera group instrumentalists and percussionists.

志愿乐器和打击乐演奏家。

234

The percussion group and the musical instrument group having their weekly training session.

每周接受志愿乐器演奏家和打击乐演奏者的培训。

福
肅靜
9

At the onset of the Amateur Teochew Opera formation, our family members were roped in to fill in the various casts.

我们的兄弟姐妹参与戏剧表演。

Many Teochew operas were staged to entertain the villagers and raised funds for charities in the 60's and 70's.

自60到70年代以来,戏团举办许多慈善演出。

Profiles of the amateur actors and actresses, percussionists and instrumentalists. They were a combination of volunteers comprising civil servants, hawkers, merchants, factory workers and students.

演员和器乐演奏者的简介。

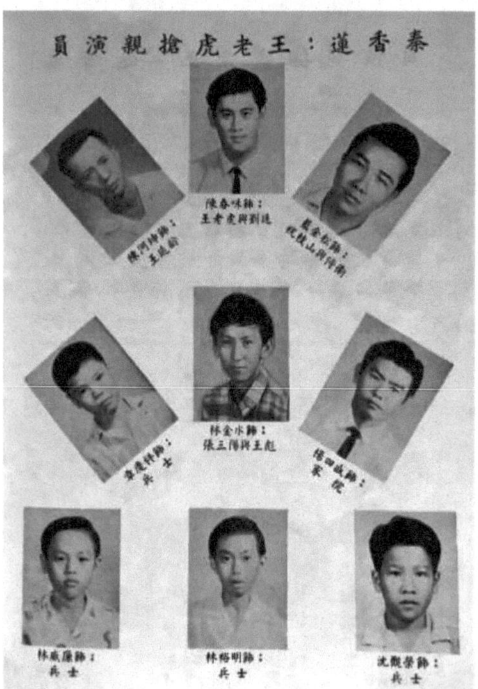

Many volunteers were English-educated and their scripts had to be translated and memorised.

许多志愿演员，器乐和打击乐演奏者都受英语教育。

The annual magazines published in conjunction with the opera performances.

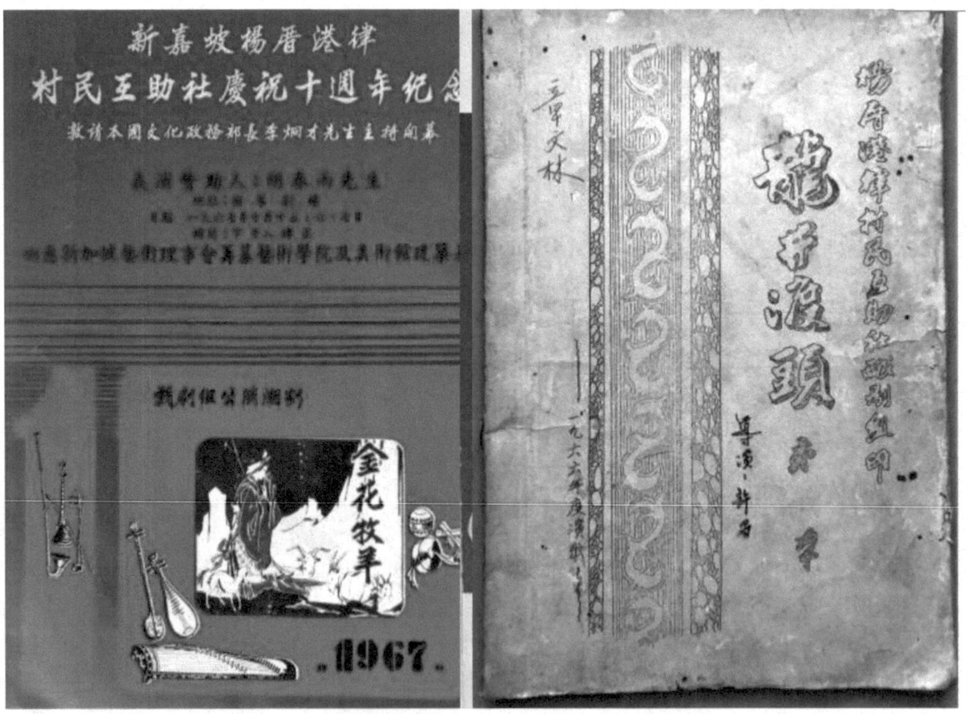

Some of the annual magazines and opera lyrics were salvaged when the association was resettled in the 80's.

CHAPTER 33

Visit By Celebrities of the Hong Kong Teochew Opera

In the 60's, Chap Goh Mei was widely celebrated throughout the island to mark the fifteenth or the last day of Lunar New Year. Traditionally, it was also known as Chinese Valentine's Day, when courting couples would propose marriage and the eligible ones would try their luck and look for their life partners either at the temples or join the festive events. The festive event usually ended with the bursting of firecrackers all over the island. The temples, shops and associations would compete to display and burst the longest line of crackers to entertain the crowds.

Our Teochew Opera Troupe was invited by the Ministry of Culture to participate in the yearly Chap Goh Mei float processions moving around the island. This event is still fresh in my mind as I remember being dressed up as a monk along with my eldest brother to participate in the float procession with live Teochew music, passing through the Istana grounds. Over the years, the name of this event had changed to the Ching Gay procession, adding more international flavour to attract tourists and younger audiences.

At the peak of the opera troupe's cultural achievements, which gained high popularity and ranking in the Teochew performing arts fraternity, many organisations invited the association troupe to showcase and assist in fundraising. The then-renowned and highly respected troupe was picked to host a visit by famous Hong Kong Teochew opera celebrities. The entourage, led by leading female artistes, Ms Tan Chor Hui and Ms Poon Kar Gek, was welcomed by the association management committee and opera artistes along with several hundred die-hard fans. The association management committee was very honoured to host the visit of these top celebrities and their entourage to this remote kampong. When the visitors arrived at the Association by chauffeur-driven vehicles, what surprised them was that the famous Singapore opera troupe existed in a small kampong. The guests from Hong Kong could not believe that the kampong could produce so many talented artistes and that quite a number of them were English-educated. To their surprise, they learned that all the artistes and musicians were volunteers and had full-time jobs.

The visit by the Hong Kong artistes certainly gave a big boost to the Association's reputation, and future recruitment of new and younger artistes were much easier.

During the 60's and 70's, the two Hong Kong artistes were at the pinnacle of their popularity and their movies and live shows in Singapore National Theatre were always sold out. Even their Teochew songs were broadcast daily by the Rediffusion and Radio stations. Ms Tan Chor Hui was more popular and well-respected. She performed very well mainly as a leading male character in many Teochew movies. The movies were recorded and produced in the form of vinyl discs and cassette tapes that were much sought after by the elderly and die-hard fans. They were lucky to escape the China Cultural Revolution, which banned Teochew Opera in mid-60's. The much sought after Teochew opera performances in China were shelved for a long time, and the limelight was only on the Hong Kong artistes. As such, Tan Chor Hui dominated the top charts of most popular Teochew operas in the 60's and 70's era.

Ms Tan Chor Hwee and Ms Poon Kar Gek arriving at the association to meet with members of the Yio Chu Kang Villagers' opera group.

香港潮剧名人陳楚惠,方巧玉和其他主要演员参观衬潮剧团。

Ms Tan Chor Hwee and Ms Poon Kar Gek arriving at the Association to meet with members of the Yio Chu Kang Villagers' opera group.

香港潮剧名人陳楚惠,方巧玉和其他主要演员参观村潮剧团。

Many die-hard fans and followers turned up to welcome their popular idols Ms Tan Chor Hwee and Ms Poon Kar Gek.

许多潮剧迷和追随者赶上来观看他们的偶像陳楚惠和方巧玉。

Most of the die-hard fans were young girls and women from all over Singapore, who turned up in full force.

大多数戏迷是来自新加坡各地的年轻姑娘和女士,她们全力以赴。

CHAPTER 34

Formation of the Chia Keng Youth Club

The Village Association functioned as a community-based organisation before the People's Association community centres made their debut in the 60's. The elders in the village were very concerned about the welfare of the young villagers who had been idling around after their school hours. A task force headed by Mr Bay Ah Hian, a District Rural Committee member, was set up to approach the Social Welfare Department to assist and support the formation of the youth wing.

The Chia Keng Youth Club was registered in 1954 as an offshoot of the Association to look into juvenile delinquency and youth affairs. The club provided free tuition classes and meaningful indoor and outdoor activities. There were a few hundred youths; many were studying in Chinese Language schools and needed help in English, Science and Mathematics subjects. More importantly, the objectives of the Association were also to instil a sense of civic-mindedness and nurture them to be good citizens and future leaders.

Besides operating the clinic, the sisters from the Franciscan Missionaries of Mary were very concerned about the poor nourishment and education of the village children. They managed to source donations of foods such as oat, milk powder, sugar and wheat flour to be distributed to the needy families. Donation of new and recycled toys, books and clothing were also collected and given out during the annual Christmas parties organised by the sisters. As most of the poor villagers had many children to feed, the rations given to them certainly helped lighten their burden.

The main objectives were to keep them occupied and give them a proper education. Children are our future leaders and need to be nurtured and given proper guidance.

Giving books to the children may not serve its purpose if they were unable to read and comprehend the texts. To complement the good work of the sisters, the Association committee started free tuition classes to boost the literacy of the children so that they will treasure the free books given to them. Ultimately, a youth club was also set up to allow the children to interact through tuition classes and indulge in meaningful and constructive activities.

The main objectives of the club were to keep the children occupied and give them a proper education. Children are our future leaders and need to be nurtured and given proper guidance. It was the hope and foresight of our village elders that they would grow up to be useful citizens to serve our society and country.

Sports activities, such as basketball, table tennis, badminton and roller skating, were also organised for the youth. By popular demand, the Association elders approached the honorary patron Mr Lee Kim Tah to sponsor the construction of a badminton court in front of the temple. On the cement court, many other activities could be organised. The youth basketball team was very strong and won many tournaments organised by the Federation of Boys' Club in the 50's.

To complement outdoor sports, indoor games such as table-tennis, carrom, and English and Chinese Chess games were also available. For the youngsters, there were a variety of card games and kampong games. With all the sport facilities available and free tuition classes, the kampong leaders hoped to draw them away from illegal and unconstructive activities. At the same time, some youth leaders could be nurtured and trained as mentors to guide the younger ones.

The hardcourt also benefitted other groups of villagers who held their annual celebrations on the ninth day of the Lunar New Year. This auspicious occasion was the birthday of the Heavenly Jade Emperor deity, and majority of the worshippers who embraced Taoism would commence their offerings and prayers on the eve before mid night. The grand celebrations would be followed by Teochew or Hokkien opera performances for the next few days. Free movies would also be screened for the youth on alternate months.

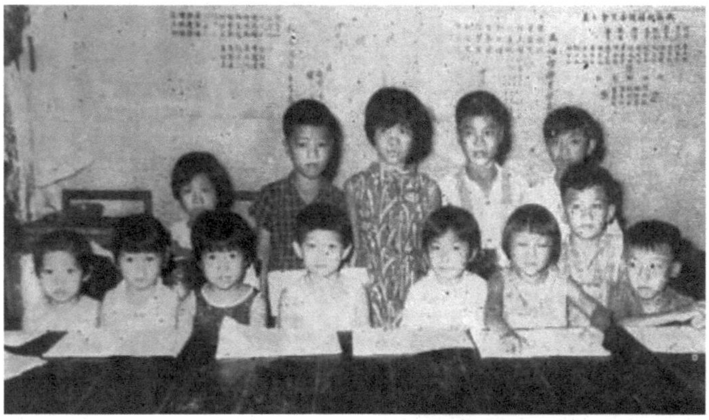

The Free Press Wednesday, August 18, 1954

Page 7

GO-AHEAD VILLAGE SEEKS AID

We want youth centre for 500 children

FIRE is the greatest worry of nearly every Singapore village and kampong, where thousands of attap dwellings are concentrated. Each one is a fire-trap.

Aware of this danger, residents of Yio Chu Kang Village formed their own fire-fighting unit early this year. Fifty villagers volunteered for service.

The Government and the City Council have already promised equipment and training aid.

But Yio Chu Kang village elders want immediate action.

When will we get the materials? they ask. When will they train our men?

—by— STEVE NEOH

Granite path

Insanitary

Time wasted

"Will assist"

THE ROAD THEY WANT TO BUILD

Sampan man drowned

Source: The Straits Times, Singapore Press Holdings Limited.
Reprinted with Permission

The Chia Keng Youth Club was formed in 1955.

车宫青年俱乐部成立于1955年。

To kickstart the Youth Club, some of our brothers and relatives joined the firefighting unit and others were deployed as amateur artistes in the Teochew opera group.

我们的家庭成员和亲戚一些被招募为初级消防员,其他被训练为潮剧演员。

Service to the Nation

为国家服务

CHAPTER 35

Fundraising and Collaborations with Government Agencies

When the opera troupe was better organised and stabilised, the Association Management Committee decided to take advantage of the performances to help raise funds for charities. Most of the fundraising events were carried out in the 60's at different locations at the requests of the management committees of different schools and community centres. The recipients were community centres from Upper Serangoon and Bras Basah constituencies. The schools included the now-defunct Chong Hwa Public School and Sin Ming Secondary School. The Chong Hwa Public School premises at Plantation Avenue was converted to a community centre and the Sin Ming Secondary School was converted to a centre for ex-offenders.

The most significant donations went to the Singapore Arts Council and the National Defence Fund. The biggest amount was raised in 1967 at the National Theatre, when the troupe along with the then Association President Mr Oh Choon Woo raised sixteen thousand dollars for the National Arts Council. The personal cheque of ten thousand dollars from Mr Oh and another cheque of six thousand dollars from the association were presented to the former Chairman of the National Theatre Trust, Dr Goh Poh Seng. Dr Goh represented the then Minister of State for Culture Mr Lee Khoon Choy to receive the cheques at a ceremony held at the Chinese Chamber of Commerce.

Other recipients who benefitted from the fund raising activities were the victims of the various major fire disasters, such as in 1958 at Geyland Lorong 3. Donations went to another fire disaster in 1959 at Tiong Bahru and also to the biggest fire outbreak at Bukit Ho Swee in 1961. The Singapore Association for the Blind also received donations from the Association in 1984.

The Yio Chu Kang Villagers' Mutual Help Association was well known and recognised by the government, and its premises was chosen as one of the venues for citizenship registration in 1958. It was carried out with the aim of achieving self-government. In the same year, it was also selected as a polling station by the Commissioner of Elections for the District Council elections.

A few years later, the Ministry of Health Division collaborated with the association to start a maternal and child clinic to monitor the infant health status and to educate the mothers on childcare and birth control.

All mothers were also given lessons on nutritional subjects and personal healthcare. Every Saturday, from 8.30 AM to 1.00 PM, the clinic would be packed with mothers and babies waiting to be seen. While waiting in the long queue, many babies would be breastfed or given pacifiers to keep them calm. Over a period of time, the turnout at the clinic was overwhelming and it needed a bigger area to cater to the increased population. It was relocated to a bigger premises nearer to Jalan Kayu area in 1969.

In early 1970, when the Vigilante Corps was disbanded and absorbed into the Civil Defence Force, their Dragon Dance and Giant Flag troupes moved in to join the Yio Chu Kang Road Mutual Help Association. Most of the former Vigilante Corps members were roped in to join as Associate members. Originally the group was based at Kolam Ayer Vigilante Corp headquarters, which was earmarked for redevelopment by the Ministry of Manpower. It was a happy ending with a win-win situation as the Association had another Chinese cultural group to draw the youth into more meaningful activities and reinforce the kampong spirit. By the late 70's, the village was earmarked for the development of a new sports complex, and that marked the end of the vibrant Chia Keng village.

Teochew Wayang performance for fundraising towards the National Defence Fund.

村潮剧班为国家防卫基金筹款。

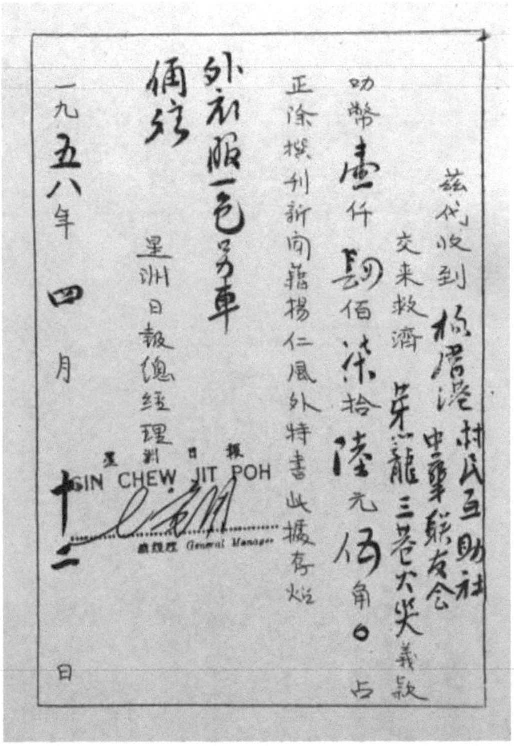

Fundraising in aid of the fire disaster at Geylang Avenue 3 in 1958.

为芽笼3巷火灾民筹款。

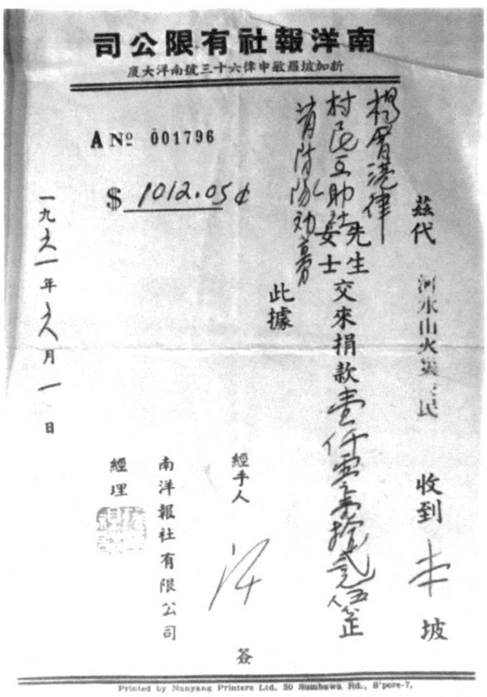

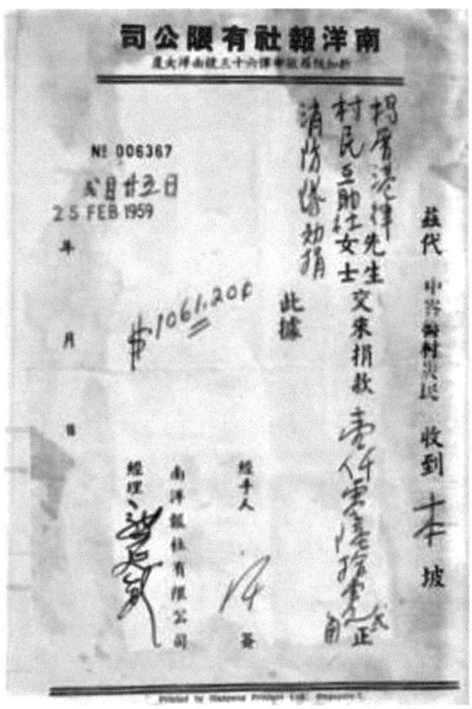

Fundraising for victims of fire disasters at Bukit Ho Swee in 1961 and Tiong Bahru in 1959.

为河水山(1961)和中峇鲁(1959)火灾民筹款。

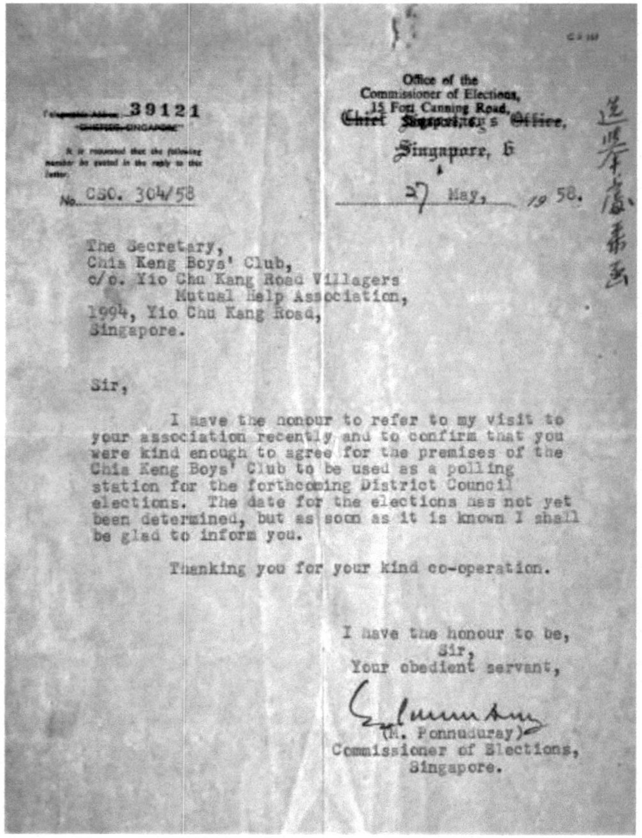

Telegraphic Address: 39121
CHIEFSEC SINGAPORE
It is requested that the following number be quoted in the reply to this letter.
No. CSO. 304/58

Office of the
Commissioner of Elections,
15 Fort Canning Road,
~~Chief Secretary's Office,~~
Singapore, 6
27 May, 1958.

选举處来函

The Secretary,
Chia Keng Boys' Club,
c/o. Yio Chu Kang Road Villagers
Mutual Help Association,
1994, Yio Chu Kang Road,
Singapore.

Sir,

I have the honour to refer to my visit to your association recently and to confirm that you were kind enough to agree for the premises of the Chia Keng Boys' Club to be used as a polling station for the forthcoming District Council elections. The date for the elections has not yet been determined, but as soon as it is known I shall be glad to inform you.

Thanking you for your kind co-operation.

I have the honour to be,
Sir,
Your obedient servant,
(M. Ponnuduray)
Commissioner of Elections,
Singapore.

The Association was selected as a polling station for the District Council Election in 1958.

1958年村委会址被选为区域委员会选举投票站。

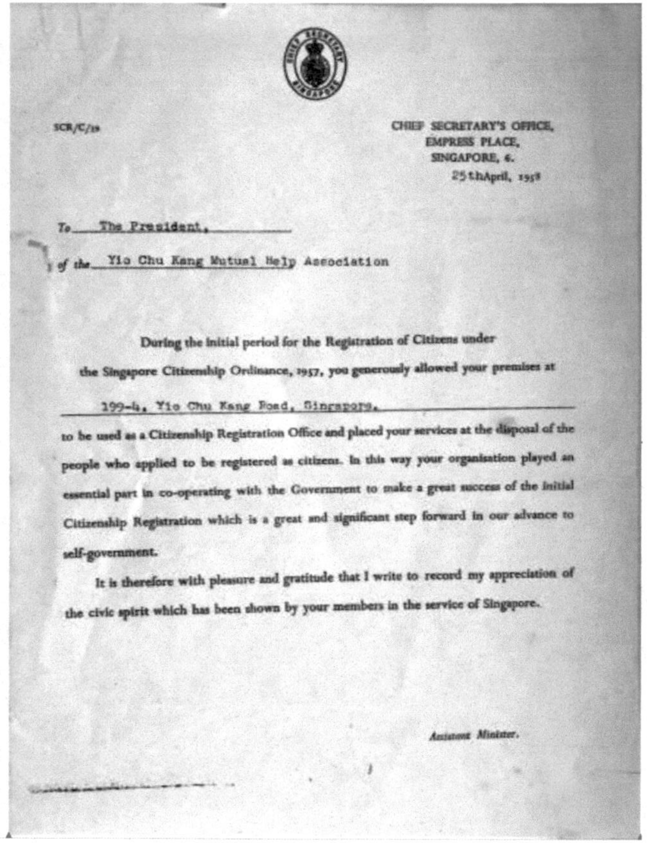

SCR/C/29

CHIEF SECRETARY'S OFFICE,
EMPRESS PLACE,
SINGAPORE, 6.
25thApril, 1958

To The President,
of the Yio Chu Kang Mutual Help Association

During the initial period for the Registration of Citizens under the Singapore Citizenship Ordinance, 1957, you generously allowed your premises at 199-4, Yio Chu Kang Road, Singapore, to be used as a Citizenship Registration Office and placed your services at the disposal of the people who applied to be registered as citizens. In this way your organisation played an essential part in co-operating with the Government to make a great success of the initial Citizenship Registration which is a great and significant step forward in our advance to self-government.

It is therefore with pleasure and gratitude that I write to record my appreciation of the civic spirit which has been shown by your members in the service of Singapore.

Assistant Minister.

The Association was also used as the venue for the registration of citizenship in 1958.

1958年村委会址也是公民注册处。

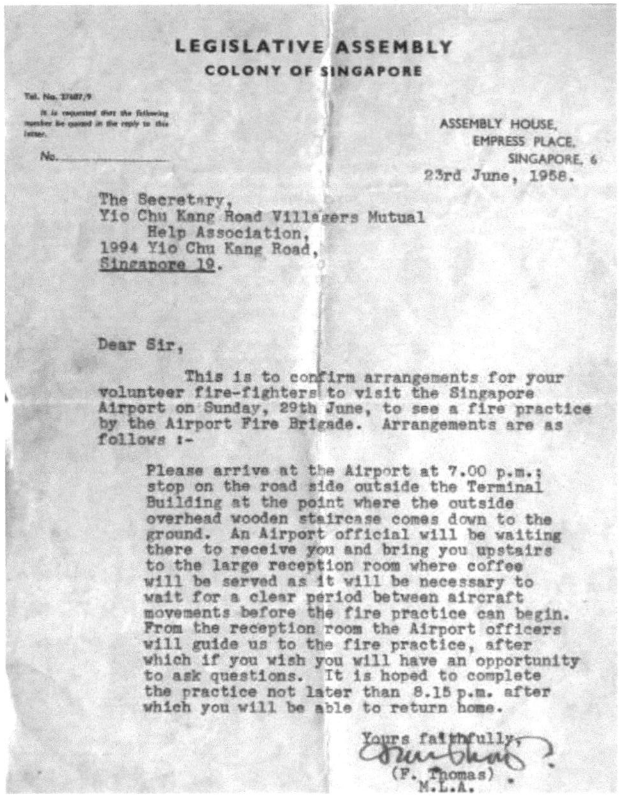

LEGISLATIVE ASSEMBLY
COLONY OF SINGAPORE

Tel. No. 27687/9

It is requested that the following number be quoted in the reply to this letter.

No. ____________

ASSEMBLY HOUSE,
EMPRESS PLACE,
SINGAPORE, 6
23rd June, 1958.

The Secretary,
Yio Chu Kang Road Villagers Mutual
Help Association,
1994 Yio Chu Kang Road,
Singapore 19.

Dear Sir,

This is to confirm arrangements for your volunteer fire-fighters to visit the Singapore Airport on Sunday, 29th June, to see a fire practice by the Airport Fire Brigade. Arrangements are as follows :-

Please arrive at the Airport at 7.00 p.m.; stop on the road side outside the Terminal Building at the point where the outside overhead wooden staircase comes down to the ground. An Airport official will be waiting there to receive you and bring you upstairs to the large reception room where coffee will be served as it will be necessary to wait for a clear period between aircraft movements before the fire practice can begin. From the reception room the Airport officers will guide us to the fire practice, after which if you wish you will have an opportunity to ask questions. It is hoped to complete the practice not later than 8.15 p.m. after which you will be able to return home.

Yours faithfully,
(F. Thomas)
M.L.A.

Collaboration with the Airport Fire Brigade in training the kampong volunteer firefighters.

与机场消防队合作为村消防队员培训。

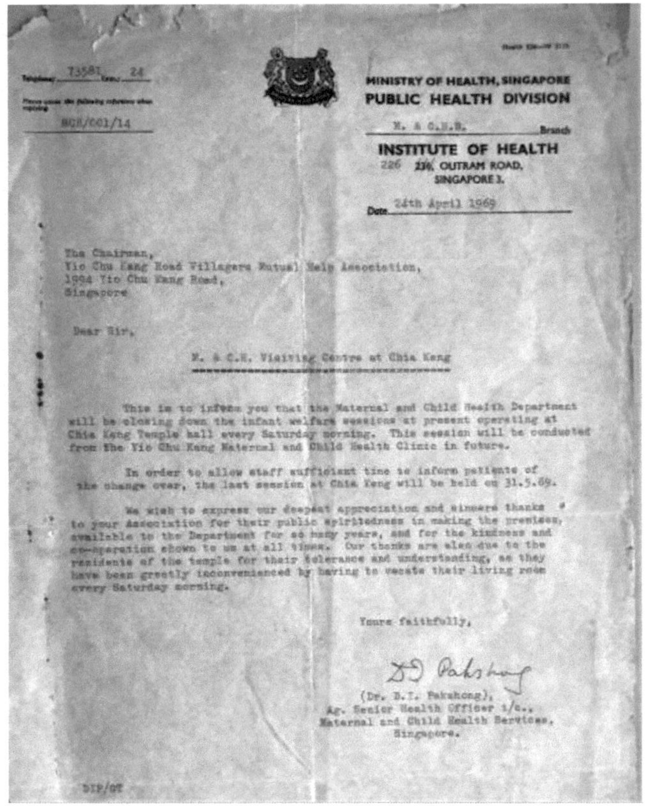

Telephone 73581 Extn. 24

Please quote the following reference when replying: MCH/661/14

MINISTRY OF HEALTH, SINGAPORE
PUBLIC HEALTH DIVISION
M. & C.H.S. Branch
INSTITUTE OF HEALTH
226 OUTRAM ROAD,
SINGAPORE 3.

Date 24th April 1969

The Chairman,
Yio Chu Kang Road Villagers Mutual Help Association,
1994 Yio Chu Kang Road,
Singapore

Dear Sir,

M. & C.H. Visiting Centre at Chia Keng

This is to inform you that the Maternal and Child Health Department will be closing down the infant welfare sessions at present operating at Chia Keng Temple hall every Saturday morning. This session will be conducted from the Yio Chu Kang Maternal and Child Health Clinic in future.

In order to allow staff sufficient time to inform patients of the change over, the last session at Chia Keng will be held on 31.5.69.

We wish to express our deepest appreciation and sincere thanks to your Association for their public spiritedness in making the premises available to the Department for so many years, and for the kindness and co-operation shown to us at all times. Our thanks are also due to the residents of the temple for their tolerance and understanding, as they have been greatly inconvenienced by having to vacate their living room every Saturday morning.

Yours faithfully,

(Dr. B.I. Pakshong),
Ag. Senior Health Officer i/c.,
Maternal and Child Health Services,
Singapore.

DIP/GT

Collaborated with the Public Health Division to use the association for maternal and child health screening in the 60's.

1960年代村委会与公众卫生处合作为妇孺检疫。

CHAPTER 36

Visit by PM Lee Kuan Yew

In 1963, when Prime Minister Lee Kuan Yew undertook his Serangoon Gardens constituency visit, the association was chosen as one of the stopover stations to meet with the village leaders and other grassroots representatives. At that time, PM Lee was 40 years old and very energetic, and he could cover visits to eight neighbouring constituencies in a day. The visits included the opening of two new community centres at Jalan Teck Kee and Kampong Cheng San.

He also combined his visits to civic and clan associations with that to schools and markets. The more important issues were to gather feedback and support on the merger with Malaysia when he spoke at the rallies. The station organising committee comprised prominent village leaders, clan and civic organisations, school principals, teachers and tycoons. They planned and prepared his visit at the Yio Chu Kang Villagers' Mutual Help Association. Many meetings were held at the association premises with the co-ordinators from other designated stations, government agencies and officers from the Prime Minister's Office in order to draw up the best and suitable programs. The streets were cleaned up and decorated with colourful flags, and welcome arches were built to give him a warm welcome. With the strong support and contributions from some notable tycoons of Kampong Chia Keng and Serangoon Gardens, the organising committee was able to defray the expenditure related to the visit.

My father was appointed as the Assistant Secretary of the Chia Keng Station PM welcoming party and helped to organise the program for that day. A Teochew Wayang performance was planned to draw the villagers to gather at a nearby open field to welcome the Prime Minister. The iconic kampong firefighters in their ceremonial uniform were specially deployed to greet him. The occasion was a good opportunity for the kampong folks to listen to his speeches on nation building and improving the welfare of the villagers.

I was 12 years old, and I followed my father and the entourage to visit several designated places and ended up in Serangoon Gardens for a tree planting event. Being young and small, I had an advantage in making my way to the front row to witness the historical tree planting ceremony. From then onwards, tree planting was earmarked as a national event to be carried out island-wide every year in the month of November to coincide with the Clean and Green Week campaigns.

The formation of a working committee represented by various schools, associations, civic organisations, tycoons and prominent villagers to organise the visit of Prime Minister Lee Kuan Yew at Chia Keng village in 1963.

李光耀总理于1963年访问实龙岗花园选区，一个由各基层组织，社团，学校，名人等组成的工作委员会积极筹备欢迎及其他事宜。

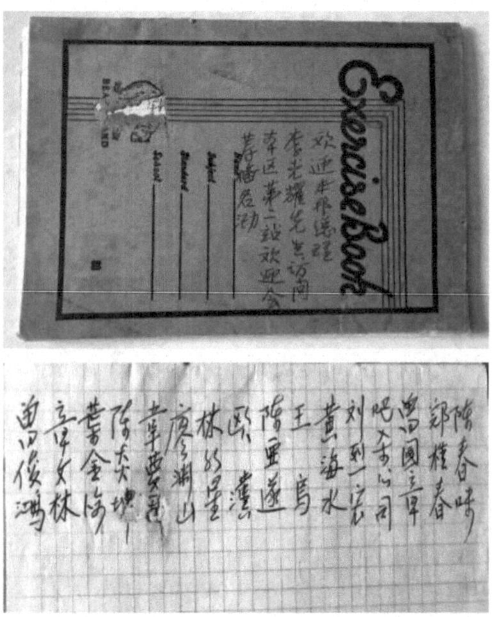

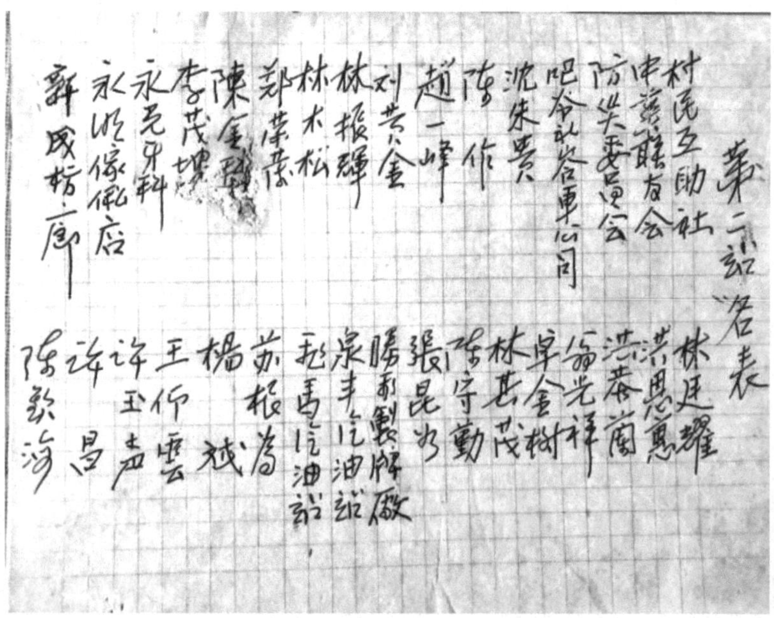

Attendance of first meeting held at the premises of Yio Chu Kang Road Villagers' Mutual Help Association on 3 June 1963.

在楊厝港律村民互助社1963年6月3日举行的第一次工委会会议。

PM Lee Kuan Yew welcomed by the leaders of Chia Keng village.

李总理受到村领导的欢迎。

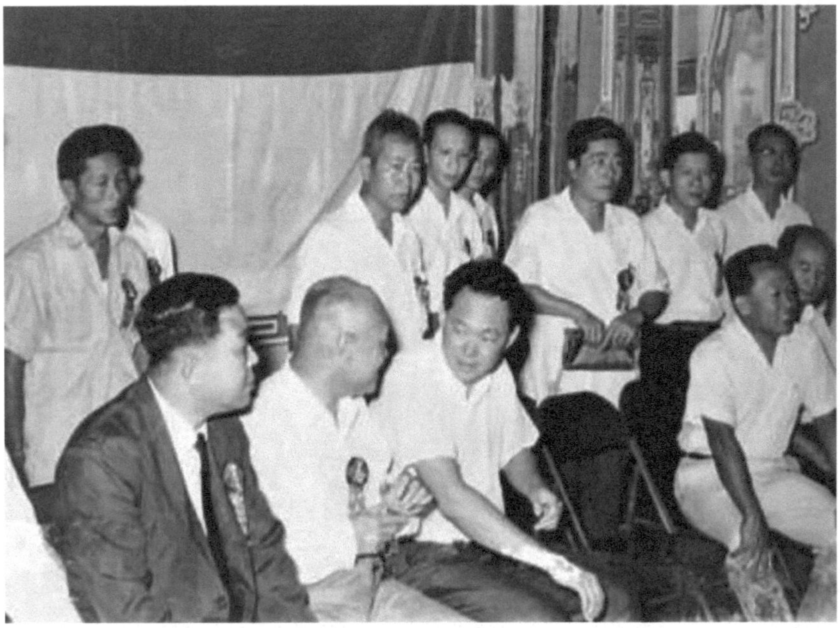

PM Lee Kuan Yew visited the Yio Chu Kang Villagers' Mutual Help Association in 1963.

李光耀总理于1963年访问楊厝港律村民互助社。

PM Lee with the village leaders before delivering his speech at Yio Chu Kang Road.

李总理在杨厝港路发表演讲前与村领导合影。

PM Lee spoke to the audience.
李总理演讲。

A group photo with the eight constituencies' working committee for PM Lee Kuan Yew's visit.

八个选区筹备李总理访问成立联合委员会合影。

In My Father's Footsteps

跟随我父亲的脚步

CHAPTER 37

Visit by PM Goh Chok Tong

My dad left behind a pair of gigantic shoes for me to fill. I never expected that one day I would be wearing them and following his footsteps to be involved in community services. History repeated itself after more than three decades, and I had to carry on his legacy. I was the Residents' Commitee (RC) Chairman at that time and was nominated as the organising committee chairman to host the visit by former PM Goh Chok Tong to Aljunied Zone E RC on 11 April 1992. PM Goh was the guest of honour to launch the Housing & Development Board (HDB) Main Upgrading Programme and was invited to view the HDB demonstration phase exhibitions at Lorong Lew Lian Estate. The Upgrading Steering Committee was formed and chaired by Mr Chin Harn Tong, MP for Aljunied GRC, to survey the residents' preferences. With a whopping 98% of the eligible dwellers supporting the upgrading programme, construction work commenced on 8 March 1993.

The Estate was one of the oldest among the blocks built before 1980 and comprised two blocks of four-room flats, five blocks of three-room flats and one block of two-room flats, which were upgraded with additional space within the units. The whole exercise took about three years and was completed in mid-1995. The completion ceremony was officiated by Minister for Information and the Arts and Minister for Health BG (NS) George Yeo after he launched the RC Souvenir Book on 25 June 1995.

On 5 November 1995, PM Goh was again invited to Lorong Lew Lian Estate to launch the Clean and Green Week Campaign held for the first time within the HDB heartland. This event was initiated by the Ministry of Environment and supported by our RC and other government agencies. Other special guests included Members of Parliament Dr Ong Chit Chung, Mr Chng Hee Kok, Mr Ibrahim Bin Othman and Mrs Yu-Foo Yee Shoon. Senior Parliamentary Secretary Mr Ho Kah Leong and Minister for Environment RADM Teo Chee Hean arrived later according to protocol. They were joined by the host MPs for Aljunied GRC Dr Ker Sin Tze, Mr Chin Harn Tong, Mr Mohamed Maidin Packer and BG George Yeo. The reasons for choosing Lorong Lew Lian was because the Estate had completed its upgrading at that time. Another reason was to take the campaign and involve the people living in the public estate.

The programmes included distributing prizes for the national cleanest precinct contest and presenting the Green Leaf Awards for winners of Gardens of Singapore Competition by Minister of Environment. The Gold Awards for the Cleanest Blocks Competition was presented by PM Goh Chok Tong, followed by planting of durian saplings by PM Goh Chok Tong along with the Minister of Environment Admiral (NS) Teo Chee Hean, Minister for Information and the Arts and Minister for Health BG (NS) George Yeo, Senior Parliamentary Secretary for Environment Mr Ho Kah Leong, Parliamentary Secretary for Information and the Arts Mr Mohammed Maidin Packer and MPs for Aljunied GRC Mr Chin Harn Tong and Dr Ker Sin Tze.

I suggested planting durian trees to reinforce the name 'Lew Lian', which means durian in the Hokkien dialect. The earlier settlers who had occupied this area were durian farmers and further down the road were pineapple plantations. As such, the upper portion of the road was named Lorong Lew Lian and the lower end was named Lorong Ong Lye.

The D24 variety durian saplings were chosen as the trees thrived best in open spaces on well-aerated grounds and required little maintenance. Under normal conditions, the trees were expected to bear fruits within six to eight years. The younger generations may have eaten durians but they might not know what a durian tree looks like. In 2012, the residents were very happy and excited when they saw the durian flowers start to bloom for the first time, and over the months more than thirty fruits were spotted. In 2015, two more trees were planted by Minister for Trade and Industry Mr Lim Hng Kiang and Seah Kian Peng MP for Marine Parade GRC to commemorate the ministerial visit to Braddell Heights.

PM Goh Chok Tong meeting HDB officials and grassroots leaders at the Aljunied Zone E RC Centre, Lorong Lew Lian in 1992.

吴作栋总理于1992年访问阿裕尼E分区居民委員会。

PM Goh Chok Tong viewing the HDB Main Upgrading Exhibitions at Lorong Lew Lian Estate.

总理吴作栋出席在罗弄榴槤住宅区组屋改进展。

Minister George Yeo launching the RC souvenir book before officiating the HDB Upgrading completion ceremony in 1995.

*1995*楊榮文部长主持居民委员会历史书的发布会。

PM Goh Chok Tong planting a durian tree at Lorong Lew Lian Estate in conjunction with the launching of the Clean and Green Week Campaign in 1995.

1995年吴作栋总理在罗弄榴樋种植榴莲树苗。

Planting of durian trees at Lorong Lew Lian by PM Goh Chok Tong, flanked by Mr Ho Kah Leong, Mr Maidin Packer Mohd, BG (NS) George Yeo, Admiral (NS) Teo Chee Hean, Mr Chin Harn Tong and Dr Ker Sin Tze.

何家良先生, Mr Maidin Packer, 楊榮文部长,张志贤部长, 钱翰琮先生和柯新治博士陪同吴总理植树。

PM Goh along with several Ministers and MPs at the launch of the Clean and Green Week Campaign held at Lorong Lew Lian in 1995.

吴作栋总理与几位部长和国会议员在1995年在罗弄榴莲村主持清洁和绿化运动启动礼。

CHAPTER 38

Visit by PM Lee Hsien Loong

Twelve years later, PM Lee Hsien Loong made his constituency visit to Braddell Heights on 15 September 2007. PM Lee succeeded former PM Goh Chok Tong as the third Prime Minister of Singapore in 2004. Prior to his visit to Braddell Heights, he also visited Lorong Lew Lian Estate in 1996 when he was Deputy Prime Minister. At that time, Lorong Lew Lian Estate was under the purview of Aljunied GRC, and Mr Chin Harn Tong was the First Adviser and Mrs Lim Hwee Hua was the Second Adviser. In 1997, Lorong Lew Lian Estate was rezoned by the redrawing of electoral boundaries and became part of Braddell Heights, with Mr Goh Choon Kang as the Member of Parliament. Mr Goh served Braddell Heights for 13 years and was succeeded by Mr R Ravindran, who was a former MP of Bukit Timah GRC in 2001. Mr Ravindran stepped down in 2006 to make way for Mr Seah Kian Peng.

As the Citizens Consultative Committee (CCC) Vice-Chairman I was tasked by Braddell Heights CCC chairman Ng Cher Yan to co-chair the working committee and plan the welcoming ceremony for PM Lee Hsien Loong. Extensive preparation and co-ordination had to be carried out to ensure the security and safety aspects and at the same time engage the community. He started his tour at station one, which covered the events at Braddell Heights Amphitheatre and the Community Hall at a nearby block.

He was invited by Mr Seah Kian Peng to light up the lanterns to mark the opening of the Lantern Festival event and visited the various exhibition stalls and flea market. He was then ushered to meet the various

Inter-Racial and Religious Confidence Circle (IRCC) religious leaders at their exhibition booths. As the IRCC chairman, I took this opportunity to gather all our religious organisations within Braddell Heights to come forward to showcase their activities and at the same time strengthen ties with one another, and more importantly, to allow our residents to interact, understand and learn about the teachings and practices of different faiths.

After PM Lee met up with the religious leaders, he was directed to join the students from St Gabriel's Primary School and Yangzheng Primary School in unveiling the park adoption plaque. This project was jointly organised by the Braddell Heights CCC and Town Council to involve the primary schools in Braddell Heights in looking after the flora and fauna of the park. Later he met the students of Nanyang Junior College to do a final touch up of a wall mural to commemorate the PM's visit. By then it was timely for PM Lee to join the Muslim community in the breaking of fast at Blk 256 Serangoon Central Drive. There he met up with the Malay community leaders, residents and family members. He undertook the breaking of fast and mingled with them before moving over to the CC to continue his engagement with other residents.

The programmes were very tightly scheduled as he had to cover many stations and was ushered to the next station anchored by another CCC vice-Chairman Ng Kim Eng to join the family telematch and sports event. He then launched the Citizens On Surveillance programme organized by the Serangoon Neighbourhood Police Centre. This brilliant project was piloted by the dedicated police officers to engage the ordinary citizens and residents in fighting crime at the grassroots level. After the launch, he was invited to witness a line dance event and interact with the participants.

Then he was invited to view the National Chinese Calligraphy contest organized by Braddell Heights Chinese Traditional Arts Programme Committee. Thereafter, he wrapped up the visit with a dialogue session with the community leaders and invited guests.

Deputy Prime Minister Lee Hsien Loong visited the upgraded Lorong Lew Lian Estate in 1996.

李显龙副总理于1996年访问改良后的罗弄榴榩村。

PM Lee Hsien Loong made his community visit to Braddell Heights on 15 September 2007.

总理李显龙于2007年9月15日访问布莱德岭选区。

Launching of the Citizens on Surveillance programme organised by Serangoon Neighbourhood Police Centre.

李总理启动警方组织的民众预防犯罪计划。

Viewing the National Calligraphy Contest held at the Braddell Heights CC.

李总理参观全国书法大赛。

A New Beginning

一 个新的开始

CHAPTER 39

Resettlement of the Village

In the mid-70's, most of the villagers received notices from the Housing & Development Board (HDB) on the redevelopment of the entire Chia Keng village, including the temple and the Association. Our family members had also moved out by the late 70's and settled down in Lorong Lew Lian HDB Estate. During this time, many other kampong folks from different parts of Singapore were also resettled here. We had to adapt to a different lifestyle as we resettled in high-rise houses and was surrounded by concrete jungle. We had to readjust and restart our networking with new neighbours who were resettled from Punggol, Kampong Wat Tanjong, Haji Karim Road and Lorong Ah Soo areas.

The Yio Chu Kang Villagers' Mutual Help Association management committee was offered an alternative site to join with other religious organisations for the building of a joint temple. In consideration of the worshippers and supporters who had been relocated, coupled with leadership succession problems, the Committee decided not to take up the offer by HDB and moved the near century-old Jade Emperor deity to Hougang Street 21 in the mid-80's. By then all the villagers were living in different parts of Singapore, and the Association had outlived its usefulness. The role of the Association became irrelevant and was taken over by the better-equipped modern community centres. Unfortunately, all good things must come to an end. It was a heart-breaking decision for the management of the Association to decide to close and deregister the Association with the Registry of Society.

The location of the temple at Hougang St 21 was not suitable for the aged worshippers as there was no lift and they had to climb three flights of stairs to worship at the temple. This resulted in a decline in number of worshippers and the donations, affecting the upkeep of the temple. A decision was made to relocate the deities to a more convenient place at Lorong Lew Lian. My parents bought a three-room flat in 1988 and converted one of the rooms and hall as an interim accommodation for the deities. The dedicated worshippers continued to pray and attend the annual celebrations to mark the birth of the Jade Emperor, which falls on the ninth day of Lunar New Year. The annual celebrations and gatherings were scaled down and went on for many years at Lorong Lew Lian Estate. With the ageing population and the demise of many worshippers, coupled with the problem of leadership succession, a decision was made to relocate the deities to the Kancanarama Buddhist Temple at Lorong Ong Lye. With the kind assistance of my good friend Tan Beng Chong, who was the former president of the temple management committee, the Jade Emperor deity was moved to the Buddhist Temple on 27 November 2016. The dedicated worshippers and followers continue to pray and hold their religious activities at the new location.

Towards the early 80's, the Ngiap Er Lian Ngee Sia and The Dragon Art Athletic Association were rehoused and shared the premises with Yio Chu Kang Villagers' Mutual Help Association.

在80年代初業餘聯誼社和藝龍體育會搬进了楊厝港律村民互助社。

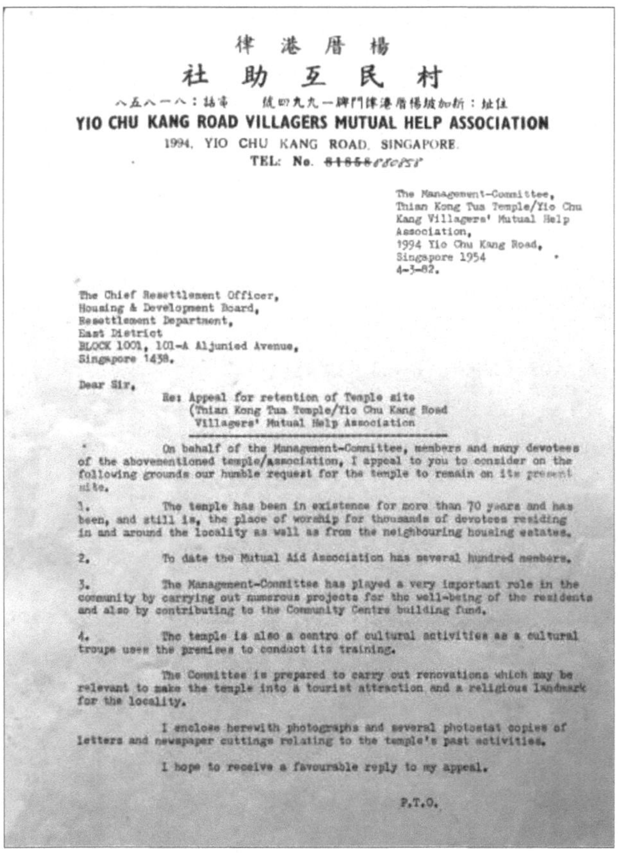

楊厝港律
村民互助社
住址：新加坡楊厝港律門牌一九九四號　電話：八一八五八

YIO CHU KANG ROAD VILLAGERS MUTUAL HELP ASSOCIATION

1994, YIO CHU KANG ROAD, SINGAPORE.

TEL: No. ~~81858~~ 580858

The Management-Committee,
Thian Kong Tua Temple/Yio Chu
Kang Villagers' Mutual Help
Association,
1994 Yio Chu Kang Road,
Singapore 1954
4-3-82.

The Chief Resettlement Officer,
Housing & Development Board,
Resettlement Department,
East District
BLOCK 1001, 101-A Aljunied Avenue,
Singapore 1438.

Dear Sir,

Re: Appeal for retention of Temple site
(Thian Kong Tua Temple/Yio Chu Kang Road
Villagers' Mutual Help Association

On behalf of the Management-Committee, members and many devotees of the abovementioned temple/association, I appeal to you to consider on the following grounds our humble request for the temple to remain on its present site.

1. The temple has been in existence for more than 70 years and has been, and still is, the place of worship for thousands of devotees residing in and around the locality as well as from the neighbouring housing estates.

2. To date the Mutual Aid Association has several hundred members.

3. The Management-Committee has played a very important role in the community by carrying out numerous projects for the well-being of the residents and also by contributing to the Community Centre building fund.

4. The temple is also a centre of cultural activities as a cultural troupe uses the premises to conduct its training.

The Committee is prepared to carry out renovations which may be relevant to make the temple into a tourist attraction and a religious landmark for the locality.

I enclose herewith photographs and several photostat copies of letters and newspaper cuttings relating to the temple's past activities.

I hope to receive a favourable reply to my appeal.

P.T.O.

Final Appeal to HDB to remain at Chia Keng Village was turned down as the land was needed to build a sports stadium

Relocation of Chia Keng Tian Kong

Dear Members and Friends

This is to inform you that Chia Keng Tian Kong@Blk 4 #02-92 Lorong Lew Lian will be relocated to a new premise with effect from 27th November 2016 (Sunday). Kindly note on this date we have made arrangements to conduct a prayer session at 10.00am at the current address@Blk 4 #02-92 Lorong Lew Lian before we start the move to the new premise at 1.00pm.

The move to the new location is inevitable as the house owner of the current premise has passed away. In accordance with the HDB regulation, the said premise has to be sold. Hence arrangements for the relocation of the Chia Keng Tian Kong has to take place.

We wish to thank you for all the support given to the temple all these years. Hope you will continue to pray and support the Chia Keng Tian Kong at the new premise.

Thank you for your kind attention.

New address:

TIAN KONG AND KANCANARAMA BUDDHIST TEMPLE

NO. 2 Lorong Ong Lye

Off Paya Lebar Road

Singapore 536358

Tel: 62886945/62878107

Email: watkan@pacific.net.com

Sincerely,

Chiang Kheng Peng

Relocation of Tian Kong Temple.

車宮天公壇庙搬迁。

The resettlement of Chia Keng village.

在80年代車宮村受发展体育中心影响被拆除。

The villagers were relocated to other parts of Singapore, and the village made way for redevelopment into the Serangoon Sports Stadium.

居民被安置到新加坡的其他地方, 车宫村让位给实龙岗体育场的建设。

CHAPTER 40

Continuing the Legacy of Kampong Chia Keng

With the experience in community service that we gained during our kampong days, we were privileged to carry on the legacy of our village pioneers and continued to contribute to the newly formed high-rise community at Lorong Lew Lian. Over here, the resettled communities had a larger presence of residents of different races and religious backgrounds. This was entirely different from the way we managed the kampong folks. We have to be mindful and sensitive to meet their needs and be more understanding to their cultures, religions and practices.

As most of the residents were resettled from various parts of the island, such as Punggol, Lorong Ah Soo, Yio Chu Kang Road, Kampong Wat Tanjong and Haji Karim and Jalan Hock Chye, the immediate task was to gel the resettled communities. For starters, the shop owners and the coffee shop stall operators initiated the formation of the Seventh Moon Organising Committee. The objectives were also to provide an opportunity for the residents to get together and at the same time identify potential leaders to lead and help in the community. The setback was that the Seventh Moon Committee might not be able to reach out to the minorities and residents of different faiths. Just like the kampong days, we had to think big but start small and find room for improvement as we progressed.

There was hope when the Residents' Committee (RC) at Lorong Lew Lian was formed in 1979. My father was approached by prominent grassroots leaders to recommend some shop owners and Seventh Moon Committee members to support and strengthen the formation. The first RC was formed under the purview of Paya Lebar Constituency, with many pioneer members recruited from the civil service and government agencies. A refreshed RC was started with the demarcation of the electoral boundary when Lorong Lew Lian Estate was rezoned under Braddell Heights Constituency. Six of us representing the shop owners and the Seventh Moon Committee were roped in to support the renamed Braddell Heights Zone A RC and the Lorong Lew Lian Community Centre Management Committee (CCMC) in 1980.

The RC was chaired by the late Mr Loke Wah Heng, and the CCMC was initially headed by Mr Tay Bak Tee and taken over by the late Mr Aw Kim Cheng. The Lorong Lew Lian Community Centre was formed due to the closure of the Plantation Avenue Community Centre as the residents there were due for resettlement. The Plantation Avenue cemetery ground, known as Pua Pak Tiong, had to make way for future HDB housing projects. Pua Pak Tiong was the term used by the Hokkien community to refer to victims who had died of tuberculosis and had undergone a post mortem before they were buried.

At that time, Braddell Heights had only eight blocks of HDB flats and the most populated area, so the focal point for activities was targeted there. The immediate task was to reach out to the residents and build a cohesive community. In collaboration with the RC, CCMC, Youth Group and the Seventh Moon Committee, extensive efforts were required to gel the residents who were resettled from various parts of Singapore.

The first target group was to reach out to the elderly residents to tap on their experience and wisdom in forming a Senior Citizens' Club. With much efforts and hard work, the working committee managed to kickstart the formation of the Senior Citizens' Club under the management of the RC. Thereafter the Senior Citizens' Club formed their own interest groups such as a Taiqi and Qigong group. To attract more elderly residents to interact during tea sessions, gatherings were regularly held at the RC Centre, and later they started their yearly anniversary celebrations.

The annual celebrations were mooted by my father, who took over the Senior Club Chairmanship in 1983. With his many years of experience in the kampong days in organising self-supporting dinners, it was not a difficult task. With the yearly successful dinner gatherings, the Senior Citizens' Committee expanded their activities to include wake visits and funeral send-off for their members, parents and parents-in-law. They also helped to raise funds in aid of the Hotel New World disaster rescue mission. After thirty-six years, the Senior Citizens' Club, currently headed by Mr Heng Joon Chaik, still carries on with various activities and anniversary celebrations.

With the successful formation of the Senior Citizen's Club, more sub-committees and interest groups were formed. I took over the chairmanship in 1986, after my predecessor Mr Loke Wah Heng suddenly passed away due to a severe heart attack. I decided to cast the net further and started more sub-groups, such as the Junior RC Club, Ladies' Club, Indian Activity Club, Malay Activity Club,

Community Safety and Security Program and other interest groups.

The kampong spirits were slowly regained with the residents gathering at the void decks for Chinese tea sessions. The Teochew and Hokkien group from Punggol and Haji Karim areas would congregate at the void deck of Blk 7, whereas the Hainanese group from the Lorong Ah Soo area would gather at Blk 4. Another mixed group, who were Chinese Chess enthusiasts, would gather at the Blk 1 void deck. There was also a group of Chinese and Malay bird lovers who would gather daily at the open space in between Blk 4 and Blk 5 to watch and compete in bird singing contests. A couple of these enterprising bird lovers would search the nearby wooded area of the Teochew Cemetery ground to trap wild birds for sale or keep them as pets.

Families with young children would fly kites in the evening at the open area of the cemetery ground. The older children would play soccer games and go spider hunting in the bushes. Others would make their way to the open canal at the fringe of the estate to fish for eels hiding in between the gaps of the concrete drain slabs. For those gluttons, the fish would end up on their dinner tables. A group of Taiqi and Qigong enthusiasts would conduct their exercises in the early morning. There was a group of school bus drivers who took advantage of the big empty carpark at Lorong Lew Lian during office hours to station their buses and have their tea break at Blk 3. It was very convenient and shady to park at this precinct while waiting to pick up the students from nearby schools when school was dismissed. As such groups had grown bigger and bigger, soon they made this place their official meeting point and started another Seventh Moon festival organising committee. This group complemented the one formed by the shop and food stalls owners. The small estate became very vibrant with closely knit residents, as the majority were Teochews from the same ethnic group.

The cemetery ground, which belonged to the Ngee Ann Kongsi foundation, was looked after by a Malay family who stayed in a small kampong near Lorong Lew Lian. It was a win-win situation for this family as they also benefitted from the amenities provided by the HDB in this new estate, and some of their family members took advantage of the opportunity to sell their home-made curry puffs in the neighbourhood.

Soon they became good friends of Lorong Lew Lian residents and integrated with our community. Over time, the family members were seen attending and helping in many of the Malay wedding functions at Lorong Lew Lian. A strong relationship was forged with the family, and members of their family informed us to keep a lookout for a peeping tom lurking around their bathroom area at night.

True enough, the intruder appeared at their house a few days later and they tried to catch the perpetrator who had fled towards Lorong Lew Lian. My brother Gary and I heard the commotion and we joined the chase inside the high lallang area. It was not easy to see him under the cover of darkness, and when we spotted him, I shouted that the police were present. The warning had its effect as he stopped running. He was outnumbered and we caught and handed him over to the police. The lesson we learned was to strengthen our social cohesion and reinforce racial and religious harmony within our own community.

By the 80's, the Ngee Ann Kongsi Teochew cemetery ground next to Lorong Lew Lian Estate was earmarked for redevelopment of new HDB housing estates. The Teochew Funeral Parlour, the Malay kampong and the burial ground had to make way for the construction of another twenty-seven blocks of flats. During the planning stage, this area was named Serangoon South. Later on, when the new roads were laid, the estates were renamed as Serangoon Central and Serangoon Avenue 1. With the new development, another thirteen blocks of flats were rezoned under the purview of the RC at Lorong Lew Lian. By 1988, the eight blocks in Lorong Lew Lian and thirteen blocks in Serangoon Central and Avenue 1 were rezoned under Aljunied GRC and the RC renamed as Aljunied Zone E Residents' Committee. With thirteen blocks from Serangoon Avenue 1 and Central added to the Zone, another Seventh Moon celebration committee was formed. It was named the Serangoon Central Seventh Moon Celebration Committee.

Across the Upper Serangoon Road, a new town was created with more HDB high-rise dwellings and the construction of a new mega community centre and bus interchange. All the small community centres (CCs) within Braddell Heights, such as Bartley CC, Plantation Avenue CC, Jalan Teck Kee CC and Lorong Lew Lian CC, were merged to form the Braddell Heights CC located along Upper Serangoon Road. The construction of the new town and CC commenced in 1983 and was hampered by the presence of a small temple known as Chap Pang Kong at Lorong Patong, as the caretaker could not be contacted to vacate the site. As such, the HDB approached the MP Mr Lee Khoon Choy for assistance. Mr Lee assigned the Citizens Consultative Committee (CCC) Secretary Mr Tay Bak Tee to seek help from the village elders who were in a better position to convince the caretaker to relocate the deities as scheduled.

As I was also a CCC member, Mr Tay Bak Tee approached me and another two community leaders, Mr Seah Wee Tuan and Kwek Kian Tong, to help relocate the deities. We were aware of the risk and prepared ourselves for an impending showdown in case there was a violent resistance by the caretaker and the worshippers. We expected to be confronted by the villagers as nobody would like to be relocated after been rooted in a place for a long time. We were also concerned with not offending and upsetting the deities and engaged a Taoist Priest to pray and appease them. Like in many resettlement cases, there was bound to be difficulties and unhappiness, but we had to explain to them that the new development was for the benefit of the majority and a way of progress for our nation and the people.

An auspicious date was chosen by the Taoist priest to pray at the temple and conduct the religious ritual for the relocation. Fortunately, the ceremonial send-off for the deities went smoothly without any glitches. With the completion of the ceremony, we accompanied the priest together with the deities in my pick-up vehicle and headed to the new location near Bartley Road. Another short religious ceremony was conducted to place the deities in the shrine and thank them for their blessings and successful relocation. The cost of the relocation and religious ceremony conducted by the priest were sponsored by the CCC Chairman Mr Aw Kim Cheng. Mr Aw was a successful businessman who contributed tremendously to Braddell Heights in terms of not only his time and efforts but also financial support for many years.

In 1984, the HDB Resettlement Department had also approached Mr Lee Khoon Choy for the clearance of two other temples at Lorong Chuan area. Their efforts to contact the management teams of Woo Tun Nia and Hock Chye Tua temples to discuss about the relocation and compensations were futile. Alternative temple sites at Kampong Ubi were offered for the relocation of the temples but they did not respond.

Braddell Heights CCC members headed by Tay Bak Tee and Tan Chin Teck were assigned to assist and understand the problems faced by the management of the two temples. With much negotiations, finally the two temples' representatives agreed to take up the site at Serangoon North for the development of the new temples. The relocation ended well and went smoothly with the help of CCC Chairman Mr Aw Kim Cheng and some other patrons, who donated generously to the construction costs.

The other challenging task was the relocation of the Lim Tua Tow Road market, which was closed in the mid-90's. It had to make way for the construction of the Serangoon Viaduct, which was opened in 2002. Braddell Heights CCC members had to step in again to help in the relocation exercise. A meeting with the affected stall owners was conducted at the Braddell Heights Zone A RC Centre regarding the allocation exercise. It was impossible to rehouse all the stall holders and shops in one location. As such, the affected owners were offered three locations at Chong Pang, Ang Mo Kio Blk 409 and 453 markets. Initially, all the stall owners were worried about whether they could sustain their business in these new areas as the residential units were not fully occupied. Over a period of time, their businesses had picked up and most of them were doing well and were happy that they had made the right decision to move on.

Resettlement of the Chap Pang Kong Temple at Lorong Patong by HDB for the construction of the new Braddell Heights CC and housing development in the early 80's.

80年代初,基层领导人协助在 *Lorong Patong*的什班公庙搬迁。

Braddell Heights grassroots leaders Tay Bak Tee, Seah Wee Tuan, Kwek Kian Tong and I helped relocate the deities to a shrine at Jalan Rindhu.

布莱德岭公民咨询委员帮助神像搬到了*Jalan Rindhu*的一座寺庙。

The last Malay kampong next to Lorong Lew Lian HDB Estate was resettled in the 80's.

80年代在罗弄榴莲祖屋隔邻的最后一个马来村被迁移。

The open canal at the fringe of the HDB estate where the children fished for eels.

罗弄榴梿的孩子在排水沟中捉鳗鱼。

Inauguration of Braddell Heights Zone A RC in 1981.

*1981*年布莱德岭A分区居民委员会的就职典礼。

The RC Senior Citizens' Club was formed to look after the welfare of the elderly residents at Lorong Lew Lian.

The appointment ceremony was officiated by Mr Danabalan, Minister for Foreign Affairs in 1984.

*1984*年，居民委员会成立了乐龄俱乐部，照顾老年人的福利. 丹那巴南外交部长见证乐龄俱乐部委员会任命礼。

CHAPTER 41

Pioneer of Singapore Civil Defence Volunteer Company

By 1984, a national drive was initiated to organise civil defence courses as the majority of Singaporeans lived in high-rise buildings. Should there be a crisis, the residents would be better prepared and could help one another to evacuate and take shelter in a safe place. At that time, within Braddell Heights, Lorong Lew Lian was the only HDB estate with high-rise buildings, and the courses and activities were conducted here.

The Civil Defence Co-ordinating Committee was formed with representatives from various grassroots organisations, volunteer welfare organisations and schools. The immediate task was to form the volunteer company to train and co-ordinate in rescue, first aid and evacuation procedures. Residents, shop owners, hawkers, teachers, students and community leaders were inducted to attend the courses and ultimately helped to pioneer the formation of the first civil defence volunteer company in Singapore. Several of our family members had also volunteered to join the Civil Defence Company. Our experience and firefighting skills from our kampong days and army training during National Service came in handy in civil defence procedures. The Civil Defence Co-ordinating Committee nominated me to head the Volunteer Company to prepare for a passing-out parade when all the trainees had completed their courses.

Intensive courses for first aid, rescue and evacuation were conducted in English and Chinese for more than one hundred volunteers. The courses and trainings commenced on 15 January and were held until early May 1984. On 20 May 1984, a passing-out parade cum mock-up exercise with simulations of a bomb attack was conducted at the basketball court at Blk 6 Lorong Lew Lian. The event was officiated by Mr Lee Khoon Choy, then Senior Minister of State (Prime Minister Office) and MP for Braddell Heights, with Mr Mah Bow Tan as our special guest.

A few months after the exercise, refresher courses and recall of volunteer practices were carried out to test the efficiency and confidence of the volunteers. We also conducted a water and rations distribution exercise on 10 March 1986 at Blk 1 Lorong Lew Lian. To sustain the interest of the volunteers, we also organised overland trips and gatherings as team-building exercises.

Mr Lee Khoon Choy officiating at the passing-out parade of the First Civil Defence Volunteer Company in Singapore at Lorong Lew Lian on 20 May 1984.

*1984*李炯才次长主持新加坡第一支民防志愿部队结业礼。

The mock-up exercises were conducted after the passing-out parade.

为居民进行民防演习。

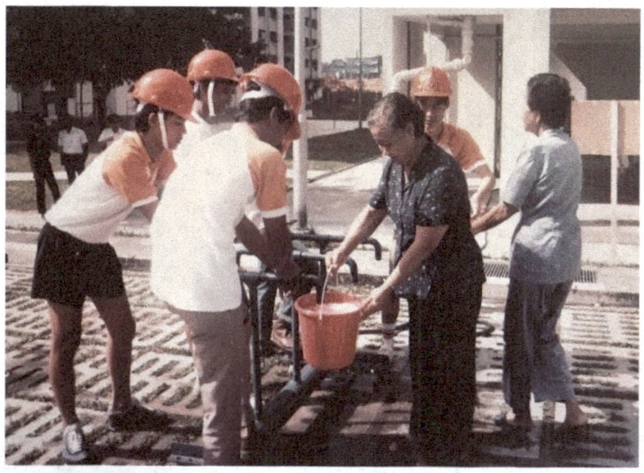

The VIPs at the parade. From left front row: Mrs Mah Bow Tan 马宝山夫人, Mr Aw Kim Cheng 胡金钟 BBM(L), Mr Mah Bow Tan 马宝山先生, Mr Lee Khoon Choy 李炯才部长, Mr Eugene Wong and Mr Gan Teng Geow 颜挺尧 BBM.

The youth members from Lorong Lew Lian. Many of them were students at that time.

罗弄榴莲青年组员，很多人还是学生。

Residents of different races and all ages came forward to volunteer their services to serve the community.

不同种族和年龄的居民参加了培训。

My third younger sister Molly, youngest brother Melvyn and niece Constance were also at the passing-out parade.

我的妹妹和弟弟也经过培训的志愿者。

CHAPTER 42

Hotel New World Disaster — 15 March 1986

With the official formation of Braddell Heights Civil Defence Volunteer Company on 20 May 1984, there was a need to sustain the interest and conduct refresher courses for the volunteers. Coincidentally, we conducted a recall exercise and water rationing procedure for our Civil Defence volunteers on 10 March 1986, and five days later, the Hotel New World disaster happened. I still remember, a few years before the hotel collapsed, our family members had been to the hotel to meet our relatives who arrived from Thailand in the early 80's. This was their maiden trip to Singapore to catch up with relatives and strengthen our bonds with our paternal grandpa's second family.

I was working at our family florist shop when I heard over the radio that a building had collapsed at Kitchener Road and Serangoon Road junction. It was very shocking news, and my heart was with those who were buried and trapped under the concrete debris. I immediately called the Civil Defence full-time officer Mr Tan Eng Wah to check whether help was needed. With concurrence from the then MP for Braddell Heights Mr Goh Choon Kang and the former Civil Defence Co-ordinating Chairman Mr Tan Eng Soon, I helped to organise a busload of trained civil defence volunteers and rushed to the disaster site. My younger brother Melvyn, sister, Molly and brother-in-law David Lim were also there. I had to call many of the volunteers individually, as in those days pagers and social media had not been invented yet. With the help of some other leaders, we managed to round up about thirty volunteers.

We reached the disaster site in the early afternoon and immediately were tasked to help in the evacuation and removal of the concrete debris. We took turns to stay at the site for a week as some of them had to go back to school, return to work or run their businesses. Initially we were deployed to rescue those trapped inside the building and help remove the debris, but when the full-time rescuers and National Service personnel from the army, fire brigade and police arrived, we stepped back and switched our duties to manage the logistics and food distribution section. Our job was to cater to the rescuers and the devastated family members of the victims who were waiting anxiously for the news of their loved ones.

Back at the constituency, my father, who was the chairman of the Braddell Heights Zone A RC Senior Citizens' Club, helped to raise funds for the purchase of toiletries, masks, medical supplies and tonics for the rescuers and the victims' families. The rescuers worked very hard and nonstop to reach out to as many trapped victims as possible while time was running out. They had to be taken care of and given moral and psychological support as they toiled day and night in the dark tunnels. The selfless rescuers also had to steel themselves to make their way through entangled steel bars and slabs of concrete, which might give way any time. We have to salute them for their sacrifices and for risking their own lives to save the trapped victims. We could imagine that, along the way in the tunnel, they would have encountered dismembered bodies and had to bear with the unpleasant odour of the decaying bodies.

The rescue mission also had to be timely and speedy as those surviving victims trapped inside the collapsed building would be starved and dehydrated. The rescuers tried many methods to remove the concrete slabs and entangled steel bars. They tried using a hydro cutter but there was a disadvantage; the water would flood the basement and drown those who were still alive. Another concern was that using the electrical cutters the sparks might ignite the leaking gas and cause an explosion. It was a blessing that at that time there were foreign tunnel experts working on our first Mass Rapid Transport (MRT) line, and they were roped in to help open up tunnels to reach out to the survivors. It was a better and faster way to move underground and search for survivors.

Our Volunteer Civil Defence Section Commander, Ms Afidah Bte Babjan, who was working with a food catering company, helped by approaching her employer to donate rice packets for the rescuers and helpers at the disaster site. It was also very touching to see many people coming forward to donate money and blood to help the victims and their family members. Others came forward to offer their tools and heavy machineries such as cranes, excavators and construction vehicles to remove the concrete debris. Contributions, irrespective of whether they were big or small, and in kind or in cash, poured in; moreover, the most commendable and heartening thing was seeing all our fellow citizens banding together to help during the disaster.

It was heartening to see that many other citizens and foreigners, especially the tunnel

Our job was to cater to the rescuers and the devastated family members of the victims who were waiting anxiously for the news of their loved ones.

experts, banded together as one united people to play their roles to save as many people as possible who were trapped inside the collapsed building. At the end of the rescue mission, seventeen lucky survivors were saved and thirty-three perished. We salute all the unsung heroes and many others for their selflessness and bravery to save the trapped victims under such adverse circumstances. This was the worst disaster in Singapore history involving the first collapsed building and was also an eye-opener to our civil defence forces and building control authority.

After more than twenty-five years, the disaster was still fresh in my mind, and I was honoured to be invited to share my experience at several events, one of which was organised by the National Heritage Board at the Ang Mo Kio Library from June to July 2012. Other speakers were writer Ms Joan Hon, Red Cross volunteer Ricky Goh, retired consultant in Anesthesia and Intensive Care Dr Edward Pang and Adjunct Associate Professor Fred Long Foo Yee from the Division of Psychology, NTU. The following year, I was invited by the Republic Polytechnic Engineering Faculty to give a talk on 22 January 2013. Another talk was conducted at the National University for the participants of the Total Defence N.E.mation contest organised by NEXUS and National Education at the Ministry of Defence on 7 September 2013.

On 15 March 1986, we arrived at the Hotel New World disaster site and immediately were tasked to help in the evacuation.

1986年3月15日，民防志愿者正在新世界酒店灾难现场提供帮助。

Many of the volunteers formed human chains and helped to remove the debris while others were searching for and rescuing the trapped victims.

我们的成员帮助清除碎片并营救被困在瓦砾中的人。

Many of our volunteers took turns to stay and help at the disaster site till the final day of the rescue operations.

许多志愿者轮流协助救灾直到最后一天。

布莱德岭 区讯

MC (P) 4/3/86 86年3月第1期

本区民防队参与新世界大酒店塌楼惨祸救灾工作

3月15日，一座矗立在实龙岗路的新世界大酒店，突然发生崩塌事件。惨祸消息一经传开后，本区国会议员吴俊刚先生，民防协调委员会主席陈荣顺先生，以及民防志愿连队长章庆裕先生等人，立即召集所有队员，积极参与救灾工作。

当日下午，共有42位民防志愿队员赶抵现场报到，展开救灾行动。他们之中有些协助拯救人员搬移乱石，有些分发食物与饮品予现场工作人员，或从事其他支援性的工作等。

队员们热心服务，自始至终，历久不懈。从塌楼惨剧发生到清理现场工作结束为止，他们轮流分批每日到场服务，深受咨委、管委、居委及妇委等基层领袖的激励与赞赏，充份表现出群体合作的精神。

女队员阿菲达的雇主深受塌楼事件所感动，特报效一千包的黄姜饭予现场工作人员食用。而乐龄俱乐部的乐龄人士，也热心捐赠一千两百件的面巾予现场拯救人员使用。

巧合的是，3月10日本区民防志愿连刚举行过"报到演习"，而队员们都能认真对待工作，表现良好。这次的参与救灾工作，他们或出自内心对受难者的同情与悲伤而在紧急救人的感召下，他们可说是忘却自我，置生死于度外。

布莱德岭人民对参与这次英勇救灾行动的工作人员，仅致以最高的敬礼及永志不忘。

16

Braddell Heights NEWS.....

NO. 1/86 MC (P) 4/3/86 March 1986

Braddell Heights Constituency Responded To New World Hotel Tragedy

Immediately after the news was flashed of the collapse of the New World Hotel in Serangoon Road, on Saturday 15th March, the Member of Parliament Mr Goh Choon Kang, Chairman of the Braddell Heights Civil Defence Committee, Mr Tan Eng Soon, the Company Commander, Mr Bernard Chiang, summoned all CD volunteers to assemble to give aid.

By early afternoon, 42 volunteers were mobilised and in spite of transportation problems were rushed to the site of the tragedy. They were deployed to help other rescuers remove rubble, man food/drink stalls and perform other supportive work.

Our volunteers were truly enthusiastic in their duties and toiled long hours at a stretch. They were there every day until it was all over. Fired by their dedication a good number of Officials from the Citizens' Consultative Committee, Management Committee, Residents' Committee and Women's Sub-Committee of Braddell Heights made time to be with our volunteers, giving them encouragement and a word of appreciation. It was team work in its true sense.

Hard working Ms Afida's boss donated 1,000 packets of Nasi Brani and Senior Citizens and volunteers donated 1,200 pieces of towels for use by the rescuers.

By a strange coincidence our volunteers held "A Recall Exercise" only on 10th March and the volunteers were most eager to put their training into practice. Some were visually moved by sadness, the thought of innocent people crushed under tons and tons of debris. But steeled by the urgency to save lives, they forgot about the risks involved.

To these gallant helpers Braddell Heights salute and shall always remember you.

Source: Braddell Heights Newsletter.

As more professionals and trained uniformed groups arrived to help, we switched our roles to providing refreshments to the rescuers and the victims' family members.

当专业救援人员到达时我们改变了职责为救助者和受害者家属提供点心和食物。

Sharing my experience learned from the Hotel New World disaster at public events.
在公共活动中分享我对新世界大酒店灾难的经验。

Ang Mo Kio Library — 13 July 2012.
*2012*年*7*月*13*日，在宏茂桥图书馆。

Republic Polytechnic — 22 January 2013.

*2013*年*1*月*22*日，在共和理工学院。

National University — 7 September 2013.

*2013*年*9*月*7*日，在国大。

CHAPTER 43

Encountering Other Disasters and Epidemics since the 50's

During the kampong days, the villagers faced a serious threat from the spread of tuberculosis in the late 40's. According to reports, it originated from the prisoners-of-war during the Japanese Occupation of Singapore. I remember in those days villagers had to cover their nose and mouth with handkerchiefs as the disease was very contagious. Tuberculosis spread through the air when an infectious person coughed or spat. At that time, it was considered as the number-one killer until the 60's, when it slowly subsided. During that period, public education was difficult as only Rediffusion broadcasts and posters were available. In 1955, The Singapore Anti-Tuberculosis Association (SATA) started their mobile treatment services to reach out to the villagers. Then in 1959, SATA also started a campaign to conduct mass X-ray camps for the kampong folks.

In 1957, when the Asian Flu struck Singapore, leaders of the kampong played their part by offering free boiled Chinese herbs to the villagers as a remedy to strengthen the immune system. The concoction of green olives and other herbs were supplied by two medicinal shops and prepared by the village leaders. The expenses were borne by the village association supporters and well-wishers. Fortunately, the flu epidemic didn't last long and subsided in a little more than a month. This was followed by the Hong Kong Flu in 1968, when all the villagers were required to have their anti-flu jabs, provided by the Ministry of Health, at vaccination drives held at the village association premises and schools. Luckily it lasted only for a short while as my cohort had been preparing for our GCE "O" Level examinations and the most memorable National Day Parade.

When I was in my third year of secondary school in the year 1967, there was a fear of Koro syndrome, a disease characterised by the sudden shrinkage of the male organ. It was believed that it would result in the retraction of the penis and its complete disappearance, which might lead to death. The public was concerned when a local newspaper reported that some people had developed symptoms of the disease when they consumed pork from pigs that were injected with anti–swine-fever vaccine. There was a report that more than ninety men with Koro had been quarantined due to eating pork. People began to panic and feared that the spread could turn into an epidemic. By late 1967, the situation stabilised, and the medical authority dismissed rumours and clarified that Koro was due to the result of anxiety and undue fear. With the assurance and public education, the fear factor and assumption of the cause by eating pork were rebutted and led to a slow change in the people's mindset. I couldn't remember whether this was the case with the non-pork eaters.

Severe Acute Respiratory Syndrome (SARS) first appeared in late November 2002 in Guangzhou City. The outbreak in Singapore started in February 2003, when three young women returning from holidays in Hong Kong were infected and spread the disease to more than two hundred others, including healthcare staff. It was the same year that the North-East MRT Line was opened, and many commuters were fearful of the close interaction with other passengers in the crowded trains. Our school Golden Jubilee Dinner at the Neptune Theatre had to be postponed from April to September 2003. Grassroots leaders headed by former Citizens Consultative Committee (CCC) Chairman Dr Goh Bak Heng were also busy, conducting house visits to educate the community on their personal hygiene and to adopt preventive measures. The morale of the healthcare workers was very low, as many of them were infected with SARS and the members of the public began to shun them. Some were turned away when they tried to take public transport, especially when they donned the nurses' uniform. This was a very serious matter as the nurses are our frontline heroines and should be respected and acknowledged for their hard work and bravery in stopping the spread of infectious diseases. As such we started a signature campaign to salute and recognise the hard work of our frontline healthcare workers in order to boost their morale and gain public confidence.

In 2004, the numbers of dengue fever cases started to surge in Lorong Lew Lian Housing and Bartley Neighbourhood Estates. A task force was organised to alert and conduct educational programmes for the residents. Grassroots leaders were roped in to conduct house visits and remind residents, especially the maids, on the potential mosquitoes breeding areas within their premises and common corridors. In 2014, the National Environment Agency (NEA) conducted courses for volunteers to be ambassadors of Dengue Prevention. Refresher courses were also organised for the earlier trained batches and thereafter the NEA and grassroots organisations also collaborated with the neighbourhood schools to reach out to the students and residents. The collaborations were encouraging and still ongoing when the need arises. Braddell Heights was awarded the 'Most Improved Constituency" in the management of dengue control during the Clean and Green Week Campaign in 2014, thanks to the foreign domestic helpers and the support from our residents. We were also grateful to have the support from the schools to involve their students as anti-dengue ambassadors.

The coronavirus disease, known as COVID-19, originated from Wuhan, the capital of Hubei in China. The virus began to spread to many parts of the world, including Singapore. Singapore had its first confirmed case on 20 January 2020, when an elderly man from Shanxi Province came here on holiday. This was the busiest period for the Chinese as they were preparing for the Lunar New Year celebrations, which fell on 25 January 2020. Many Chinese nationals also used the long holidays to return to their villages to have reunion dinners with their loved ones. Others would take this opportunity to travel abroad to meet their relatives who were working in foreign countries. Travellers from Wuhan, who arrived in Singapore for various reasons, were unknowing carriers of the coronavirus. Those who were infected had no obvious symptoms as the incubation period was about two weeks.

Lorong Lew Lian Estate reported its first case of COVID-19 on 29 January 2020, when an elderly couple from Wuhan flew into Singapore from Guangzhou to stay with their relatives here. They arrived on 19 January 2020 and developed symptoms about a week later. The couple took a taxi to Tan Tock Seng Hospital, where their infections were confirmed, and were later transferred to the National Centre of Infectious Disease. When the news released, the residents of this estate did not believe it and were shocked that the coronavirus had appeared at their doorsteps. People started to panic and many wanted to know which block the infected persons lived in. Business in the estate was affected as residents avoided going to shops and eating houses as there was a possibility that the infected couple could have patronised those establishments.

Our immediate response was to start an action plan to protect our residents and family members and provide them with surgical masks and hand sanitisers. Coincidentally, the relevant Ministries and the People's Association (PA) also came up with similar plans, and we were eagerly working out on the distribution dates on 1 and 2 February 2020 at the Braddell Heights Zone B Residents' Committee Centre. Each household got four surgical masks on production of their identity cards.

This was followed by the distribution of hand sanitisers sponsored by Temasek Foundation from 23–29 March 2020 at the Braddell Heights CC. Another round of reusable mask distribution took place from 5–12 April 2020, this time including work pass holders and other residents from private estates elsewhere. The mode of identification was further improved by scanning the barcode of the identity cards with a handphone application, and it took just a few minutes to complete the collection procedure. We were fortunate that many of our members, volunteers and friends from the Residents' Committee and Inter-Racial and Religious Confidence Circle came forward to help us.

Several other rounds of mask distribution were also conducted using the 'Do It Yourself' method through vending machines. At the time of writing this narrative, the latest was the distribution of Trace Together tokens at the Braddell Heights Community Centre scheduled on 22 December 2020.

In 2003, Anti-SARS ambassadors distributed educational flyers and sanitisers to residents. We also rallied our residents to sign their names in support of healthcare workers.

2003年,反SARS大使向居民分发传单和消毒剂.
我们还召集居民签名以支持医护人员。

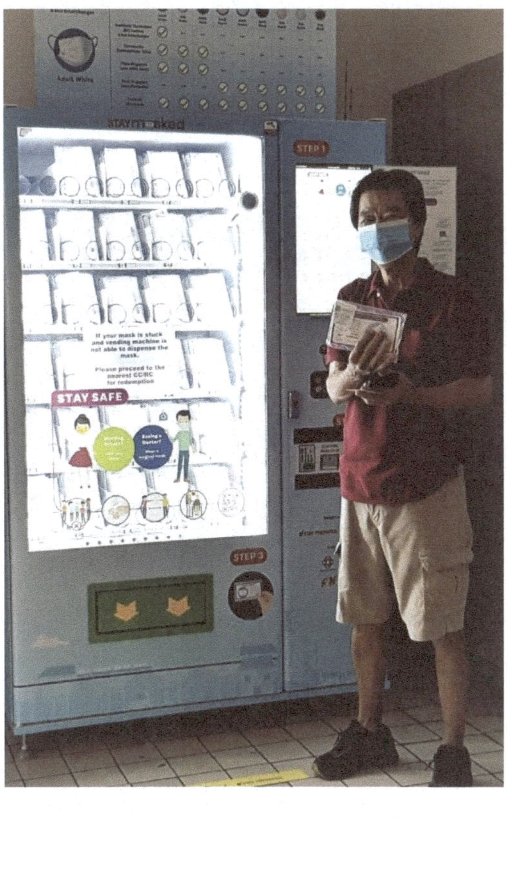

Braddell Heights Zone B RC and IRCC members helped to distribute face masks to the community at Blk 6 Lorong Lew Lian on February, April and September 2020.

在2020年2月，4月和九月我们的志愿者帮助分发口罩给居民。

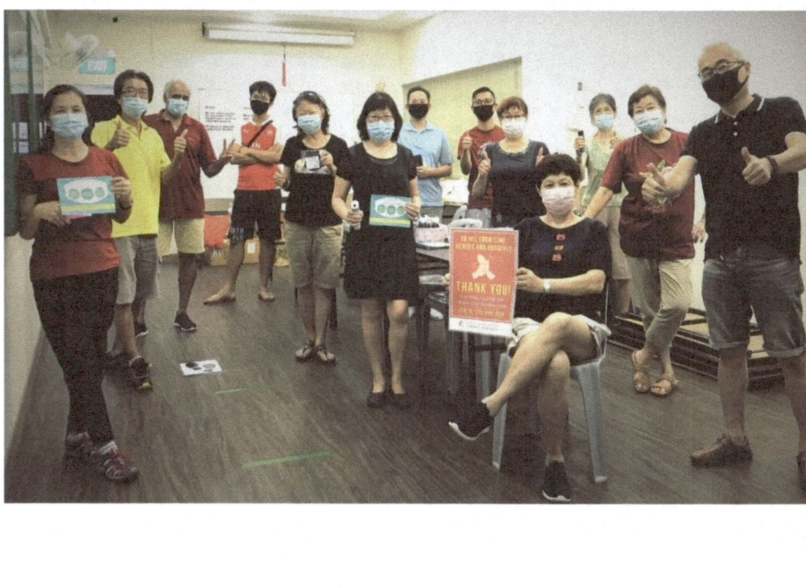

WEDNESDAY, APRIL 10, 2019 | THE STRAITS TIMES

HOME | B7

While the pioneer leaders were the architects of Singapore, everyday heroes helped to build society here. Members of the 'Merdeka Generation' – those born in the 1950s – persevered through a tumultuous period. The Straits Times meets one man who has been contributing to his community since his younger days.

MerdekaGeneration

Community service runs in his blood

Cara Wong

At the age of 12, while his friends were playing "masak masak" – a cooking game – Mr Bernard Chiang had a more serious pastime.

As a member of his local volunteer firefighting team, he would help to put out blazes that the thatched attap houses of the time were prone to.

"I would be the first one to climb up the kampung's observatory tower and tell them where to go," said Mr Chiang, now 67. "I was very adventurous back then."

Mr Chiang was the sixth son of 10 children. His parents ran a provision shop, selling milk, rice and pig feed in Kampung Chia Keng – now the site of Serangoon Stadium.

While he has fond memories of his early days, they were also a time of great difficulties and even danger.

"There was no electricity, no running water in our houses, and we had to use candles, kerosene lamps and take water from a common standpipe outside," he recalls.

"We were also living in danger – once there was a fire, there was a possibility that it would wipe out the whole kampung."

It was for this reason that the kampung leaders, including Mr Chiang's father, decided to set up a civilian firefighting unit.

It was made up of around 30 volunteers who were trained by the Singapore Fire Brigade. "We saved quite a number of people by dousing those fires," said Mr Chiang.

Members of the unit doubled as security personnel for kampung residents during festive events, protecting them from pickpockets and gangsters who roamed the area.

As the son of a kampung leader, Mr Chiang was involved in many other community activities.

He and his siblings helped to operate a free clinic in the kampung twice a week, and they would register patients and set up the space for doctors and nurses to treat kampung residents.

When Mr Chiang was about 12, the kampung – which did not offer many recreational activities – set up its own Teochew opera troupe.

"We felt that there was a need to bring people together, so we started a Teochew wayang to bring the residents together for entertainment," said Mr Chiang.

His family had to "start the ball rolling" and Mr Chiang and his siblings were among its first actors and percussionists.

"Some of us even had to dress up as female characters, until we could get enough female cast to join," he recalled.

Mr Chiang would play supporting roles, and professional directors would help to run the shows.

As a member of St Gabriel's Secondary School's brass band, Mr Chiang joined the troupe's percussion band, playing the cymbals.

After completing secondary school, Mr Chiang studied at the Nanyang Academy of Fine Arts and in the 1970s, he met his wife while working as a store detective at department store John Little. "I was supposed to detect wrongdoings in the store, but I detected her instead," he laughed.

It was also during this period that the authorities resettled kampung residents into Housing Board flats.

Mr Chiang, along with his family, moved into a Housing Board flat in Lew Lian Gardens. His brother opened a florist shop there, and Mr Chiang went to work in the shop.

However, Mr Chiang remained active in the community at his new residence, joining the Braddell Heights Residents' Committee in 1980.

He was a founding member of the Braddell Heights Civil Defence volunteer company – a group of civilians trained to respond during emergencies – and was the group's company commander during the Hotel New World disaster in 1986.

The six-storey building collapsed suddenly on March 15, leaving 33 people dead.

"I was in the shop doing work when I heard about it on the radio," said Mr Chiang.

"It sounded very serious so I quickly called the commander of the national civil defence team to ask if they needed help."

Mr Chiang rounded up a team of about 20 volunteers – including hawkers, housewives and students – to go to the site to help clear debris and look for survivors.

When experts arrived on the scene, the volunteers took the backseat and helped to distribute food and tended to the family members and helpers at the site.

They remained there for about a week, taking turns to care for the people there.

"It was very devastating, but also very memorable," he said.

Mr Chiang, who has two children and two grandchildren, continues to work as a florist in Lew Lian Gardens, where he still lives today.

He is also still active in his role as a vice-chairman of the residents' committee, helping to organise community activities "to get the people together". He added: "I'm still very active in helping to build a cohesive community."

carawong@sph.com.sg

LIVING CONDITIONS

There was no electricity, no running water in our houses, and we had to use candles, kerosene lamps and take water from a common standpipe outside. We were also living in danger – once there was a fire, there was a possibility that it would wipe out the whole kampung.

MR BERNARD CHIANG, on the living conditions in the kampung and the constant risk of fire

Mr Bernard Chiang is a vice-chairman of the Braddell Heights Zone 8 Residents' Committee. His father was a leader in the former Kampung Chia Keng in Serangoon.
ST PHOTO: CHONG JUN LIANG

Mr Chiang (with a clipboard) led the Braddell Heights Civil Defence volunteers who responded to the Hotel New World collapse in 1986.
PHOTO: COURTESY OF BERNARD CHIANG

Source: The Straits Times, Singapore Press Holdings Limited. Reprinted with permission.

My service records in the grassroots organisations and alumni association.

我在基层组织和校友会的服务记录。

1980: Braddell Heights Residents' Committee
1982: Braddell Heights Citizens' Consultative Committee
1982: Braddell Heights Community Centre Management Committee
1984: Braddell Heights Civil Defence Co-ordinating Committee
1990: St Gabriel's Old Boys' Association
1991: Aljunied Town Council
1997: Marine Parade Town Council
2005: Braddell Heights Inter-Racial and Religious Confidence Circle
2008 — NACLI Adjunct Faculty
2011: Serangoon Moral Family Service Centre

CHAPTER 44

Fostering the Kampong Spirit in the HDB Estate

With all the training and experience gained over the years from our kampong days, we were geared to handle several cases of house fires occurring in the Housing & Development Board (HDB) neighbourhoods. House fires were common and occurred in the flats of those not used to high-rise living as the cooking apparatuses and kitchen setup were different from those in the kampong days.

Over the years, we had handled several cases of house fires in the HDB flats. Some residents were very careless and left their boiling water and food unattended while they ran errands and forgot to turn off the stove before leaving the house. With continuous boiling, the food got burnt and caught fire, which and then spread to the cabinet area.

On 22 September 1986, a few of us from the neighbourhood shops helped to stop a house fire at Blk 2 Lorong Lew Lian. The owner had been cooking and left the house without turning off the gas stove. The food was burnt and the fire spread to the cabinet. My older brother Gary, the former neighbourhood Chinese medical shop owner, Mr Heng Chee Yong, and I managed to break open the wooden door and stop the fire.

By 1988, another redrawing of electoral boundaries had taken place and another thirteen HDB blocks from the newly built estate were added to the Lorong Lew Lian precinct Residents' Committee (RC). As such the RC boundary was enlarged and renamed the Aljunied Zone E RC under the purview of Aljunied GRC.

Another incident happened on 12 July 1991 at Blk 415 Serangoon Central. My brother Gary and I tried to save an old lady who was trapped in her room which had caught fire. Unfortunately we couldn't reach her as the metal gate was locked and there was no way to cut the padlock without proper equipment. Only the firemen, with special hydraulic cutters, could cut open the iron-grill gate and break down the front door. By the time they gained entry to the unit, it was too late; she had already succumbed to toxic smoke inhalation.

On another occasion, a Malay family which lived at Blk 417 was devastated when a baby was locked inside a room as the door was accidentally locked up by the force of a strong wind. The grandmother was panicked and helpless and approached me for help. I used a ladder to climb over the balcony in order to gain access to the baby's room and unlatched the lock. Luckily the baby had only had a fright and was crying loudly but not hurt.

In 2007, the whole of Singapore island was struck by metal parts theft due to high demand of copper and metal in China. The price of scrap metal had gone up threefold, and drain covers, handrails, signboards, joss-stick urns and even the lightning strips protecting HDB dwellers were not spared. This was a very serious matter, and was described by MP Seah Kian Peng as 'More Serious than Michael Fay'. The lives of people living in the flats were at stake and we had to put a stop to it. We rallied our residents to keep a close watch and work with the police to nail down the perpetrators. The thieves were very bold and even struck openly during daytime. On the afternoon of Christmas Eve, I chanced upon a suspicious character attempting to remove the lightning strip right in front of my eyes at the gable end of Blk 416. Without wasting any time, I quickly contacted the police to carry out an ambush and managed to arrest the elusive culprit. The police reacted rapidly and efficiently and arrested the culprit who had attempted to run away.

On another occasion, sometime in January 2008, some residents informed me that they had seen a group of mischievous students in uniform at the Lorong Lew Lian multi-storey carpark playing with home-made explosives. The explosive was improvised by strapping a bundle of sparklers to a bottle of compressed gas to turn it into a bomb. They managed to ignite the sparklers but failed to detonate the gas cylinder, which they had placed under one of the parked vehicles. It would have been devastating and disastrous if the explosion was successful, as it would have caused extensive damage to the building and the surrounding vehicles, not to mention the possibility of heavy casualties and fatalities. Together with the residents, we managed to restrain the culprits and took down their particulars before letting them off. Their names were handed over to the police for investigation while the special bomb units arrived to investigate and gather evidence at the multi-storey carpark.

The lessons we learned from this episode was the importance and effectiveness of community policing and reinforcing the kampong spirit. The residents are at the frontlines and would be the first to know what is happening before the law enforcers arrive. They can also provide information and feedback regarding the safety and security issues within and around the housing estate. Coincidentally, Braddell Heights Division and the Serangoon Police Centre initiated the Citizens On Surveillance (COS) Program in 2007. The programme was part of the Community Safety and Security Programme launched by PM Lee Hsien Loong, when he made his community visit to Braddell Heights on 15 September 2007.

When the Mass Rapid Transport (MRT) North-East Line was fully operational in 2003, there was a demand for rental units in Braddell Heights for migrant workers and foreign students. The presence of foreign workers, family members and students had gone up over the last few years due to the availability of new condominiums and HDB units at Lorong Lew Lian. This was a prime location with the convenience of transportation, shopping mall, neighbourhood shops and other amenities. Initially, with the arrival of foreigners in this HDB estate, there were many cases of fire in the rubbish chutes. Many foreigners had not been high-rise flat dwellers in their countries of origin and were not careful when discarding leftover burning charcoal into the rubbish chutes, which resulted in the sudden surge of bin chute fires.

By 2009 and 2010, when the MRT Circle Line and NEX mall opened, respectively, there was more demand for residential units in this region. More condominiums had sprouted in the next few years, and the grassroots leaders and residents were expected to face new challenges with the additional of many new developments in the area. By 2013, the old Jade Tower Condominium built around the same time as Lorong Lew Lian Estate was sold en bloc and rebuilt as two ten-storey residential blocks. The latest private redevelopment around this area was at the former Paya Lebar Police Station, where seven blocks of twelve-storey private residential units would be built. Work has been in progress since 2016 and the expected date of completion was scheduled for 2021. The narrow road at Lorong Lew Lian had to be widened as the vehicle traffic would be increased and there would be more visitors parking in the HDB carparks.

By the year 2025, Singapore's biggest polyclinic would have been built at the location of the former Braddell Heights community centre, opposite Lorong Lew Lian Estate. This good news was disclosed by the MP Mr Seah Kian Peng, who shared that it would be an integrated facility consisting of a polyclinic, active ageing hub and kidney dialysis centre. The building of the polyclinic is timely and beneficial to the majority of the Pioneer and Merdeka generations living in Braddell Heights. By then Lorong Lew Lian Estate would be almost 50 years old. Braddell Heights' ageing population would increase tremendously, and more elder-friendly amenities have to be implemented to make Braddell Heights a better and safer place to live.

Friends of Braddell Heights Gathering was initiated by Mr Lee Khoon Choy and Mr Gan Teng Geow in 2005.

2005年李炯才先生和颜挺尧先生发起的布莱德岭之友年度聚会。

Reappointment of Braddell Heights CCC members.

布莱德岭公民咨询委员会任命仪式。

Celebrating Deepavali with our Indian residents.

和我们的印度居民一起庆祝屠妖节2019。

Celebrating National Day with our grassroots leaders, leaders of religious organisations and friends.

与我们的基层、宗教领导马来居民和朋友一起庆祝国庆节。

Fostering the kampong spirit and bonding with the grassroots leaders and residents.

培育甘榜精神并与基层领导人和居民建立联系。

CHAPTER 45

Fostering Racial and Religious Harmony

As Chairman of the Residents' Committee, I was approached to defuse a very tense situation involving a Chinese and Malay family in 1990. Both families were long-time residents of Blk 5 Lorong Lew Lian Housing Estate. The Malay family had booked the void deck a few months in advance to organise a ceremonial wedding. Preparations for the wedding were ready and invitations had been sent out to relatives and friends. They were shocked when they saw that a wake was taking place at the same void deck which they had booked for the wedding celebrations.

The Chinese family was unaware that the Malay family had already booked the same void deck for a wedding ceremony. They occupied the far end of the void deck, which was above their unit for the wake. It had been a weekend, and the deceased family had no access to the Town Council Office. The situation was urgent so they went ahead to use the void deck first and had planned to follow up and register with the Town Council on the next working day.

The Malay family was very upset and wanted the wake to be relocated to a nearby block. I was approached by the Town Council to mediate this very sensitive issue. Along with another Malay community leader, we visited both parties and offered an alternative site to either party but both sides refused. We were in a very difficult position and had to be very sensitive and respect both parties' decisions. Each family had very strong reasons for not moving to another location. The Malay family, who had a stronger case, insisted that they stay on as they had already sent out their invitations to their relatives and friends. Whereas the Chinese family, who had been unaware of the pre-booking of the void deck by the Malay family, reasoned that shifting the coffin was very inauspicious.

Fortunately, after a lengthy discussion, we managed to convince the grieving family to get their tentage vendor to use a tarpaulin to partition the wake area from the wedding venue. Both parties accepted our proposal, and the wedding celebration and funeral ritual events were carried out smoothly. We had experienced the racial riots in the 60's, and therefore we were aware that such a situation could get out of hand and result in serious consequences.

The lesson we learned from this episode was not to take peace and harmony for granted as we have to respect and understand one another's religion, culture and practices. We went through an unforgettable and painful experience to achieve peace and harmony to gain progress and prosperity for our nation. With the progress in information and technology, we would be more exposed to many, undesirable, extremist ideologies online, and a weak-minded individual could be easily radicalised. We have to keep a close watch for such radicalised individuals and ensure they don't harbour any ill intentions of breaking up the delicate social fabric of our society. Over the years, we also noticed the presence of new citizens and foreigners living in the HDB heartlands, and felt the need to integrate them into our multi-racial society.

I served as RC Chairman for sixteen years and moved on to helm the Braddell Heights Inter-Racial and Religious Confidence Circle (IRCC) in the year 2005. The IRCC was formed in 2002, and the first chairman was Mr Gan Teng Geow, followed by Benji Ng in 2003, under the purview of the Braddell Heights Citizens Consultative Committee (CCC). When I assumed my role as the new chairman, I immediately reorganised the committee structure and recruited more leaders from religious and civic organisations, school principals, voluntary welfare organisations and former grassroots leaders to broaden the areas of representation. The initial outreach was challenging as we had to work very hard for the recruitment in order to gain their trust and confidence to be volunteers and come on board the IRCC.

Initially, it was very challenging to get the religious leaders to come on board the IRCC. They were worried and concerned that the authority would interfere in their management and intrude upon their privacy. With many friendly networking sessions and gatherings, we managed to overcome the psychological barrier and fostered a good working relationship. Ultimately everyone understood the importance of strengthening our social cohesion and resilience in time of crisis. The IRCC also served as a platform for all the leaders of the religious organisations and other civic organisations to gather and know each other better.

We worked very well and prepared ourselves under the new direction of the IRCC, and by the year 2006, when the then Ministry of Community Development, Youth and

Sports wanted to reposition and restructure the IRCCs, we were ready to kickstart our project in the new direction. As we were ready and established ahead of many other IRCCs, we were nominated to share our success story at the National IRCC Conference in 2007. With the restructured management, we were also picked to host several GRC-level table-top exercises. I was also invited to join the IRCC Newsletter Editorial Committee after the launch of the first publication by Minister Lawrence Wong in 2013.

With the strong support of our dedicated members and partners, I was fortunate to be selected along with another two other IRCC chairmen, Chia Keng Hian and Sarjit Singh, to be recognised for outstanding performance at the Colour Awards. Our IRCC partner, Bartley Christian Church, represented by Pastor Kenneth Teo, was awarded the Ambassador Award. The awards were presented by Mr Lawrence Wong, Minister for Ministry of Community, Culture and Youth (MCCY) in year 2015. The success of the IRCC was due to the concerted efforts and passion of every member, along with the support of the adviser and other grassroots leaders.

The Braddell Heights Inter-Racial and Religious Confidence Circle was formed in year 2002.

布莱德岭族群与宗教互信圈委员会成立于2002年。

MCCY Appreciation Dinner 2017 graced by Minister Grace Fu and Senior Parliamentary Secretary Mr Baey Yam Keng.

傅海燕部长和高級政务次长马炎庆先生出席文化社区及青年部答谢晚宴。

The Management Committee of Serangoon Moral Family Service Centre and staff welcomed the visit by President Halimah Yacob, MP for Braddell Heights Mr Seah Kian Peng and grassroots leaders on 6 March 2018.

2018年3月6日，实龙岗德教家庭服务中心管委和职员欢迎哈利马总统和国会议员谢键平先生到访。

Religious leaders and IRCC members at the Harmony Trail.

宗教领袖和族群与宗教互信圈成员在和谐之旅– *17.3.2019*。

Racial Harmony Day Dialogue with Mr Othman Wok, Mr Lee Khoon Choy, Mr Joe Conceicao and Mr Seah Kian Peng at the Harmony Centre — 18 July 2009.

在种族和谐日与三名前国会议员和国会议员谢健平先生进行对话。

Marine Parade GRC and Macpherson SMC IRCCs Reappointment Ceremony officiated by ESM Goh Chok Tong.

族群与宗教互信圈委员会成员的新任期由國務資政吴作栋主持。

20.7.2019

Harmony Fun Run with DPM Teo Chee Hean organised by Al-Istighfar Mosque — 2018.

张志贤副总理参加由一所回教堂主办的和谐竞走。

IRCC National Day celebration at St Gabriel's Sec School — 2018.

族群与宗教互信圈委员会在生加密中学庆祝国庆。。

Left: Dr Ho Chee Lick and I were featured in the IRCC newsletter in 2016.

Source: IRCC Newsletter

Bottom picture:

Right Clockwise — Chandraseharan Vijayakumar, Albert Lee, Chia Keng Hian, David Choo, Leo Kwang Lin, Abdul Rashid Ibrahim, Neo Miao Chin and Bernard Chiang (Newsletter Editorial Committee formed in 2013).

成立于2013年的族群与宗教互信圈新闻编辑委员会。

Dialogue with Inter-Racial and Religious Confidence Circle Chairpersons organised by MCCY at the Maghain Aboth Synagogue on 21 Feb 2019.

2019年2月21日族群与宗教互信圈主席的对话与交流。

Bonding of our multi-racial youth through bowling.

通过保龄球比赛将我们多种族的年轻人联系在一起。

Braddell Heights Inter-Racial and Religious Confidence Circle

布莱德岭族群与宗教互信圈。

- *2004: Member of Braddell Heights IRCC*
- *2005–2014: Chairman of the Braddell Heights IRCC*
- *2013–2017: IRCC Newsletter Editorial Committee*
- *2015–2023: Co-chairman of Braddell Heights IRCC*

HOME | THE STRAITS TIMES | MONDAY, AUGUST

life dedicated to fostering harmony

ecently recognised for his efforts to idges between races and religions

STAYING THE COURSE

The journey to peace is long and painful, and shouldn't be taken for granted.

MR BERNARD CHIANG

Source: The Straits Times, Singapore Press Holdings Limited
Reprinted with permission.

Vanishing Landmarks

消失中的地标

Vanishing old landmarks around Braddell Heights.

甘榜和选区附近的地标消失。

Former Paya Lebar Police Station.

前巴耶利峇警察局。

Upper Serangoon Road before the construction of the overhead bridge.

修建天桥前的上实龙岗路。

The former Paya Lebar Outpatient Dispensary.

前巴耶利峇政府诊所。

Pre-war shop houses at Upper Serangoon.

在实龙岗路上段的战前店屋。

4th milestone Tua Pek Kong Temple at Upper Serangoon Road.

实龙岗路上段四英里的大伯公庙。

Shop houses at 5th milestone.

实龙岗路上段5英里的商店。

The former Braddell Heights CC at Upper Serangoon Road.

在实龙岗路上段前布莱德岭民众俱乐部 。

Shop houses at the entrance of Lorong Lew Lian.

罗弄榴槤入口处的商店。

Back view of shop houses at Lorong Lew Lian.

罗弄榴樋店屋的后巷。

Building used by former Singapore Civil Defence Force.

前民防部队使用的建筑物。

Tian Kong Tua Temple at Yio Chu Kang Road.

車宮天公壇。

Chap Pang Kong Temple at Lorong Patong.

什班公庙。